MARSHAL LAW

William Kinnebrew

ISBN: 978-1-942451-48-8
eISBN: 978-1-942451-49-5

DEDICATION

This book is dedicated to all the men and women who pick up the badge and are willing to put their lives in harm's way for the sake of freedom, especially the men and women who have gone before us. We salute you.

PRELUDE

The Deputies of the United States Marshals Service are some of the greatest men and women to ever walk the face of the earth. They are the line that evil will not cross. This is their oath: I do solemnly swear that I will faithfully support The Constitution of the United States, will enforce the laws thereunder, and execute the duties of the office of Deputy United States Marshal during my continuance in office. So help me God.

CHAPTER 1

February in Oklahoma was a cold and gray month, with everything dying or dead. Each day crept along slowly while dark clouds, holding the sun at bay, maintained a guarded vigilance of its warm wonderful light. The ground was frozen and hard, but the night seemed a little warmer than usual with the wind blowing out of the Southwest. The campfire had reduced itself to nothing more than glowing embers that grew a little brighter every time a gust of wind rolled over the remaining coals. The dream had come as it always does with her coal black hair shining in the sun. The tide was high, the color of the water graced her beautiful blue-green eyes, and they danced on the beach, rocking each other gently somewhere peaceful and warm. They danced for a moment in time as the sun dropped into the ocean. Once the light started to fade, he opened his eyes. She was gone, the ground was cold, and he was alone.

The sound of something rustling in the leaves alerted his horse Patton, and he stomped his foot as if to let him know that it was close to him and he didn't like it. Patton earned his name for being stubborn and strong willed from the beginning. He came to Sam as a wild bag of bones from an old horse trader who told a tragic story about a hunter shooting his mother by accident while deer hunting. The colt was too young to eat solid food, had nothing to nurse, and the trader was out of options. The trader really wasn't much of a trader settling for a case of beans, some jerky, and a bottle of whiskey, barter being the method of exchange since the almighty dollar had fallen. In 2017, most markets had crashed, and the United Nations created a world market with one currency. The only people who used it in America were those left on the east coast. In the more dense populations, it had become more difficult to function without a monetary unit of exchange.

Sam gained the trust of Patton quickly by using crushed carrots and apples covered with molasses. After that, it was easy getting him to eat solid food. Once he was full grown, he was like a puppy, following him around begging for attention and eventually becoming a huge, seventeen hands high chestnut beast of a horse that still acts like a spoiled little baby but can outrun the wind. As luck would have it, the rustling leaves happened to be a rabbit who, unfortunately for the rabbit, ambled into camp and made a quick and convenient breakfast for Sam as he enjoyed watching the sun rise over The Winding Stair Mountains.

Riding horseback through the mountains sometimes gives a man the ability to see the world through God's eyes, providing a perspective of purpose that brings peace and wisdom to the problems at hand. Sam moved to Oklahoma in the '90s after becoming a Deputy Marshal, and discovered his love for horses and the outdoors. He frequently escaped to the wilderness, staying lost in a world of seclusion for days at a time and returning to what was left of civilization only when his job required it. After the Fall, petroleum became scarce and horses soon became the most popular mode of transportation as automobiles became a thing of the past. After the Trade Center fell, the country was lost to a progressive attitude and was soon regulated and taxed into a third world death. The powers that ruled the land continued politics as usual while the reigning elite in Washington portrayed themselves as royalty. The rest of the country had become a war zone regulated by militias, separated by blood and barter. Shortly after the last U.S. presidential election, ISIS gained the support of many of the countries being controlled under Islamic Sharia law and launched pandemic attacks using illegal immigrants as disease carriers, slipping them through the porous Mexican border.

The population was decimated from sea to shining sea in a matter of months. The extremely contagious disease was developed in a laboratory by using a unique genetically altered strain of bovine spongiform encephalopathy, or mad cow disease. The disease in its original form was easily prevented and cured, but the biomedical engineers that composed the new strain made it extremely contagious and fast acting. This created a new twist by causing it to not only attack the brain and spinal cord, but cause rapid organ failure as well. Within days, the lungs begin to fail, fill with blood and cause coughing spasms which allow the disease to go airborne. In two months, the Center for Disease Control (CDC) discovered a cure, but by the time it was administered the world had lost half of the population – almost four billion people.

Cemeteries filled, and crematoriums ran twenty-four hours a day, seven days a week. Some of the more populated areas of the country had to take more drastic action, burning mass graves full of bodies. Other countries were not so lucky. Once it gained ground in Europe and Asia, there was no way to produce the cure fast enough to satisfy the enormous demand. What was left of the rest of the world joined forces, recognized an opportunity, and jumped on the United States like a wounded animal.

ISIS took control of the Iranian Nuclear Program and began detonating dirty bombs throughout Europe. China launched missiles at four locations along the Gulf Coast trying to take out the Strategic Oil Reserve. North Korea attacked U.S. bases in Alaska, attempting to further cripple the U.S. by strangling and depleting energy resources. Russia launched the most aggressive attack in naval history on the U.S. Navy, concentrating their efforts against what little defense was left and drove America to her knees, but America didn't break. When things couldn't get any worse, the West Coast, decimated by disease and famine, washed into the ocean as earthquakes drowned everything west of the San Andreas Fault.

In an act of desperation and survival, the U.S. nuked Hong Kong, Moscow, North Korea and the majority of the Middle East. America was divided geographically by politics and religion.

A decade later, the east coast had begun to re-establish the communication infrastructure but was still limited to 1970's technology. Some analog towers allowed cell phone use with very limited coverage while most people used land lines. The country had looked to our leadership for answers, and the answers were consistently lost in political whitewash. Everyone west of the Mississippi seemed to adjust a little more quickly than the east coast holding fast to God, guns and Old Glory.

The rest of the country began calling the middle of the country – basically the heart of the old USA consisting mainly of Texas, Oklahoma, Kansas, Nebraska, Missouri and Arkansas – "Neverland." Neverland still recognized the authority of the U. S. Constitution, but that may be short lived. The elite in Washington had wanted America to join the United Nations and finalize the one world government, but Neverland threatened rebellion and refused to put away the U.S. Constitution.

As the sun crept into the sky, Sam stepped into the stirrup, swung his leg over the saddle and pointed Patton toward Tulsa. Tulsa had become the unofficial capital of Neverland due to the oil. Oil had become our gold. Tulsa not only had the oil and natural gas, but maintained the refineries to process it, giving Neverland the leverage it needed to maintain its position politically and economically. Early during the collapse, the sitting President thought to flex his military muscle, but soon realized that what was left of the military and the conservative population had fled the idiocracy on the east coast, seeking refuge in Neverland. It was quickly decided that even though the elite in Washington wanted to take the oil and every resource Neverland possesses, to do so would be catastrophic to both sides and cause a modern day civil war. They in turn chose patience and decided to wait, engaged in a political chess match that has so far been in Neverland's advantage.

Patton stopped in the creek to take his fill of water, and Sam paused, looking up the mountain to the old Queen Wilhelmina Hotel. It was in ruins now. People had no use for vacations anymore. Most were fighting for their next meal. Sam always preferred the solitude of the wilderness and the freedom of the mountains over the restrictions of the civilized world.

The old trails through the Winding Stair Mountains were much more enjoyable and discreet than following the main roads. Avoiding the routes of the old highway system was necessary for someone traveling alone. A solitary traveler in desperate times often made an easy target for those who looked to benefit from evil ways. Sam traveled for several days, turning north along the outskirts of Tahlequah, then heading west through the Cookson Hills. He stopped for the evening and made camp on a ridge, his back to a bluff. It helped to block the wind which had shifted out of the northwest, bringing the cold, cutting chill that penetrates to the bone. Protection from the elements is extremely important, and shelter is critical when establishing a camp, not only from the wind or rain but from those who may seek to steal what travelers may have. A fire can be seen at night for miles and can attract the wrong kind of attention. A wise traveler may run a cold camp without a fire, or use a fire for cooking at one location and move a safe distance from it after eating.

The bluff to the rear provided protection from the wind and kept the flames from being seen in three directions, while a small clearing in front provided an adequate field of fire. Beyond the clearing was a steep hill that created a small canyon, giving Sam added protection from the south. Sam finished eating and rested his head against the tree on which he was leaning. He was tired from his ride, and the flames of the fire kicked and danced until his eyes could no longer stay open. Of course she came to him again in the dream, dancing a slow dance, this time at night with the light from a fire flashing in her eyes. There seemed to be a million stars in the sky with a quarter moon setting over the ocean. He kissed her softly and she smiled, putting her head against his chest. She looked up gazing into his eyes and said, "It's time to wake up Love." Sam awoke startled with Patton standing close, having pulled lose from his tether. It was daylight, something was wrong. Someone was coming, and they were getting very close.

CHAPTER 2

Sam looked at Patton, who was alert and cocking his ears toward the meadow. He rolled to his side and crawled to Patton, putting the horse between him and his threat. He slowly rose at Patton's side and slid the AR-15 out of the scabbard, then glanced down the hill and saw four people on foot rapidly approaching him. They seemed to be more interested in what was behind them than where they were going. Sometimes it doesn't matter how hard you try to hide or escape the reality of life, trouble can and often will find you. This was beginning to look like much more than what Sam wanted to deal with on this trail ride. As the leader of the group approached, Sam crouched behind a large tree, more curious now than threatened. They had not even seen Patton yet, which spoke volumes about their ability to survive in the wilderness. Survival was ultimately being aware of everything around you.

As the leader of the group topped the hill, he turned back to those following as if to hurry them along, backing right into Patton. Patton, as surprised as the leader, started and reared backward making a loud protest and scaring the leader so badly that he fell backward to the ground, frozen in fear. Those following popped up over the hill brandishing sticks as if they were long swords in defense of their leader. Sam admired their tenacity. They were fearless in spite of their lack of tactical skills and weapons. Patton had bolted back against the canyon wall behind Sam, who trained his AR-15 in the group's general direction.

"Drop the sticks," Sam commanded almost smiling.

"And let me see your hands, now!" They looked at one another, and one by one dropped the sticks on the ground.

"Remove your hoods and hats," he said. "Let me get a look at who is invading my camp."

The leader stepped forward almost in defiance, prompting Sam to point the AR-15 in his direction. Hesitantly, the leader pulled the hood back, removed the hat, and long black hair fell about her shoulders.

"You three, do the same." Likewise, they all removed their hoods and hats to reveal their identities. Sam thumbed the safety on and let the barrel drop, letting it hang from his shoulder strap. "Sit down. I'll build a fire and get some coffee going."

Travel in a wilderness area requires a certain amount of skill and preparation, more so in the winter. Most rational people would not run into a wilderness without a plan, unless they have fled something far worse than the dangers of starvation and hypothermia. Running into outlaws was something Sam was always prepared for. Running into four girls in the middle of nowhere was nothing he had prepared for. The coffee started to boil as the rag tag group huddled by the fire, fighting to get warm. Sam pulled some jerky out of his pack and let them pass the bag around. They attacked the jerky as if they had gone days without eating. Their hollow eyes had dark circles revealing exhaustion and dehydration, a dangerous combination for winter survival. Confident they would not have lasted another day, all four girls continued to glare at Sam with fearful eyes, not yet knowing whether he was a friend or foe.

He asked the leader, "What is your name?"

"Theresa," she replied.

"Are you hurt?"

She thought for a minute while chewing a piece of jerky, eyes lost in the flame of the fire…. "We all are."

"Where are you from?"

Again she paused, seeming to gain comfort and confidence in the conversation.

"We are all from different places," she replied looking back into the fire.

"Who is following you?"

She looked up now with a totally different look in her eyes, a vengeful look of hate that seemed to capture the flames of the fire and cast them directly at Sam.

"Men!"

She spat the word at Sam as if he had been her tormentor. He looked at her and the other three with compassion, and could not imagine what they had been through. They looked like hell. Realizing there was not much more that he could do at the moment other than offer help, Sam looked at Theresa and said,

"No one will hurt you anymore."

She glanced toward the other three, looked back at him and replied,

"We'll see."

Sam let the conversation go for a while, realizing that they needed to learn to trust him. These "men" she spoke of were probably not very far behind them, and Sam felt it best that they be on their way. With the exception of the rifle scabbards, Sam removed the packs off of Patton and loaded them onto his back. He kept the AR-15 at the ready with the big bore 450 Marlin still in its scabbard. The 450 was a belted magnum beast of a bullet that can punch through almost anything, shooting 400 grains at almost 2000 feet per second. The AR-15 shoots a small bullet at high speed with a good range, and also holds the capacity for a lot of ammunition. Sam carried a Glock 23 .40 caliber for close quarters, a Ruger GP100 .357 magnum as a backup, and an old knife if things got really bad. The knife was a Bianci Nighthawk his dad had given to him for his high school graduation. The blade was Solingen Steel which was virtually indestructible. Sam's training, weapons, attitude and personality all made him the warrior that he had become over the last twenty-five years. Any fool willing to engage him would quickly learn that a man who had reached old age in a profession of violence is best left alone.

Sam helped the girls get as comfortable as possible on Patton, letting the three younger girls ride first while letting the older girl walk beside him. Their lack of speed worried him considering whoever was pursuing these girls could easily overtake them if they knew how to track. This part of the country along the Illinois River was like Sam's back yard. Before the Fall, the river was a fountain of youth, a garden of fun, a playground offering an all summer adventure for those who wanted to play in her waters. In his younger days, Sam had spent days on end hiking, swimming and fishing along her banks, not realizing that one day she would provide him not only with the wonderful memories, but also an opportunity to save a life or two. While canoeing one day, Sam discovered a portion of the river that was shallow enough to cross with a rocky bluff on the western side. The bluff appeared to be a solid granite cliff running for at least a quarter of a mile along the river. About half way down the cliff was a cut-through in the rock that water and erosion had created over the centuries, making a perfect trail up to the old Oklahoma State highway 10 running from Joplin, Missouri to Tahlequah. The highway is rarely used anymore except by locals who cross it getting water from the river.

Several miles away from the secret path, Sam started crossing the river at shallow spots, sometimes walking up the river in hopes of slowing whoever may be trailing the girls. He had yet to see any indication of anyone on their back trail, but with years of experience he had grown paranoid. In fact, he was more cautious than ever because if they were back there, they knew the girls were no longer traveling alone. Paranoia is a term that sometimes carries a negative connotation. If you were labelled as paranoid in some settings, you may need counseling or medication. In survival situations, paranoia might save your life. Sam had become a healthy paranoid from being in law enforcement for thirty years, chasing murderers, sexual predators and any other type of depraved person involved in evildoings that would make a normal person's skin crawl. The current perspective of being paranoid meant that you were alive, that you were cautious enough to protect yourself, your loved ones and anyone else you deemed worthy of protecting, with the ultimate goal being survival.

The girls had accepted the fact that Sam was trying to help, but still chose to remain silent with a guarded attitude, indicating lack of trust. Theresa had spoken very few words since their first encounter, but had begun to be more polite, responding with a smile and a "thank you" or a "yes sir."

As they approached the secret path, Sam started humming an old hymn his Mom had taught him when he was very small. Theresa smiled and finished the song: "After I'd wandered in darkness astray, Jesus my savior I met." Theresa looked at Sam and for the first time since they had met, she seemed somewhat comforted. The hardness in her eyes had softened, and her expression was somewhat normal. Theresa looked to be about nineteen or twenty. The other three were no older than sixteen. It was apparent that they looked up to her as a big sister. Sam caught them at times speaking in hushed tones, but the minute they realized he was listening they would stop.

They arrived at the crossing and were almost into the woods on the other side of the river when Sam heard the clatter of shod horse hoofs on river rock. He looked downstream, spotting six men on horseback looking up and down the river – he knew immediately what they were searching for. The one in front looked directly at him and spurred his horse, urging him to charge in their direction. Sam quickly led Patton and the girls through the woods to the secret path, and as he removed his defense from their scabbards he shouted to them, "climb!" Theresa grabbed the reigns of Patton and coaxed him up through the path.

"Theresa!" he yelled.

She stopped and turned, tossing her his hat. He smiled and calmly said,

"Hold on to that. Go to the top of the bluff, turn right and find a place to hide. I'll be along shortly."

Sam turned and walked back toward the bank of the river as he rotated the AR-15 on the sling to his chest, allowing it to hang. He took the 450 marlin and trotted back to the edge of the river. The men on horseback were still a little more than seventy-five yards away. Shouldering the big bore rifle, he yelled, "U. S. Marshals, stay where you are." They continued to advance. Sam watched as the men drew closer and knew that he would not last very long if they stayed in the saddle. Sam loved horses, but this was life and death, and they were using those horses as a weapon against him. He squeezed the trigger on the lead horse. The 450 screamed as a deafening explosion of smoke and flame produced a freight train of lead from the end of its barrel. The first horse went down in a pile, and the rider fell hard into the river. Sam worked the lever, charging another round into the chamber and squeezed the trigger. As the second horse fell, Sam cycled his weapon and fired on the third, and then the fourth, and a few seconds later he was standing alone knee deep in the river. The river bottom was full of smoke, and the smell of burnt powder hung lazily in the air. Sam discarded the 450 and walked deliberately forward through the water, shouldering the AR-15 with a thirty round magazine. The six men were in a temporary state of shock, crashing to the ground as their horses fell. They were obviously not used to having a victim that would fight back.

"U. S. Marshal. Drop your weapons!" Sam yelled. Three of the men had yet to gain their feet. Two of the men were up but staggering, regaining their composure. One was standing, glaring at him with a gun in his hand. Sam aimed at the man and yelled, "Drop the weapon!" His friends were getting up, and he took a step. Seeming to gain confidence, he took another, and then he was running. He screamed, "Allaaahu Akbaaar!" As he ran, he lifted his rifle and Sam shot him, then shot him again and again until he fell, face down into the cold Illinois River.

Well, that was different, Sam thought.

The dead man's friends had gathered themselves behind his lifeless body, advancing with guns drawn. Sam leveled the gun at the closest one and started firing with immediate results. Bad guy leader number two went down, but his friends had started returning fire. Sam moved to the right looking for cover just as he felt a horrible, stabbing pain in his left shoulder. He went down just as he reached the bank, but raised his rifle with his right hand and continued to fire. Two men were down, floating the rapids downstream with four remaining and gaining ground. Sam crawled to a fallen log and tactically reloaded the AR-15. He crawled around the end of the tree, changing his position. He peeked around the stump and saw all four of the remaining men approaching the bank at the point where he had crawled ashore. Sam slowly moved up and into a shooting position. The idiot who elected himself to be bad guy leader number three leaned over the log Sam had previously been hiding behind, and immediately took a round to the head. *Three down three to go*, Sam thought.

Two men were frozen in fear, standing in the river staring at their dead friends and wondering where the shot had come from. Taking advantage of their hesitation, Sam finished them quickly. Sam then turned to see bad guy number six as he ran up the bank on the other side of the river into the bushes. Taking lead in the shoulder had minimized Sam's motivation to pursue a thug over the river and through the woods, so he laid there and bled. Minutes passed, and he knew two things: more bad guys may be on their way, and the girls needed his help. So, he gathered himself and staggered to the hidden path. He looked up toward the trail head and thought, *her face, but how? I can't be dreaming, not now, but it's her. How could she be here?* He stumbled as she reached out to help him … then darkness.

Dreams always confuse me. Why her? Why is it always her? Love is never simple. You see a person and feel different. Your heart leaps, you get chills, you long for that moment when they say, "I love you too." You build a dream, attempting to take your life in a deliberate direction. You think you have it all, the world by the tail, and life comes crashing down. A broken heart, an injured soul, each time building an armor over the emotions, pain creating a shield, a protective layer that gets harder and harder to penetrate. But why her? I haven't seen her in thirty years. How on God's green earth do you stop a dream?

CHAPTER 3

The sand was still comfortably warm under the setting sun as they danced. She was the most beautiful woman he had ever met. She was the essence of every flower, with black hair flowing to her waist and blue-green eyes that fed a thousand oceans. Sam could never completely describe her personality, mysterious and intelligent with a hint of bubbly cheerleader. They met on the beach at a concert in Biloxi, Mississippi. Their eyes met, and something happened that rarely happens in a lifetime. They shared the day and danced all evening until the sun set and the music stopped. As the roadies were breaking down the stage, the two were still wrapped around each other, dancing in the sand. *I wish that day had never ended*, Sam thought. They dated for a while, but life got in the way when Sam was hired by the U. S. Marshals Service and sent to Basic Training at the Federal Law Enforcement Training Center on the south Georgia coast.

By the time Sam had graduated from the Academy, she had disappeared and Sam assumed she must have married someone else. There were no cell phones then, or Internet. He never saw her again except in his dreams. Life as a Marshal was pretty complicated. The early 90s brought new missions to federal law enforcement. The increase of crime and the federalization of laws created a need for deputies to travel to special operations. These operations, in turn, created trials that Deputies ultimately had to support.

In 1993, a group of terrorists rocked the very foundation of the United States of America by driving a bomb into the basement of the Trade Center in New York City. Terror was attacking us on the home front. But it was just the tip of the iceberg. Islam was at war with the United States and wanted to destroy all that western civilization stood for, and in the era of political correctness no one would admit that an age-old enemy was still threatening us. Islam would not rest until Christianity was totally destroyed, and Islam maintained world control with their theocracy. On September 11, 2001, they succeeded further by crashing two airliners into the Twin Towers. That, combined with a perfect storm of political failure lasting for more than two decades, eventually brought Camelot to its knees.

Wow, Sam thought. *Love, politics, and where the hell am I?* Sam's dream had turned into a rambling chain of memories and thought. Strange, being asleep and being aware of being asleep, dreaming and being aware that it is a dream. Or did I die and this is hell. "Wow," Sam said out loud. He blinked and gasped for air, rolled out of his bed, and landed roughly on his knees. *A bed?* He thought. Sam sat there on the floor for a moment gathering himself, grasping at realty, trying to remember the last thing he could fathom. The mountains … the girls … The gunfight! *Oh hell, my shoulder*, he thought. Lord it was sore. My wound was bandaged. Where were the girls? Where the heck was I?

Looking around the room, Sam realized he was in someone's home. He picked himself up and limped to the window before he realized he was naked, and clean! His mind was racing; his shoulder was stitched and bandaged. *What in the world is going on?* He thought.

Suddenly, there was a knock on the door.

"Come in," he said, diving underneath the covers of the bed.

Theresa opened the door and walked in the room, having taken this opportunity to shed her winter clothes and remove the dirt from weeks of surviving in a frozen wilderness. She was a radiant, beautiful young woman with striking features.

"You're staring," she said….

"I'm sorry," Sam replied. "It's just that you remind me of someone… from long ago." Theresa smiled, walked to the bed and set the clothes down. They were washed and repaired, patches closing the rips and holes left over from the fight in the river.

"Who was she?"

Sam paused, looking for a way to answer the question and finally said, "She was a very special lady from my past. I wished things would have turned out differently but life got in the way."

"Are you hungry?"

"Absolutely," Sam replied.

"Dinner is ready".

She turned and gracefully walked out of the bedroom as if they had done this a hundred times before. Still in shock and very sore, Sam gingerly put on his clothes and found his way through the house and into the kitchen. Sitting at the table were the three other girls, an older man, and there was Theresa. The man rose as Sam approached the table.

"Call me Tom, Tom Eagle Feather," he said.

"Welcome to my home."

Tom was an older man, maybe in his early seventies with long gray hair braided down his back, wearing a plaid flannel shirt with blue jeans and cowboy boots. The table appeared to be set for Thanksgiving dinner with the exception of a turkey. Instead there was a large roast, an enormous chunk of meat that could last for several days.

A wood stove burned in the corner of the kitchen, giving a soft aroma of oak. On top of the stove were two pans. In one pan, Theresa stirred wild turnips seasoned with black pepper and bacon fat. In the other pan, pinto beans lay simmering with wild onions. It smelled like heaven. Sam stood at the edge of the table with his mouth open and drooling. *I haven't seen a spread like this in over a decade*. He thought.

"Tom, where did the meat come from?"

"Well, me and several friends were comin back from Tahlequah when we heard W-W IV break out down in the river bottom. After the dust cleared, we saw these young ladies leading that horse of yours up outta that trail. We offered to help, and Miss Theresa ran back down the trail so I followed her down to the river. We picked up your guns for ya, and these young ladies cleaned and oiled 'em. They're over in the shed with the rest of your gear. I put your horse out in the pasture behind the barn. Do you really need me to tell you where that roast came from?" he said as he smiled a crooked smile.

"No," Sam laughed, "I guess not." Fresh meat was hard to come by these days. Six fresh killed horses could feed a small town for a couple of weeks.

"Just don't get any ideas about my horse," Sam laughed.

They all sat down, Tom said grace and they began to eat. All that could be heard was the clinking of utensils on the plates, and the occasional sigh of someone getting a full belly. It had been too long since Sam had eaten like this.

"Tom, are we safe here?"

"You betcha," he replied. "My ranch here is in the middle of the res. Yor bad luck brought us meat. Me and my brothers won't forget that."

"What tribe is this?" Sam asked.

"Back when anyone gave a damn, this was Cherokee land; but none of that matters anymore, does it?"

After dinner, Tom put on a pot of coffee. Sam sat across the table from Theresa and her three friends. He tapped his finger on the table for a few seconds, seeming to be lost in thought. He then pushed his chair back a bit, folding his arms as he rolled a toothpick across his mouth.

"I think it's time that we start talking about who you are, where you're from, and who is chasing you," Tom said.

Theresa looked at him. "I'm pretty sure we can trust you, but I don't even know your name."

Sam blushed and stumbled for a second. "I'm sorry miss, I spend a lot of time alone, and social skills sometimes escape me. My name is Samson Crow. My friends call me Sam."

Theresa sat staring at him for a moment with a puzzled yet curious look on her face. "That's a very unique name … Sam Crow … really?" She continued to look suspiciously at Sam, or as though she were keeping something hidden.

Tom broke the awkward silence as he returned to the table with a pot of cowboy coffee and cups.

"How long you been a Marshal, Sam?"

"Too long." Realizing this man who had basically saved their lives deserved a better answer than that, Sam added, "Almost thirty years. Although it hasn't been much of a job since the Fall, we are happy to let the locals enforce the law. The Government in D.C. still wanted a Federal presence in Neverland, and Marshals were the only law enforcement authorized by the Constitution. Although there are agents here from the FBI and ATF, they just help out in investigations." He looked back to Theresa. "Can you tell me where you're from?"

"I'm really not sure," she said. She hesitated, then and started to rise as if to leave the table, but instead settled in her chair and took a long, deep breath. She began talking and soon her story unfolded, describing a relatively short life of hardship and pain for all four girls.

"I was born in a place that's hard to describe. It's like a compound or a military installation. Mom was one of many women who were kidnapped at an early age. They were chosen because of their youth and beauty and taken to a place where they were made into slaves." She stopped for a moment, obviously gathering herself and controlling her emotions.

"Please, take your time but tell me more about the compound," Sam asked.

"It's huge. It's about the size of a town and has stores, a school, parks and even a hospital. Some of us are taught a profession, but most are just taught how to be better slaves. We're trained with weapons, how to use and maintain them as well as clean them. We are also trained as combat medics. I not only cleaned your weapons, but tended your shoulder. As slaves, our primary duty is to keep the men happy," she paused again looking down at her hands, and she started to shake. "In every way." She continued, "The girls were taken from all over the country. Once processed, they were given to the men in camp, beginning with the highest commanding officer. If he liked what he saw, he could keep a slave for as long as he wanted, but once he got tired of her, he could pass her down to the next in command. This only stops when a slave becomes pregnant. Once pregnant, the slave is taken to a different part of the compound and no one is allowed to touch her. If the baby is a girl, she is raised within the compound to be a breeder. Records are maintained so that no inbreeding occurs, but if there is a deformity or an undesirable trait, the infant is immediately killed and cremated. If the baby is a boy, he is raised as a soldier, trained in their ways, waiting for their army to be complete." Theresa had tears in her eyes. "I wanted to get pregnant. I really did. Just so that they would leave me alone."

Sam shook his head as his eyes started to tear up, feeling every bit of her pain. Tom's mouth was hanging open in shock. The other three girls were looking at their friend, seeing her through their own pain and tears.

"What does 'trained in their ways' mean?"

"Islam," She replied with her anger returning, "Jihad. They will not stop until every infidel head is bowed to Allah, or severed."

"How many soldiers do they have?" Sam asked.

"Thousands, they have been kidnapping kids for years. If you can't have children, then you are sold as sex slaves to people in other countries. We had been bought by someone in South America, and were being transported to the airport during a storm when our van crashed. The guards looked unconscious, or dead, so we ran. Because of the storm, the wreck wasn't discovered until it cleared the next day. By then we were several miles away. I hoped the storm would take care of our tracks, but I knew they'd probably find us."

"How many girls are enslaved there?"

"At least one for every man, some commanders are rewarded by having multiple girls, or boys."

"So, let me get this right ... Somewhere in Arkansas there is a hidden city of Muslims, a city that sustains itself, that's heavily fortified, and is a training camp for the future destruction of America?"

"Not destruction," she said. "Conversion," she continued. "It's my understanding that it is not the only city. There are several. I'm not sure exactly where, but they are located throughout the country, hidden in mountainous regions or old military bases."

Sam stood briefly in silence thinking about Theresa's comment. His past included working with the Anti-Terrorism Task force and handling past Islamic terrorists. What Theresa had not mentioned was the fact that these girls were probably being enslaved and raped as early as six years old. Pedophilia and child brides are well accepted within the Muslim culture. Muhammed himself was a pedophile, marrying his wife Aisha when she was only eight years old.

"How has this gone unnoticed?" he asked.

Theresa replied, "I remember when I was young, a sitting President toured the facility." Tom choked on his coffee and had to clean it off his shirt. Theresa looked at him and said, "It's been here much longer than you can imagine. Children have been going missing for years and their pictures placed on milk cartons, but they were never seen again. That's how they recruit." Theresa then looked directly at Sam and said, "My mother was taken in Biloxi when she was nineteen, and that was thirty years ago. I think you know her."

Silence filled the room. Sam blinked a few times, trying to process her words. He shook his head and looked at Theresa in denial, seeming to hold his breath. He leaned forward, gathered himself and took a deep breath before saying, "Tom, got anything stronger than coffee?"

Tom rolled his eyes as though this were a stupid question, looked at him with his crooked grin and said, "You betcha. Be right back." Tom left the room and returned moments later with a large Mason jar with a clear liquid in it. He poured a shot and slid it across the table to Sam. Tom offered without any prompting, somewhat proud of his concoction, "It's muscadine moonshine, an old family recipe."

The moonshine made Sam's eyes water as it warmed the back of his throat. Sam closed his eyes tightly as he sat the glass down, and in the darkness he still saw her face with that warm beautiful smile. As he opened his eyes facing Theresa, he realized at that moment there was no doubt that she was Jennifer's daughter.

Sam leaned back toward Theresa and asked, "What about your mother?"

Theresa looked back with tears in her eyes and said, "I don't know. I haven't seen her in almost six months. I think they realized we were too close and moved her to one of the other compounds somewhere in Colorado. We are not supposed to know who our mothers and fathers are."

"What's her name?"

"Jennifer," she replied. "Jennifer Boudreaux."

Sam was now at a loss for words. A thousand "what if's" were racing through his mind. Imprisoned for thirty years by terrorists, used for God knows what. He rose slowly, left the room and walked outside. The cold winter wind hit Sam in the face, and he embraced it and welcomed the feeling, hoping that somehow it would dull the thought of where Jennifer may be right now…or if she were even alive. He leaned on the porch railing and realized how tired he was. He suddenly felt the soreness in his shoulder, and asked himself what the hell was he going to do with these girls. Home was two days by horseback from here, he thought.

It was obvious that the only option was to take them home and try to find out where they were from, maybe find their relatives.

Sam returned to the house and saw Theresa sitting there. She looked at him and said, "Mom used to tell me about you when I was little. She would make up stories of a man she met on the beach. Hoping and praying that one day he would come. She stopped telling me those stories, but I know she never lost hope. She told me once a long time ago that you were in Tulsa, and that's where we were headed after the crash." Sam looked squarely at her. "We'll find your Mom, but first I need to get home. We leave at day-break tomorrow."

CHAPTER 4

As morning broke, they bid farewell to Tom and started on their way. Tom loaned Sam two pack horses for the trip, hoping that with all the girls on horseback they could make it home by sundown. They traveled north to Oklahoma Highway 412, then turned west. The highway at one time had been a turnpike, and was well maintained. It had become neglected over the years, but a company called World Pro was working a deal with the States to help maintain it. It was one of the only regularly used highways due to commerce between Western Arkansas and Tulsa. Basically, Tulsa needed goods provided by the company formerly known as Walmart. Once international trade crumbled, the biggest corporations recognized the need to return to home grown manufacturing and production. Walmart changed their name as well as their entire business plan, and started production instead of just distribution which created a surge in an otherwise failing economy. They now call themselves World Production and Manufacturing, or World Pro. Northwestern Arkansas is one of the only regions in the world that has shown consistent economic growth since the Fall. World Pro still has a few stores, but only in the biggest communities unlike back in the day when Walmart was on every corner.

Life had treated Sam well over the years and he loved his work. His job kept him occupied and left him with not much of a personal life, but as life goes he met a younger beautiful woman named Melissa. They dated for almost a year and on Sadie Hawkins day, she asked him to marry her. Sam laughed and said, "Why not." They were married by Judge McClintock in a small ceremony, and later bought a small ranch. They rode their horses and enjoyed a simple, unassuming life together, not paying attention to the chaos that existed in the world around them. Melissa was a petite, passionate woman who loved Sam more than life itself. The first wave of the pandemic took Melissa from him, but while she still fought for her life in the hospital, they found out she was not alone.

Losing Melissa and the child caused an emotional void in Sam that made him cold for a while; he lost himself in his work and created a world for himself where love was impossible, thinking that love had slipped through his fingers for the last time. His job became his wife, and at fifty-three he was looking for a way out. *Retirement would be somewhat of a divorce*, he thought. *I just hope they don't take half of my stuff.*

The house was large enough to provide the girls with plenty of room for a while, and as they grew to know each other, Sam started to enjoy them. Each had a unique personality, and they all seemed to complement one another. The three younger girls started opening up a little. In fact, their constant chatter became somewhat over the top at times, but after what they had been through, they deserved it. The oldest was Elise at sixteen, Tiffany at fourteen, and then Sara at thirteen.

Sam's house was solid brick with a hidden safe room under the kitchen. The microwave pushbutton panel provided access to the security system and safe room. The limited electricity the solar system provided made running a microwave somewhat wasteful. The panel of the microwave was wired into the bunker door, allowing access by pushing the combination on the microwave. The kitchen was designed years before the Fall, initially as a storm cellar, but as the world became progressively worse, Sam recognized the need to use it for protection from things other than weather. It also provided a place to store defenses, food and valuables.

Neverland had to be a model for everything Socialists and Communists hated. Everyone pulled their weight in one form or the other. Crime rates plummeted, and life was flourishing without the nuisance of federal intervention. Unfortunately, even though Sam was close to retirement, he still had to report for duty every now and then. It was one of the few occasions on which he was allowed to drive the government vehicle. In 2019, the president decided to make all federal vehicles electric. Sam was lucky enough to keep his older hybrid, maintaining a little good old fashioned fossil fuel torque under the hood. The younger deputies were fighting over the new all-electric cars, not realizing what a hassle they can be.

Sam left for work at sunrise, arriving early enough to make the first pot of coffee. He typed the report on the Illinois River shooting, excluding much of the non-essential information related to Theresa and her friends. There was no way to know how many people were involved in this Islam Conversion Conspiracy, and Sam was not going to take any chances. His retirement paperwork lay on the desk next to his name plate, requiring only a signature. He glanced at it as he walked by and smiled. *Time sure flies*, he thought. *What would life be like without a badge? The internet along with much of the cell phone grid, was gone. New York City and Los Angeles were supposedly back up and running, but who cares? They can have it. I started this job without a cell phone or internet, and it looked as if I would leave it the same way.* Land lines connected the main offices, but since there was no security on land lines, they had basically reverted to a system of communication by horseback. Sam smiled again and thought, *Sixty years ago we landed men on the moon, but after the Fall we were basically back to the Pony Express.*

As lunch approached, Sam called an old friend on the second floor who worked at the National Security Agency. Doc answered his phone as usual and Sam said, "What's up Doc?"

"Oh hell, Sam, that never gets old. How ya been brother?"

"Lovin' life man, I have a tale to tell. You wanna run down the street and grab some Coney's? I'm buying."

"Well of course I do. Free food is good food. Race you to the front door."

Doc had been around federal law enforcement forever, it seemed. Starting with the Border Patrol around 1980, then transferring to ATF and then the FBI. With three years remaining before mandatory retirement, he transferred to the NSA, who let him extend for ten more years. He started working for the government more than a decade before Sam, and he was an enormous resource for information. If he didn't know it, he knew someone who did. As they walked toward the Coney Islander he asked, "What are you digging for?"

"I am looking for a secret facility in Colorado that is either former military or nonmilitary."

He stopped, looked at Sam with his head tilted sideways and said, "This doesn't sound much like a Marshal's jurisdiction".

"It isn't, and it's going to upset a whole bunch of people when this story blows."

They turned and continued walking. They ordered the Coney's and found a bench away from the crowd, where Sam told Doc about the Illinois River shootout. Nothing usually fazed Doc, but he took the situation with the girls pretty hard. Doc had lost a wife and two daughters during the pandemic, and like most emotional scars they ran deep and never seemed to heal. Doc promised to make some calls and added, "You know this could be a career ender."

"I know," Sam said, shaking his head.

"You also should be prepared for the worst. Once they find out who you are, they will come for you with everything they have."

"I know that as well."

"Take care," he replied. "I'll definitely be in touch. Oh, and watch your back, brother."

Sam took the elevator into the basement, squeezed into the hybrid and headed home. As he pulled into the drive he saw three horses tied to the fence over by the barn. He quickly parked the car on the other side of the house and walked inside, mindful of Doc's "watch your back" comment. The house was quiet and appeared empty, so he stepped outside onto the back porch and heard voices coming from the barn. Drawing his Glock, Sam approached the barn door using a row of trees for cover. Once outside the door, he could hear one of the girls giggling. He stepped through the door, gun drawn, and there was Tom, the girls, a man he did not know, and Bad Guy Number Six wrapped in duct tape hanging by a harness from the rafters. The girls had formed a circle around him and they were pushing him back and forth, swinging him across and watching him spin. The girls were enjoying this way too much. "Do you girls know this guy?" Sam asked.

"No sir, but I think he deserves a little torture," Elise, responded bobbing her head side to side.

"I agree," Sam said. "But you girls need to leave." They reluctantly left the barn and Sam looked at Tom. "Where did you find him?"

"Well a couple of days after ya left, my buddy David here came to the house complainin' that he had been missin' some eggs. You had told us about the one that got away, and we all thought that he would probably run back home. We had taken a map and a compass off of one of the others, but this guy being a young pup was probably just along for the ride. I guess he couldn't find home, so he started helpin himself to David's eggs. So David set a trap. He put a latch on the outside of the chicken coop that would fall into place after the door closed, moved the chickens into the barn and put his Rottweiler in the coop. Number Six got a big surprise. He and Ronald got intimate for about five minutes before we could drag him out of the coop. We patched him up, tied him up, and brought him to ya."

"Ronald? Who's Ronald?"

"David's dog," Tom replied.

Sam looked at David. "You named your Rott Ronald?"

David shrugged. "Named him after Reagan." Sam reached up and ripped the duct tape from the young man's mouth. He looked at the boy as he was working his mouth back and forth. That had probably hurt a bit with that semi-peach-fuzz beard of his. "How old are you?" The boy glared at Sam in defiance and seemed to tighten his lips in a show of fortitude. Sam laughed, tilted his hat back, looked at Tom and said, "What do you think Tom? Should I kill him?" Sam still had the Glock in his hand, and Number Six glanced down at it.

"Well at least we know he speaks English. Tom, do you and David want to spend the night here? The girls usually cook a pretty good meal, and I've got a bottle of whiskey I haven't broken the seal on yet." Number Six was getting upset that he was no longer the center of attention.

David and Tom looked at each other and responded without hesitation. "Yes sir," David said. "We would love some good company this evening."

Sam turned to Number Six and said, "Young man, I don't have much time for you. I will give you time to think about an opportunity, one chance only. You can help me and do what's right, or you can choose a very hard road. Ultimately, I will win either way. It is totally up to you to figure out what you are willing to endure." Sam took him down from the rafters and put leg irons on him with belly chains, hand cuffs and a black box. The black box fits over the hand cuffs, preventing excess movement and access to the key holes. He tied him back up, making a more secure harness out of the rope and hoisted him back into the rafters. He then took another small strip of duct tape, placed it over his mouth and asked, “Did you understand everything I just said?” He glared back at Sam, indicating that he was a little angry. “Young man, this will end only one way. You can give me the stink eye all you want, but I will win, with or without your help. Now I am going inside to enjoy a meal with my friends. I’ll come back in a little while to see if you are willing to change your mind. If you still choose to be stubborn, I am going to stake you to a log and cover you with pig guts. Then I am going to pour gasoline on you and light you up. Now to make sure you understand what that means ... you die covered in pig guts, you’re not making it to paradise, and you won’t see your virgins either. You got that?” His gaze softened a bit and he nodded affirmatively. Sam turned abruptly and walked back to the house for supper. He walked through the door and smiled. They were having ribs.

CHAPTER 5

After supper the men returned to the barn. Sam walked through the barn door first, checking on Number Six as Tom and David waited outside. He seemed content enough, still swinging a bit from his useless struggle to defeat Smith and Wesson's finest handcuffs. Sam looked up at him and winked. Sam had intentionally left the barn doors open so that Number Six could look across the yard and see how much fun they were all having as they enjoyed supper. Apparently the wind was right because the smell of the smoke from the ribs and the yeast rolls Theresa had made still lingered; they smelled wonderful, even with a full belly. Sam reached up and pulled the tape from his mouth, grabbed a chair, spun it around to face him and sat down, leaning on the back of the chair. He stared at Number Six for a minute and waited until the silence made him uncomfortable. His eyes darted from Sam, to the door, over to the house, back to Sam.

"How old are you?" Sam asked.

"Twenty," he replied. He looked it. *Young, indestructible, living for the here and now, full of a false sense of badass, just like me a long time ago,* Sam thought. Number Six was five feet eight inches, one-seventy maybe. A brown mop for hair, light skinned but tanned, a rough complexion indicating typical male hormones for his age.

"What's your name?" Fatigue was wearing him down. It's amazing how quickly you can lose your mean button when you're tired, dehydrated and famished. The smell of those pork ribs had to be killing him, even if he was a Muslim. "I'm going to ask you one more time. What's your name?" He looked directly at Sam and started to say something, but paused. He mustered some strength and hit the mean button again, glared at Sam and looked out the barn door. "Tom," Sam called loudly. Tom rounded the corner and walked through the door pushing a wheelbarrow full of seasoned oak. On top of the pile was a can of gasoline.

Tom stopped just inside the door and said, "Where you want it?"

"Better take it out back of the barn, probably close to where we burned the last body."

Tom walked straight through the barn out the back door and disappeared into the darkness. Sam looked back at Number Six, and no amount of mean button could overcome the look on his face. He even started twisting in his restraints again. "Six," he said, "you know those cuffs won't give. Settle down. Dave, go get the pig." Minutes later they could hear Dave coming with the squealing pig, getting louder as he got closer. Sam looked at Six, and he was pale, mean button disengaged.

"Where ya want him?" Dave yelled from outside the barn.

"Out back," Sam said. "Look for Tom back there." Dave stayed outside the barn and walked toward the back carrying a screaming pig. "Lord that is a horrible sound. Six, one last try buddy … talk, or trade your virgins for a pig. What'll it be?" He hesitated and Sam yelled, "Dave, gut that pig!" The pig squealed for a moment, then silence. Six wavered a bit, as if he would faint. Sam reached up and cut him down, letting him drop to the ground. Sam then grabbed the leg irons, turned and started dragging him to the back of the barn.

"No, No, my name is Daniel," he cried. "I'll talk, I'll talk, I don't want to die."

Sam set him up against a stable door post and said, "Well son, for now you have a reprieve, but one lie or one hesitation and it's gonna be a barbeque." He sat there, licked his chapped lips and started talking. "I didn't even want this," he said. "I was eight, homeless, living in a shelter in Shreveport when they came and took me. They promised a life of everything I ever dreamed of." He paused, caught his breath and licked his lips again.

"Daniel, they sold you a lie, and I believe you know it." Sam walked over to the well pump and got him a cup of water. He grabbed a chair and placed it in front of him, sat down and leaned in close. "This bunch you've been runnin' with is pure evil! They will fall, and their false god can't stop it."

"I grew up in a church mister, at least until everybody got sick. Mom and Dad died, and I tried to help my little sister but she died too."

"Daniel, where is the compound you were living in?"

"Buffalo National River, close to Ponca," he replied.

"That's a long river, and some very big country."

"Yessir, it is, easy to get lost in. That's why it took us so long to catch up to the girls."

"How did you find them?" Sam asked.

"The first guy you killed was a master tracker, he's mean, kills for fun … the girls are lucky you came along. We weren't there to bring 'em back. They were gonna die that day."

Sam looked at him, shaking his head. "And you'd just watch?"

"Dude, I was surviving. I didn't say I liked it or agreed with it. I couldn't stop the tracker if I wanted to, and there were four others with him."

"Dude? Did you just call me Dude?"

"No sir, I mean yessir, I'm sorry sir." He stammered. Confused and desperate, Number Six slumped into a worn out young boy with not much left but a whimper.

Sam lifted his head and gave him some more water.

"Daniel, I need a few more answers before we are done. Can you help me? How many of those guys are there?"

"Hundreds," Daniel said flatly. "And they have lots of guns and weapons. Everything you can think of."

"Where do they get them?" I asked.

"The military mostly," he replied. "Trucks arrive all the time loaded with pallets full of guns, ammo, everything you need to fight a war. They even have a few tanks."

Leaning back, Sam rubbed his face with both hands, took his hat off and scratched his head. What was left of the elite in Washington were pooling their resources, manipulating defense spending and funding terrorists in our own backyard. They had created strongholds of evil throughout this country, preparing to end the American Dream forever. "Daniel, one more thing, is there another installation, maybe in Colorado?"

"Salida," he replied. "I've been there. It used to be a mine. After I got picked up in Shreveport, that's where they took me first. It's where they used to process the new guys.

"How long were you there?"

"Fifteen weeks. Back then it was mostly underground. They do some really terrible things there, brainwashing kids and all. I learned pretty quick how to act. If you adapt quickly they leave you alone. The sooner you adapt, the sooner you get to leave. I was there long enough to see the Sheikh. He likes young boys and picks the prettiest ones for his own. Glad I'm not that pretty."

"Where does he stay?" Sam asked.

"During the winter he lives in the Florida compound, but they say he can't stand the humidity during the summers down there, so he moves to Salida."

"What month was it when you saw him in Salida?"

"June, two days before my birthday," he replied.

"How long has it been since you've been there?"

"Oh it's been awhile, five years maybe."

"Do you think you can find it again?"

He looked at Sam as if he had lost his mind. "Dude, are ya crazy? I mean sir, so sorry sir."

"Focus," Sam said. "Get back on topic."

Daniel paused to gather his thoughts and said, "Well yeah, it's easy. North of Highway 50 at the base of Aspen Ridge. But the whole valley is part of the compound now."

Salida was a beautiful town nestled in between the eastern and western slopes of the Rocky Mountains in central Colorado. It was a town created by the railroad more than a century ago that supported mining and the related trades of prostitution and gambling. Apparently not much had changed in a hundred years, just a different kind of bad.

Sam removed the restraints from Daniel (all but the handcuffs), untied the ropes and stood him up. His legs all but collapsed beneath him. Sam lifted him, bringing him to his feet and steadied him against a rail. Daniel almost seemed thankful, but was still fighting with his mean button, and it was obvious that he was torn between the deception he had lived for the past decade and reality.

"Tom! Dave!" Sam shouted. "We're good." They strolled through the barn walking side by side, both with a big grin. As they passed by, Dave did his best pig call… "WEEEEEEEEEE, WEEEEEEE!"

Daniel turned red, embarrassed. "Just so you know. The pig thing wasn't scaring me. It was the dying part that I didn't agree with."

"Daniel," Sam said. "One more thing … would you like some ribs?"

CHAPTER 6

Monday night was a full house with four girls, one semi-bad guy and three old men. Daniel was handcuffed and leg-ironed with the chain of the leg-iron threaded through the handle of a 75-pound kettle bell. Daniel may be able to lift the kettle bell, but he would not be able to get very far. Even though he had eaten his fair share of pork ribs, Sam still hesitated to trust him. As he sat in his recliner listening to the conversations of his company, his mind was elsewhere contemplating the nature of Islam and his experience with those that he had dealt with in the past. Islam is a strange religion to the West. Where Christians spread the word of God to save souls, Islam spreads the Quran with the intent of world domination by theocracy using fear and intimidation to manipulate the ignorant. Islam has been at war with everyone who is not Islam for almost 1500 years. Islam has made it clear that, given the opportunity, they will eventually take over the world and destroy any resistance. The problem with trusting Daniel is that within Islam, there is a practice called Taquiyya. Taquiyya allows a follower to do anything he can to further the mission of Islam. Muslims are allowed to deceive, cheat, even pretend to be Christian to move Islam forward toward the ultimate goal, without condemnation. So Daniel could eat pork and deny Islam to deceive without being held accountable, because he would be furthering the mission of Islam. Islam's mission is evil. Its purpose has always been to convert or destroy. Sam never had a doubt that God put him here for a reason, and he could not imagine that God ever created men like him to turn the other cheek when evil was advancing. No, Sam thought. It would be quite a while before he could trust Daniel.

The sleeping arrangements were not that difficult. The girls were in their rooms, Tom and David shared Sam's king size bed, Daniel was on the couch with his kettle bell, and Sam was in his recliner. Daniel turned on the couch trying to get comfortable locked in his chains. He looked in Sam's direction and Sam was leaned back with his feet up reclining. He had a double barrel shotgun across his lap, looking directly at him.

Tuesday was typical. Sam woke and rubbed his sore neck. *Hell, everything is sore when you reach fifty*, he thought. Theresa was in the kitchen making a pot of coffee. Sam walked in and looked at the clock, "Five a.m.? Why are you up?" He asked.

"Habit, I suppose. We all get up at five at the compound. Our day starts early, we all have jobs. Kids are in school, the rest of us work at whatever we are assigned. We not only had mandatory school, but a workout schedule that we followed until we were too old to reproduce. After that we cooked and cleaned. Ya know, slave stuff."

"Theresa, how has your mother stayed there so long?"

Theresa fumbled with some dishes for a minute, grabbed a towel and dried her hands. She grabbed a cup of coffee and sat down in a chair.

"I think she was one of the first to be taken. The Imams, the leaders, have always looked for special people, you know. They like smart, pretty people. That's why they took Mom. She had it all, but I guess you knew that." She smiled.

"Go on, why is she still there?"

"Well pretty girls are a dime a dozen, but IQs of 175 are pretty rare. She was given a career placement test, and blew the tops off the scores in medicine. They were more than happy to send her to a private medical school in South America owned by the Saudi's. She was the Senior Chief of Staff in the hospital on base and was in charge of all the medical training. Well, she was until they moved her. I was recently scheduled to attend medical school as well."

"Medical school?" Sam said, very surprised. "How old are you?"

"Nineteen. The education program is accelerated. We graduate high school at fourteen. If our placement scores suggest college, we have a bachelor's degree by eighteen. They have cut out all the unnecessary classes, and by controlling our career placement we don't waste our time taking classes we don't need. They streamlined the process and made it much more efficient."

"For a machine," Sam said.

"Wait, what? I don't follow....why does that make us like a machine?"

"Well, it's pure communism. From birth, your life is not your own. You are a slave to whatever they want you to be. You have no choice in anything you do. The first real choice you made was the day you ran away from the wreck. How does it feel here knowing that if you do not want to get out of bed, just snuggle up and get comfy, if you don't want to cook or clean, that is fine? Life is about the freedom of choice, being free to make the right choice, knowing that you will be held responsible for the wrong choice. Living a life without choices isn't life. It is slavery."

Sam paused, sat quietly for a moment in thought and finally said, "Theresa, was your mom ever uh, in the, uh, with someone?"

Theresa laughed and stopped Sam before things got any more awkward. "No, once she began school, she was never required to take part in the process of satisfying the men. In fact, no one was allowed to approach her that way. It has been very lonely for her."

Sam looked at her, his expression asking the obvious question he had been trying to ask.

"Oh, yeah, me, I see your confusion. Well, Mom is just like anyone else. She did have a 'moment' with a fellow Doctor. They had worked together for several years without any problems. He was an orthopedic surgeon. One day there was a terrible accident where a kid lost his leg. They both knew that if they didn't save him and his leg, he would be killed. They both worked on the boy for hours when his heart just quit. He was unable to fight any longer. Mom was devastated. After they finished, they cleaned themselves up and went to her office to finalize the death report of the boy. They somehow found comfort in their common cause, had a romantic moment, and one thing led to another. Then boom! Here I am."

"Where is your father?" Sam asked.

"Dead," Theresa replied. "After Mom started showing, they put two and two together and sent him to the Florida Base. He was there for six months when he was diagnosed with a very progressive case of prostate cancer. Two months after he started chemo, he died. I was born two weeks later."

"Wow, I'm sorry."

"Don't be," she replied. "He was no one to me."

Sam could tell she cared more than she wanted to show. She had not known him, but she wanted to. Every baby girl needs a dad. Sam gave her a hug and then glanced at the clock, realizing he needed to get moving. He showered, dressed, and bid farewell to Tom and David. He then hopped in the faithful old hybrid, and once on the road realized it was time to make a plan. This was much bigger than he initially thought: multiple compounds as big as small cities existing under our noses, funded somewhat by our own government, not to mention the kidnapping and slavery that was occurring all in the name of Islam. There was no doubt in his mind. There was going to be war.

CHAPTER 7

Sam turned right onto Denver Avenue and continued past the Tulsa County Court House. He crossed 4th Street and waited in the turning lane. In the oncoming lane approaching from the north was Doc, grinning as he turned ahead of Sam and cutting him off, then pulling down the ramp leading down into the parking garage. Doc rolled his window down and threw a peace sign as he produced his security card to open the automatic door. As the door slowly rose, Sam caught movement in the corner of his eye up and to his left. Standing at the rail above the entry ramp was a man in a ski mask. He racked the action of a shotgun, leaned over the railing and started pumping rounds into Docs car. Doc's body jerked with the vicious assault, and his head slumped forward. Sam drew his gun, but the shooter had already moved from the rail.

Sam jumped out of the hybrid, ran up the hill to the ten minute parking lot and saw an old Honda motorcycle as it sped away south on Denver Avenue, already passing the Tulsa Library. Sirens were blaring, people were screaming and Doc was dead. Sam walked down to his car, leaned in his open window and turned off his ignition. He went to sit on the concrete wall next to the ramp, and wept. Doc was the last of many good men Sam had known and worked with throughout the years, and as he sat there watching the emergency teams arrive, he realized his mission.

Sam got up and moved his car out of the way so the emergency crews could pull in, then drove around to the back parking lot and entered the building through the front door. He greeted the guys at the metal detectors and walked around to the garage ramp where Doc still sat in his car. Police and crime scene investigators were pawing over every inch of ground close by. Another hybrid pulled into the ten minute parking lot, and the door opened. It was the last remaining FBI agent in Tulsa. They left him alone because, like Sam, he was too old and mean to move anywhere else. Also, they had to keep an FBI agent around for this very reason. The FBI's jurisdiction included leading the investigation for the murder or assassination of any federal law enforcement agent, regardless of agency.

"It's been awhile, Sam. Not many people go hunting law enforcement in Neverland anymore. This is pretty strange."

"I know, Ben." Sam looked at the ground and then glanced up at the American flag flying on the pole on the corner of 4th and Denver. "I have a feeling I know why this happened."

Ben looked at Sam over the top of his reading glasses and replied, "That so … why don't you tell me about it?"

"Not here, let's go for a walk when you're done at the crime scene. I'll meet you at the 21st and Riverside bridge parking lot at noon."

Sam walked away, left Ben to his work and returned inside the Federal Building. As he passed his old P.O. Box he thought, *what the heck.* He opened the door, and the hinges cried in protest. Mail only ran once a week now, and Sam had not received mail in a very long time. Now he only checked it once or twice a month. Not many people maintain a P.O. Box, and because they have so many vacant, they let the Deputies have one for free. There is probably some sort of policy violation here, but there is no one left who cares. Surprisingly, inside the box was an 8 x10 manila envelope. It was rolled to fit into the box. No return address, one simple word on the front: "Sam," in Doc's handwriting. He quickly tucked it inside his jacket, closed the door to the box and walked to the elevators.

Sam walked into the main area of the United States Marshals Service Office without a word, continuing past his office and into the Chiefs office. He sat down and looked across the desk at his Chief. His eyes were red. He had just finished typing a memo to Headquarters, informing them about Doc. Doc was a legend in his own right. Heroes do not always show up on the front page. Most often they are found in the background, fighting the fight against evil where no one can see. Every person Sam knew in law enforcement was a patriot, sworn to uphold and protect the Constitution. Every now and then a bad one comes along, but most brothers and sisters of the badge are heroes. They fight evil for low pay, cheap equipment and long hours. The reward, more often than not, is a divorce from a person leaving you with not much more than your job and a bottle. Your friends are your coworkers, the only ones you trust, even if there are some you dislike, they still always have your back. It is a family bound by blood and stronger than steel, with Doc being one of the best.

"What do you want, Sam?" Chief sounded tired, and it was only 11:00 a.m. Chief was a hardcore, old school cop. He played baseball in college at Oklahoma State University and was drafted in the third round, only to blow out his knee during his first season in the minors. Peter Campanova applied to the U.S. Marshals about two weeks before Sam, and went through basic in the class ahead of him. They worked for years in different offices, but together many times on the same cases or special assignments. Chief was born to work, and sometimes seemed a little over the top when it came to motivation. He was always a great boss, and even a better friend. Once he was promoted, he insisted that Sam still call him by his first name. Sam disagreed and told him, "You earned this title, Chief. I'm not going to call you Chief Peter, that just sounds a little wrong and Chief Campanova is too long, so I'll just simply call you Chief."

Across the desk, Chief Campanova stopped typing his report and turned to face Sam. "Chief, a lot has happened since the Illinois River shootout, and I think it's all related. I also think that Doc's murder was part of it."

Chief looked hard at Sam, turned to his typewriter and finished the signature line. He then ripped the memo from the machine, walked into the front office and signed it. He placed a post-it on the front of the memo that said "Mail to HQ," and put it in the outbox. We walked out of the building onto the sidewalk. He turned to Sam and said, "Washington has been trying to shut us down for months. I think they are going to try and make a play to take over Neverland. I think Doc's death is related. What do you know?"

Sam told him about the meeting with Ben at noon, so they walked to the parking garage, grabbed a car and drove to the park at 21st and Riverside. Ben was seated on the trunk of his car smoking a cigar, waiting for them. Ben greeted Chief Campanova and they walked south on the running trail under the bridge, down to the first set of benches. The breeze out of the south still had the lingering chill of late winter, but the sun was bright and warmed the group as they walked. Sam sat down with his back to the Arkansas River and started talking. He told them everything about the girls, Daniel, the compounds, and finally the hardest pill to swallow: our government funding the whole fiasco and the possibility of the U.S. Congress and POTUS being involved. Sam told Ben about the conversation he had with Doc the day before, and mentioned the letter in his P.O. Box. He reached into the pocket inside his coat, producing the folded envelope and slowly opened it. As Sam pulled the contents out, he noticed two pages. The first page was a copy of the U.S. Constitution. The second page read, "They will have it in Salida …The POTUS is going to be there July 4 signing an executive order enacting martial law. During the ceremony they will burn the U. S. Constitution and relinquish all authority to the United Nations." It was signed, "See ya on the other side … Doc."

He was a wise and foolish man. He knew they were coming for him. *He knew it was a suicide mission when he made the call, and he still showed up for work*, Sam thought. The inquiry he made must have set off multiple alarms with all sorts of bells and whistles screaming at the NSA Headquarters. Sam imagined there were probably a few bodies at that end as well. He looked at Ben and Chief, then said, "We have a problem. Because of Doc's inquiry, do you think they realize that we received his message and know their plan?"

Ben replied, "I don't think so. They got him first thing in the morning, before he had a chance to contact anyone. I don't believe they counted on his ingenuity."

Chief said, "I agree, and from the sound of things this bunch is so damn arrogant they don't think anyone will even contest them." Chief added, "I need to get back to the building and issue a press release for the paper. No doubt we are being watched. We need to act 'business as usual' and play Doc's murder suspect as a former bandit Doc arrested, maybe a meth dealer he prosecuted when he was with the DEA."

"Good idea. Meanwhile, we need to get the message out to other offices." Sam listened to Chief and Ben chatter about what they needed to do and that was fine, but he was ready to move. His mind was already working toward his plan. He had never been one to sit twiddling his thumbs when bad things were knocking at the door. There was no question that the primary mission was to save the Constitution. There were about two hundred original copies of the Constitution printed so that the document could be passed around for others to read, and at least thirty copies are secured by the National Archives and private collectors. But the significance of the ceremonial destruction precedes the actual destruction for all that it represents. If we delayed to have another Crusade to finish the job this time, our children would be dealing with this forever. Sam looked at Chief and said, "Chief, I am going home to grab some supplies, saddle up Patton and get lost in the wilderness for a couple of months, maybe three. I may be back after July Fourth, or I may just keep riding."

"And what are you going to do?" he asked.

"I'm gonna go crash their party!"

CHAPTER 8

Sam pulled the Hybrid out of the back parking lot and pointed it toward home. As he slowly drove by the ramp to the basement, a tow truck was dragging Doc's car out into the street. Sam knew what he had to do, and it would be a long, hard road. He arrived home and greeted the girls working diligently in the garden. The house and yard had not been this clean in years. Daniel was still cuffed and leg ironed to the kettle bell. Sam walked into the living room and sat down. "Dan," he said. "Do you remember much about Salida?"

"Well, it has been a while, but I can't imagine them changing too much. Buffalo River has pretty much stayed the same since I've been there."

Sam thought for a moment. He was unsure of how he was going to do it, but he had to get inside Salida, take the Sheikh down, secure the Constitution, and determine if the President was a patriot. It sounded easy enough. He returned to the kitchen, poured a cup of coffee and said, "I am going away for a while, maybe for about three months. I was wondering if you girls could house sit for me."

Each of the girls looked at Sam at first with curiosity then concern, and then at one another. Finally Sara grinned and giggled, "You're going after Theresa's mom aren't you?"

"Well, yes, that's part of it. There is a lot more at stake here than a man saving the girl of his dreams. I need to tell you guys a few things. If things go bad there, I may not make it back. If that is the case, you guys can stay here as long as you want. If I do not succeed, it's not going to matter much anyway."

One of the pots on the stove started boiling over and Theresa turned to take care of it, so Sam took the opportunity to go shower. Once clean and in some sweats, he returned to the living room. "Daniel, would you like to get cleaned up?"

"Oh heck yeah, I mean yessir."

"Well, you're starting to stain the air with your earthy fragrance." Sam removed the restraints, escorted him into the bathroom and threw him a towel and bar of soap. ''I'll be right here with the door open holding my gun. You have three minutes!"

Daniel quickly showered and said, "I'm done."

"Wrap the towel around you. I'm coming in." Sam handed him a basket for his rank clothes, and placed a folded stack of fresh ones that were left over from years gone by when he was a little younger. Sam took the basket and led him back into the living room, where he placed the restraints back on him.

"Will this ever end?" he asked.

"That is up to you. You and your bad choices earned those cuffs. Now you have to earn your freedom."

"How can I do that?"

"By helping me do what needs to be done. You help me take down the Sheikh, and I will make sure you get what you deserve."

"Aaand what exactly do you want me to do?"

"I'm going to Salida and I'm taking you with me. You will have an opportunity to prove yourself there. If you try me one time on the way, I will shoot you and leave you where you lay." Sam left him on the couch with his kettle bell and walked into the kitchen. The girls were setting the table for supper, and they all sat down to eat. Sam motioned to Theresa and asked, "I haven't thought much about your raising or upbringing with the Muslim influence, but would any of you like to bless the food?"

Theresa said, "Certainly, let us pray." The girls bowed their heads to pray, and Theresa led the blessing. "Dear Heavenly Father, thank you for this food, and bless it for our bodies. Please be with us tomorrow as we help Sam prepare for his journey. In Jesus' name we pray…amen." As Theresa opened her eyes she noticed Sam looking at her over the top edge of his reading glasses with a confused look on his face. "I fully expected a Muslim prayer." Theresa replied with a smile. "Mom taught me to read from a Bible that she kept hidden. She taught me the stories of Jesus, how he died for our sins and rose from the grave so that we may live. She also taught me the deception of Islam. We were careful to keep it hidden just to survive, but I think it's time our faith goes public."

"Amen!" shouted Daniel from the living room. In the back of his mind, Sam thought Dan was trying too hard, and his earlier comments about quickly adapting to survive kept tapping Sam on the shoulder. Sam rose from the table and walked into the living room to remove the leg irons. He brought Daniel to the table and sat him down with one leg chained to his chair. The girls had cooked a delicious venison roast with potatoes, and everyone ate their fill. Daniel continued to eat, obviously compensating for his days in the wilderness without food. Sam sat contented with a full belly, and imagined how fat he would get if this lifestyle continued. As the end of the evening drew near, they laughed and enjoyed each other's company knowing that very soon, they would all be facing new challenges.

Sam woke everyone up before the sunrise by ringing the bell on the back porch. Smiling as they all ran from the bedrooms, Sam put each of them to work, including Daniel whom he sat at the kitchen table packaging jerky and other dehydrated foods for the trip. The girls had put together enough food to last a few days, but it would not last long. They would soon be on their own. Sam prepared the packs for his other horse and loaded him with everything needed to get to Salida: jerky, coffee and an abundance of ammunition.

Sam demonstrated how to open the safe room in case the girls needed a place to hide. He pressed the security code on the microwave and the center island slid to one side, exposing a reinforced metal blast door. It could sustain a blast from anything most people had. The girls seemed impressed with the bunker, and somewhat excited to climb into the darkness. Once inside, he flipped a light switch on the wall. It was a very bright LED light which was powered by a separate solar panel on the top of a tall pole over by the barn. The house could burn down and there would still be a light in the bunker. Once down the ladder, they were very cautious not to touch anything, seemingly fearful that Sam would disapprove.

"Ladies," he said, "I feel confident that you know your way around most of this. Feel free to help yourselves. If you have any questions just ask."

There were enough weapons in there to supply a small army. The girls seemed very confident with the handling of these weapons, and Sam was starting to feel sorry for anyone who crossed them. Tiffany smiled and picked up a Glock 30. The Glock 30 was a large semi-automatic handgun, and it looked huge in her tiny hands. It would be interesting to see how she handled a .45. She properly cleared the weapon, racked the slide back and checked it for rounds. She looked at Sam, grinned and said, "Dibs."

The Bunker was solid. It was built to survive if the house took a direct hit from a tornado or a bomb. The ladder leading down was fifteen feet long. Once inside the bunker the walls were seven feet tall, the floor measuring twenty feet by twenty feet. On one wall was a work bench with every tool you would need for pretty much anything. The wall opposing it had gun racks with a dozen long guns, six AR-15s, and others of various calibers. Sam's favorite was his old deer rifle, a Remington model 7, 300 Short Action Ultra Mag. It was a short bolt action that made a good tree stand gun or saddle rifle. It was compact and light, but with magnum power rivaling the 300 Weathersby in ballistics. It would kill anything on this continent and then some, making it the perfect hunting rifle.

The table beneath the long guns held several handguns and some revolvers, but mostly semi-automatics. Shelves under the racks held magazines, ammunition and other supporting equipment, such as suppressors, stocks and holsters. There was a small chest to the side that contained several grenades, flashbangs, teargas canisters and other things that go boom. The next wall had shelves of canned food, canisters of rice, beans and bottled water. The other wall had a bunk bed, and in the middle of the room was a sofa bed. Sam turned to Theresa and said, "There is an escape tunnel that you can use in case of an emergency. The door is behind the bunk beds, and it will take you all the way over to the backside of the barn. The exit comes up behind three old storage drums, so you will still have some cover there as well. This bunker was set up to house four people for three months." Tiffany asked "Where is the bathroom?" There was a hole in the far corner that Elise was looking at, and Sam walked over, reached beneath a shelf to its right, retrieved a two foot pipe, and placed it into the hole. He then returned to the shelf and pulled out a custom-made toilet seat, then set it on top of the pipe and pressed down, snapping it into place.

"Do I need to explain further?" She just shook her head, laughing.

They returned top side and secured the bunker. As the center island slid into place, Sam went in to the living room, sat down with Daniel and said, "I need you to start thinking about security procedures and logistics of the base in Colorado. I need you to realize that if we do not succeed, there may never be another chance for an America again."

He was looking at the floor in front of him, and it was obvious his mind was comprehending this situation.

Sam continued, "Daniel, have you ever seen the victims of Islam and the results of what they think is punishment for breaking the law?"

"Sharia law," he mumbled.

"Yes, America will be nothing more than a memory if they win. And," Sam added, "You have a chance to be a hero."

He looked at Sam and said, "This must be one of those good choices you were telling me about."

Sam shook his head and smiled, "You betcha!"

CHAPTER 9

Tom Eagle Feather shook hands with David and said, "See you tomorrow, old man. Keep your powder dry."

"Always," David said with a grin.

Tom turned his horse down the road to his home. The trees were budding a little early, and the afternoon sun felt warm on his face as he rode past his brother's house. Strange, for a pretty day like today you would think the kids would be playing or doing chores. Tom took the saddle off of his horse and slapped him on the flank as he pushed him through the gate to the pasture. "Thanks old friend," Tom said out loud. "Take a break." He walked into his house for the first time in three days, and was ready for some peace and quiet. He put some kindling and logs in the wood stove, and coaxed a fire to burn with a little help from a rat's nest he had found in the log pile. He walked into the kitchen to get the coffee pot and stopped in the doorway.

"C'mon in," said a man sitting at his kitchen table.

Tom's heart was racing. He thought about trying to run out the door, but just as that thought entered his mind a voice behind him said,

"Don't even think about it."

Tom eased himself into a chair facing this man at his table.

"Decent people don't enter a man's home or sit at his table until they are invited," Tom said.

The stranger looked out at him coldly from under the brim of his hat and said with a crooked smile, "I've never pretended to be decent."

Tom said, "What do you want?" The stranger got up, walked over to the counter and, seeing the Mason jar, twisted the lid and took a sip.

"Not bad, got a little bite on the back side but I'm not here for the whiskey....I'm here for the girls."

The stranger sat quietly for a moment watching Tom, looking for a reaction.

"Now you're going to tell me where they are."

Tom sat there in silence for what seemed an eternity, then looked the stranger in the eye.

"Mister, I've got it figured I won't see the sunset, no matter what I tell you. So you can go to hell."

"Sir," the stranger said, "I will not go to hell now or later. The destiny of those who follow the Prophet is Paradise. But that is not the answer to the question, now, tell me," he said slowly with clinched teeth, "where are the girls?"

Tom shook his head. "I can't, I won't, go ahead and kill me now!"

The stranger grinned again and leaned in close to Tom's face. "Oh....I'm not gonna kill you." He nodded to his associate standing in the doorway and disappeared into the other room. He returned with a little girl, about eight years old. Tom's heart dropped as he saw his niece brought into the room.

"I'm so, so sorry Mary....Let her go!" he shouted.

"I will, just as soon as you tell me where the girls are."

The stranger took another sip of the whiskey, licked his lips and said, "It kinda grows on you. Now where were we....oh yeah."

He drew his pistol and pointed at the young girl's head. Pausing, he looked at Tom waiting for a response, then pulled the hammer back. Mary started crying, sobbing loudly. The stranger looked at Tom again. "Well?"

CHAPTER 10

Sam swung his leg over Patton just as the sun was breaking. It was a beautiful sunrise. Sam had his pack horse loaded, and Daniel was riding a light bay mare that Sam found abandoned several years ago in the stall of a barn by Oologah Lake. She was skin and bones, and just needed a little food and water. Sam named her Honey, and after she got healthy she proved her worth. She was not as big or as strong as Patton, but she had no quit in her. Close to home there was not much concern, so Sam stuck to the highway and took Oklahoma 412 traveling west from Inola. By three in the afternoon, they were skirting downtown Tulsa. Sam wanted to avoid the city for fear of being seen heading west. By sunset, the two were on the outskirts of Sand Springs, and Sam decided to stop and make camp. So many things were running through his mind about the coming weeks. So many unknown factors, two men traveling across a third of the United States to face an army alone – a true modern day story of David and Goliath. Sam just needed to find the right stone.

The period between the sunset and complete dark is a beautiful time of day. The wind dies down, and everything seems comes to a stop. Before the Fall, everyone was accustomed to noise. There was always noise from planes, trains or cars. Even inside, businesses played music or advertisements. True silence had become a very rare occurrence. People who have ever hunted appreciated the silence and the peace it brought to that special time of evening. It was when good things happened. A time that can create an unforgettable experience as the peace and quiet of a late afternoon completes the day with nothing but the sound of nature. They camped on the South side of a high hill overlooking Keystone Lake, or what was left of it. After the pandemic, they realized that without someone regulating the dam, the lake and river levels could eventually create a disaster. So the dam was opened to maximum output to prevent the upper river from flooding, or damage to the dam structure later. With the exception of a few ponds and lakes, Keystone Lake had disappeared.

Sam built a small fire to shake the cold off and then ate some venison jerky. The moon was almost full and rising above the old lake bed. It left them with an incredible view as coyotes howled praising the moon for its light in honor of their hunt. Sam unrolled his bed and saw that Patton and Honey were happy. Daniel sat by the fire, all cozied up with his leg irons chained to a tree. Before he lay down, Sam took a short walk down the back trail to see if anyone by chance was headed their way. Generally, no one travels at night, but if someone had a motive to stop them, the moon would definitely give them a chance to catch up.

Sam topped the hill facing Tulsa and looked back toward home. Home … years ago home meant a house, a place where you were raised, a neighborhood baseball team, high school football and the loyalty of team spirit. Home … home was once part of a different America, a simpler place, a place for a dream, a place where you were secure, a place where you were safe. Later, home became a place you had to defend; you were no longer safe because in the name of progress, laws protected the criminals and limited how you could protect your home, or yourself for that matter. In Neverland, home means what it is supposed to mean. Home is your reward. It is your castle, a castle you can defend.

As Sam looked back toward Tulsa, the lights of the few who had electricity flickered on as the sky grew dark. Years ago, Tulsa would light up the night sky. The radiance from night activity would glow for miles. Looking back east toward the Tulsa skyline, there were very few lights. Only those with solar ran lights, or those who were wealthy running generators to fuel their homes revealed how far we had fallen. Our infrastructure had crumbled, as did most everything else. As he sat on a large rock looking back, Sam suddenly caught the sound of rocks grinding under foot. He paused and held his breath. *There it is again,* he thought. He was sure that something, someone was behind him.

Sam eased down the south side of the highway keeping his profile below the shoulder of the road and waited. Silence, then wind blowing, there! He heard it again, except now much closer. Someone was riding a horse up the North side of the highway on the shoulder. They were trying to stay in the grass to avoid the noise of gravel or pavement. He peered over the crest of the center median. The moon was bright, allowing him to see at least a hundred yards or more.

Then Sam saw him. Not on his horse, but walking beside it. *That's not a bandit*, he thought. A bandit will ride a horse into the ground, and no one travels on horseback after dark unless it is an emergency. As they drew closer, Sam was more curious than fearful. He was alone walking his horse. Within minutes he was directly across the highway from Sam, his horse stopped, lifted his head and looked directly at Sam crouching just below the crest of the hill. He crouched lower and took off his hat.

"Is that you, Deputy Dawg?"

Well damn, it should have been obvious, Sam thought.

"Yeaah, it's me. I had forgotten how much your horse liked me, James."

James Bolton was a Deputy from Muskogee. His nickname was Jam because when things went bad, he jammed. Just don't get in his way. Jam had been around for about fifteen years, but had spent the previous ten years as a Navy Seal doing God knows what for his country. He was big, black, and strong as a bull. He was the sort of man for which legends were made. At six foot five, two hundred and seventy pounds, he was built like an NFL middle linebacker, but leaner and meaner.

"Glad you could make it, brother."

"Wouldn't miss it man," Jam responded. "Uh, do you have any food?"

Sam laughed. The man could eat his weight. It would be a chore just keeping him and his stomach happy.

"Not much, we didn't cook tonight. I have some jerky. You're welcome to it." He sat down and Sam threw him a bag he pulled from his pack. Jam started chewing. As Jam devoured the bag of jerky, Sam brought him up to speed on Daniel, then asked, "How did you find us?"

Jam replied, "Your Chief called my Chief, and here I am. Everybody else is bein' called in and reassigned to this detail. Whoever can, will try and catch up. I'm not expectin' much, but ya never know. I do know that your

Chief sent super-secret messages by couriers that he's payin' out of his own pocket to several friends of his in Kansas and Texas. If possible they'll try to meet us in La Veta. That will give us about a month to get there."

"Detail, I have a detail now?"

"It was explained to me like this: we swore an oath to carry this badge and protect the Constitution. Our job basically exists solely on the authority of the U.S. Constitution, so we better go save it!"

"Good point, Jam. Glad you are here. Here is some more jerky so I don't have to listen to your belly rumble all night. Now, get some sleep."

Morning came too soon. The wind had shifted out of the south and had the smell of spring with it. The group made their way back to 412 highway and continued west at a good pace. By ten a.m. they had reached the exit to Cleveland, having yet to see anyone. "They have probably seen this enormous man on an enormous horse and have run for the hills," Sam said laughing. Jam shook his head and said, "Lots of people make fun of the big guy until it's time to get busy."

"True that, Jam, true that," Sam replied.

Jam was a very confident looking fella on a very large horse. He had found his horse at a farm in Cherokee County. The farmer was selling his Belgian draft horse because he was moving back east and had no need of him anymore. Jam thought the horse would be just right for him. He had a history of wearing horses out before their time. A two hundred and seventy pound man on a horse with his gear can weigh as much as three hundred and fifty pounds, depending on what he is wearing and carrying. Jam named his draft horse Kong for obvious reasons. The two of them together looked very intimidating. Patton and Sam looked like a kid on a Shetland pony standing beside them. The group of three looked somewhat out of the ordinary as they continued to ride straight up the highway.

It was sad to see how rapidly the highway was deteriorating. Mother Nature was an amazing woman. Nothing that man can build could withstand her force; and everything, no matter how solid or technical, will eventually crumble and return to her. As the sun was setting in their eyes, they were approaching the Stillwater exit. A man on horseback rode out of the trees and up onto the highway facing them. Seconds later, another pair of men on horses emerged from the woods and joined their partner on the highway.

Sam stopped Patton approximately fifty yards away, Jam and Daniel pulling up on either side of him. “State your purpose!” he yelled.

“Are you Deputy Crow?” they asked.

“I am.”

“Reporting for duty, sir.”

Sam urged Patton forward with Jam and Daniel following. They approached the three men. They were young, not much older than Daniel.

“And who might you three be?” Sam asked.

The one that was nearest seemed to be older, and the leader of the bunch stepped forward and began to speak.

“My name is Jensen. This is Johnny, and Tim. We are deputy sheriffs here in Payne County. Dad, I mean Sheriff Clayton had a pony express rider come in last night from Tulsa County with a message from your boss asking for volunteers on a top secret mission with the U.S. Marshals Service. Sheriff Clayton knew we could be trusted because he’s our dad. We jumped at the chance to work with the Marshals.”

Sam sat in the saddle quietly and listened. His first inclination was to send these boys home, but he thought better of it. He knew they were going to need numbers to win this, and maybe some spit and vinegar is what they could use. “C’mon,” he said. “We have a long way to go.” They rode for another hour, then decided to give the horses a break and let them water in a stream that ran under the highway. They sat by the stream for a few minutes and Jam said, “Hey, quiet. Do you guys hear something?”

Sam shook his head. “My old ears couldn’t hear a thing.”

Daniel said, “It’s a motorcycle, no, wait….its several motorcycles.”

Being in this part of Oklahoma was unfortunate for them as there were not many places to take cover. Sam stepped into the stirrup and said, “Saddle up. We don’t want to be on foot if things go bad.” They rode the horses up the rise and onto the highway. The motorcycles were still a mile away, but they knew it would be useless to run. None of these horses could jump the turnpike fences designed to keep livestock off the highway and, *Hell*, Sam thought, *I was too old and tired to run.* As they got closer, Sam could see they had about ten riders with them, a relatively small group, which indicated that they were a scouting party hopefully just looking to scavenge anything they could find of value. Sam had seen gangs like this on occasion, even had a couple of scraps with them. They cruise the barren areas looking for trouble. Sam looked at his crew and said, "Guns out boys, but let's be nice."

A display of power often took the steam out of people who merely thought they were bad. Sam figured this group was probably running a truck stop off of I-35. That would be the only way they would have gas to run their bikes. Sam pulled Patton to a stop, swung the sling of his AR-15 around so the rifle was resting on his chest, and had his right hand on the grip. Using his thumb, he moved the safety lever to the fire position. Jam pulled his gun out of the scabbard on Kong and rested it across the saddle horn. Sam's mouth dropped open. "Where on God's green earth did you find that?" he asked.

Jam grinned. "Momma gave it to me for Christmas." Sam laughed. Daniel and the new guys sat on their horses in silence. They were not sure what to make of Jam and honestly seemed scared to death of him. Jam had somehow found an AR-12. It was basically an AR-15 platform designed to feed 12 gauge 3 inch magnum shells, and he had a thirty round drum-fed magazine. If these fellas wanted trouble, Sam thought, just sit back and turn Jam lose. The word jam is an old '80s word for smack down and that is what Jam could do very well.

Sam watched as the bikes approached. He could not imagine what was going through their minds as they stood there waiting on them with that huge black man on that enormous horse, holding that gun with the really large hole in the end of the barrel. *I personally would have turned around,* Sam thought. *But that's me.* Unfortunately it wasn't them.

CHAPTER 11

Theresa and the girls watched Sam and Daniel ride away, and Theresa quietly said a prayer for them. She really wanted to go, but knew the girls needed her more. Taking care of Sam's ranch would be a nice break from life in the compound. *Life on the ranch would be just fine,* she thought shaking her head. She turned, went back into the house and started cleaning the kitchen. They had made Sam and Daniel a going-away breakfast of sorts: eggs, bacon, biscuits and gravy. Not worrying about gaining a few pounds anymore was definitely a good thing. Sam had set his home up on a solar system years ago, and although it was great to have electricity, there were still limits to what you could use. Wood was primarily the source for heat and cooking, with the electricity reserved for lights at night and Sam's alarm system. Sam's ranch was at the end of a dead-end road and nestled in a large forest of old growth trees backing up to a large hill to the North. Sam called it his mountain.

Theresa, Elise, Tiffany and Sara had a lot to do. This ranch did not run itself. Sam did not have much, but it was still enough to live on if properly managed. There were six cows, two other horses, several pigs (one that was about to have a litter), and chickens. The garden had been tilled, and Theresa knew it was about time for planting. It was a relatively small garden, so they spent the morning turning the soil and making rows. They found seeds in the barn stored in old coffee cans, each labeled and ready to plant. They spent the rest of the day planting corn, okra, beans and peppers. There were tomato seeds as well, but Theresa decided to plant them in the big whiskey barrels that were cut in half by the back porch. She was excited. For the first time in her life, she was free. As the sun started to set, Tiffany looked to Theresa and said, "Do you think we'll ever see 'em again?"

"Yes, as a matter of fact I do. I don't think God brought us all this way for it to end here."

Sara asked, "Did y'all see that old truck parked in the corner of the barn?"

Theresa said, "What truck?"

Sara replied, "Yeah. It's in the back corner with a tarp pulled over it." Theresa was curious. They had hummers and military vehicles still running in the compound, but most vehicles had basically just rotted in place after the Fall. Gas was not available, and if it was, use of it was limited to big semi-trucks transporting goods to market, military or law enforcement. The girls walked to the back of the barn and peered under the tarp. It did not look that old. Sam had obviously been taking care of it. Sara pulled open the door and hopped in the driver's seat. "Hey, the keys are in the ignition!" she said excitedly. She turned the key and the lights on the dash lit up, illuminating the huge grin on her face. The old CD started playing. "Chug a lug it up one side glide down the other, I'm a lover of the other side of the hiiiill!"

"Cool, see if it will start!" Theresa said. "Sara, turn the key on." Sara rotated the key, and the starter turned slowly, then gradually picked up speed. The old diesel motor roared to life.

Tiffany said, "Let's go for a ride." Theresa reached over and turned the key off. "No, if we broke Sam's truck or even scratched it I would hate myself." Sam had bought the truck new in 1999. It was the first and only truck he had ever bought new. It was a 1999 Dodge, had a 24 valve, Cummins turbo diesel with fuel injection, four-wheel drive, and would go almost 700 miles on a tank of gas.

Theresa said, "Let's put the tarp back over it and go eat. We'll look at it more tomorrow. But, nobody is driving it!"

Theresa lay in bed as she watched the sun rise through the bedroom window. She had never slept past sunrise before. Feeling somewhat guilty for being so lazy, she swung her feet over the edge of the bed and onto the floor. She shivered as her bare feet hit the cold tile. She walked into the living room and stirred the coals in the wood burning stove, placed three logs inside the stove and walked into the kitchen. She prepared a pot of coffee and returned to the living room, placing it on the stove. Elise stumbled into the living room and stood by the stove trying to absorb the warmth. Theresa pulled the drapes open to let the rising sun into the house, and its beams cascaded across the floor. Oklahoma has as much diverse weather as it does geography. Spring mornings can begin with a heavy frost and later bake you with eighty-five degrees by afternoon. Theresa told Elise to get Tiffany and Sara out of bed, then walked to the back of the house to open the drapes there. As she fumbled with the cord, she looked out the window and her heart stopped. Two men with guns were standing in front of the barn looking directly at her. She dropped the drapes as bullets shattered the window and hit the wall across the room. "Get Down!" she shouted. As she crawled back toward the bedrooms, Elise, Tiffany and Sara came crawling around the corner. Rounds were pouring in from all sides.

"How did they find us?" Sara yelled above the noise.

"I don't know, but get to the bunker!" The girls crawled into the kitchen where Theresa reached up to the microwave and quickly pressed the numbers for the code. The center island slid over to reveal the entrance to the bunker. They opened the reinforced door and climbed in, closing the door behind them. After a few seconds, the center island returned to its natural position. The girls, once situated in the bunker, sat quietly on the bunk and sofa. They looked up trying to hear anything topside. There were several feet of dirt and foundation between the bunker and the house, so sound eluded them. They were not sure what was happening up there, so they waited.

CHAPTER 12

The bikers pulled up within about twenty-five yards and stopped. They all turned their engines off and paused, looking at the small group of heavily armed men and mumbled quietly to each other, not seeming to know what to do. None had drawn their weapons. They were either very foolish, or very confident. The leader walked within ten yards of Sam and said, "Gentlemen, it's kind of rare we see anyone on the highway anymore. It's even rarer that we see a crew like you guys. Y'all appear to have the makings of a posse."

"No sir," Sam said. "We are just prepared for any degenerates that may want to take our belongings, or our lives."

"I understand," said the leader, with a smug look on his face. "They are about."

"We'll be on our guard," Sam replied.

The leader continued, "Where are you guys going?"

Sam looked at him, growing tired of the small talk and getting ready to go hard when he said, "Oh never mind, I'm being too nosey for my own good. You fellas have a safe trip."

He turned and walked back to his bike, turned it back west, and they left in a cloud of dust and exhaust. Sam looked back at Jam. He had the AR-12 pointed right in their general direction.

Sam laughed and said, "And here I was thinking all that fear and intimidation was just little old me."

Jam laughed. "Ya know they'll be back."

"Yeah," Sam replied, "with reinforcements, I'm afraid."

Sam was familiar with the I-35 intersection and knew it was just minutes away for a motorcycle.

"I'd wager their headquarters was pretty close to the intersection ahead," he said.

"What's your call, Sam?" Jam asked.

"Well, there is not much cover out here, I was hoping to find an old home or a barn; but, hell, at this point a good tree is hard to find. I say we ride right at 'em."

The small group of patriots continued on at a much quicker pace, looking for any opportunity to avoid confrontation. They did not need to waste time, energy or ammunition while en route to battle. Also, if the bikers were of the notion to wait until morning, there was the possibility that they could slip by in the darkness of night and be on their way. They rode for a couple of hours as the sun dropped below the horizon. They crested a small rise and saw the lights of the truck stop about a mile ahead.

This particular truck stop appeared to be a functioning station. A semi-rig was pulling out from one of the bays. Its lights swept across the group in a broad arc. The truck pulled out of the parking lot traveling across the overpass of I-35. It turned and pointed south toward Oklahoma City. You could hear the driver grinding gears and accelerating as the tail lights disappeared over a hill. Sam smiled, looked at Jam and said, "You think they have any whiskey?"

Jam dropped his chin to his chest shaking his head and said, "Lord, give me patience this day."

Sam looked at Jensen, being the oldest of the three boys from Stillwater and said, "I want you to go straight north for about a mile." He reached into his saddle bag, grabbed a pair of fence pliers and handed them to him. "I don't care if you have to cut fence. Try to stay out of sight until you turn back west. We will meet you back on the highway by sun up. If we don't make it by sun up, stay out of sight and work your way west to the outskirts of Enid. We'll cut your track and find you there."

Jensen took the pliers, gave Sam a grin with a "yessir," and pointed his horse north. He seemed a little excited to finally contribute to the cause. Supplies and weapons were critical to the mission, and they were to be protected at all costs. Sam did not know the nature of these bikers or their intent, but he knew he did not like the leader of the scouting party. He looked at the pack horse way too many times.

Jensen cut a hole in the highway fence, and the boys led their horses north as they soon disappeared into the darkness. It was almost midnight when the two Marshals turned their attention toward the truck stop. A few lights were on, and only a couple of people were leaning against their bikes outside. There were still more horses tied up outside than motorcycles. Sam slid off of Patton and tied him to a post, then walked through the doors with Jam following closely behind him.

It was a typical truck stop building which had been turned into a bar. Smoke from cigars filled the air. Cigarettes had become a thing of the past. Most people grew and rolled their own tobacco, using it in pipes and cigars. In a virtual apocalypse when survival is a necessity, people will still find a way to satisfy their vices. There were about fifty people inside, one girl for every five men. There was a counter to the right of the door with an old fashioned cash register. Beyond that, a bar ran across the wall along the south end of the building. Behind the bar was a grizzled old man pouring beer and slinging whiskey. A juke box by the dance floor was playing Stevie Ray Vaughn, and a couple of ladies who had too much to drink were proving to the crowd how badly they really could dance.

There was one exit other than the front door, and it was to the left on the north end of the building. A large group of people were at an enormous round table on the east end of the room, and as Sam's eyes adjusted to the poor light and smoke, he realized that he and Jam held their attention. Sam recognized the leader of the scout group they had met on the road earlier. He leaned down and was talking into the ear of the person who was obviously his boss. Sam looked directly at them and walked straight to the bar. The bartender grinned as Sam approached, as if he knew that Sam may be the star for this evening's main event. Sam started to order and the bartender held his hand up saying, "All we got is beer and whiskey. You look like you're gonna need a whiskey." He laughed, slammed a shot glass on the bar and poured Sam a whiskey. Sam put a silver dollar on the bar, but he said, "That's no good here." Sam replied, "It's 1962, solid silver." He picked it up looked at it, turning it in the dim light, nodded his head and said, "Good enough."

Jam had followed Sam to the bar and ordered a beer. The tiny mug looked like a tea cup in his giant hand, and the drink did not last very long as he slid the empty mug back to the bartender. "That was real good," he said. "I'll have another." The group at the table had continued to watch the newcomers, and finally the leader motioned Sam over to the table. He approached the group, while Jam remained at the bar sipping on his second beer.

"My man here tells me he ran into you guys on the highway today and invited you to drop in. I'm curious where the rest of your group is," the leader of the group asked, with a fake possum smile which he exaggerated and held way too long. He spoke like a used car salesman who had no conscience about selling a car that was sure to fail soon after it was driven off the lot. He would smile, shake your hand and then stab you in the back.

He motioned for Sam to sit, to which Sam replied, "No thank you, I won't be here long."

"Why don't you tell your friend to come on over?" he asked.

"He goes where he wants."

There was an awkward pause.

The leader pushed his chair back, stood and placed his hand on the handle of the gun in his belt. His possum smile was gone. The scout leader moved over and stood next to Sam. His rotten breath overwhelmed the smoke from the cigar as he leaned in and whispered, "Sit down…now."

Sam reached back with his left arm hooking under his shoulder. He lifted him, tossing him over and crashing him down onto the table. Before the scout leader could move, Sam had drawn the Nighthawk and planted the blade into the table beside his head, nicking his ear. He drew his Glock and held it inches from the leader's face. Glancing back at Jam, curious to see if he would help, Sam was slightly irritated to see him still leaning back, resting against the bar grinning with a beer in his hand.

Jam raised his glass as if toasting the occasion, smiled and said, "Proceed." Rolling his eyes, Sam looked back at the leader and said, "We are passing through. That's all. We don't want trouble, but we are willing and very able to oblige anyone who wants to try us. We can leave your place here one of two ways. I prefer the way where nobody dies. Your move!" Sam moved the Glock a tad bit closer to his face for effect. Everyone in the bar was frozen in time, motionless with the exception of the smoke that danced its way up to the ceiling from the cigars. The leader slowly moved his hand away from his pistol and eased back down into his chair.

"I think I'll be having me a drink."

The door of the truck stop opened, and five men entered looking hard, tough and ready to fight. They spread out scanning the club as if they were searching for someone. They glanced at Jam who had not moved, seeming to enjoy the show. Looking straight at Sam, they locked on a target. Regardless of the fact that Sam was still holding a gun, the first man through the door strode across the room and stopped directly in front of him. He looked at Sam and asked, "Is there a problem here?"

"I don't think so. Not now anyway," Sam replied, then looked back at Possum. "Are we good?" Possum nodded slowly, not really sure how he had so quickly lost total control of the situation. Sam looked at Possum knowing that he had not only deflated his ego, but had made him look bad in front of everyone that ever had any regard for him....

"Hello, Sam," the newcomer said.

"Howdy Charley, it's been a while."

Charlie was a Deputy in Oklahoma City. Sam had known Charlie for years after helping him in a biker gang sting. The Comancheros were slinging meth all over the Oklahoma City area. Law Enforcement always seemed to be short with manpower, so they pulled deputies in from all over the area to round up the bad guys. Since then, they had worked together on many cases, including a special assignment to Puerto Rico where they enjoyed the last few days sitting on the beach of a private island smoking some really expensive cigars.

Charlie was another gentleman who was larger than usual. He had an uncommonly large head, earning him the title "bucket-head" among his friends. Other than his size he was not much to look at, but he was fun in a fight.

"Glad to see you brother," Sam said. "What brings you north of the city?"

"Your boss sent a pony message that said I need to find you and render aid. I grabbed my favorite compadres and here we are. Now, what the hell is going on?"

Sam looked back at possum who was grinning like he got way more than one drink, but now in addition to the grin, his eyes were closed.

"Possum, hey Possum!" He opened one eye.

"What?"

Sam leaned inside his comfort zone and spoke into his ear quietly. "We are U. S. Marshals. I am Deputy Sam Crow, and we need a private room. Top secret stuff." Sam reached down and grabbed Possum by the arm. He slowly stood and looked at Sam with a lot of doubt and a little regret.

"My office, behind the bar," he said.

Jam, Charlie and his posse, Possum and Sam crammed their big bodies into the small office. Sam looked hard at Possum. "Listen close." He seemed to straighten a little, somewhat fueled by the atmosphere of being in a top secret meeting.

"I need a few patriots, people who love this country for what it was and what it will be. I don't care what you've done or what you're doing. I care about what you are going to do! Right now you are part of something that may determine whether America lives, or dies. Which do you prefer?"

Possum glanced at Sam, and without hesitation said,

"Lives!" Sam gave Charlie the nod, and Charlie addressed the men in the room.

"We came here at the order of the U. S. Marshal and the U. S. Attorney. The Marshal ordered us here to support you with the information he received that the U.S. Constitution was in trouble, and that you have an informant who claims the POTUS intends to destroy the U.S. Constitution, aiding Islam and the implementation of Sharia law."

"Yes sir, that is true," Sam replied.

Possum, who was no longer grinning and seemed to be instantly sober, asked, "Y'all aren't kiddin are ya?"

He looked directly at Sam and said, "This means everything we stand for will no longer exist."

Sam added, "Freedom will be destroyed, the American dream will no longer exist, and you will convert or die."

"What do you want me to do?" Possum asked.

Sam said slowly, "Support us, that's all."

Possum looked at Sam and then at everyone in the room. With no lack of confidence he said, "I have been many things of late that are not desirable. But I am and always will be a Patriot."

Sam looked back at Charlie and then at Jam, both nodding.

Many things were discussed that night in that tiny room, but for the first time since Sam could remember, he felt hope. Not the empty crap that politicians promise, real hope. One man believing is a seed that once planted, spreads and grows. *This country's not done yet*, Sam thought. *Not by a long shot!*

Sam took Possum by the arm and said, "Walk with me." They exited his office, and Sam let Possum lead him back to his table so that all in the club could see them together. Once back at his table, Sam shook his hand and told him in a louder than normal voice,

"Thank you. You are a real American hero!"

Possum smiled and nodded, then sat down upon his mighty throne. Those who were snooping nodded in approval. Possum's status had been restored. He had saved face, and in some ways had gained new respect.

CHAPTER 13

The sun rose over the Rocky Mountains, creating an explosion of colors which was impossible to describe.

God, they are beautiful, Jennifer thought as she sipped her coffee.

She gazed at the mountains through the window in her office and daydreamed about being anywhere else but here. Daydreaming had become her only escape from this madness that was her home. She had just returned from Salat (Muslim prayer), and wanted a few moments of peace before her day began. She hated faking this life, pretending to pray to a god she did not believe in, all in the name of survival. Each time she prayed, she prayed that she would wake up and this had somehow been a horrific nightmare.

Her life was a prison. It was better than that of most here, only because she had found a place where her talent was of better use to them than breeding soldiers for their holy war. Now they were planning to take over this once beautiful country and turn it into the hell that they created for themselves in the Middle East. Europe was now mostly Muslim. England and France were both working theocracies. The last hope for freedom in this world was about to be sold out from under We the People by the Washington elite, and no one would have a clue until it was too late.

April was still winter at seven thousand feet in the mountains. It was cold and dry. Salida was not known for having much snow, or rain for that matter. Nestled between the eastern and western slopes, it was somewhat protected from the severe winter storms that are normally associated with the high country in Colorado. Average precipitation was not much more than ten inches a year. The compound was created in a secret government facility that had once been an abandoned mine. As the compound grew, the people of the town were forced to accept Islam, and many chose the gruesome alternative. Their heads were severed and their bodies were buried in a mass grave outside of town. The town itself was the perfect setting for a mountain fortress. In its pristine beauty, it was surrounded by mountains, difficult to access without detection and easily defended. Since Sheikh Nu'man Mahannad had inherited the throne, he had managed with the promise of Middle Eastern oil and wealth to purchase the Washington elite, and anyone who had stood in protest had been assassinated. Salida was a fully functional town now, with electricity and many other conveniences that the rest of the country had not experienced in years.

"Well," she thought. "So much for the peace and quiet of a morning gazing at the mountains, I have work to do."

"Doctor Boudreaux," a man called to her from around the corner. "You are due in your classroom now."

Jennifer slipped her burqa over her head and entered the hallway. Ali ushered her down the hall toward an open door where a classroom of young men in their early teens were being taught the skills of becoming combat medics.

"I am so sorry, Ali. I have been dealing with a severe headache. Please forgive me?"

Ali nodded. "It is certainly a shame a woman such as you is tormented by headaches. Maybe you have outlived your usefulness to us," he said coldly.

Jennifer slipped by Ali into the classroom and began her lecture on wounds and battle dressing.

How can I continue, she asked herself.

Her daughter had kept her going for so long, and now they had been torn apart. It had been at least six months now since she had seen her. The thought of never seeing her again was killing her from the inside out, and it was showing in her performance. Theresa had been her only connection to a normal life, and now that was gone. Jennifer handed out a worksheet to the young group and sat down at her desk as they poured through their books trying to locate the answers. Doctor Boudreaux buried her face in her hands and cried silently under her Burqa.

CHAPTER 14

The silence of the bunker started to wear on the girls. Theresa finally decided that sitting still was not the answer. She whispered to the other three girls.

"I have no doubt that they will eventually find the bunker. Load as many guns, ammo and grenades as you can into these go bags, and take them through the tunnel to the barn."

Without hesitation, Tiffany, Elise and Sara started grabbing the gear and putting it into manageable loads. They made two trips to the base of the ladder underneath the back of the barn. Theresa shoved a Glock 23 into her belt, and with an AR-15 slung over her shoulder she climbed the ladder. She turned the handle and eased the lid up, looking and listening for any potential threat. She slowly climbed out of the hole and looked over the top edge of the barrels covering the entrance to the tunnel. She peeked around the corner of the barn and could see the men through the windows of the house, ransacking the inside and frantically searching for what was no longer there. Theresa quietly moved up to the front of the barn, slowly closed the barn doors and tied the handles together so that it could not be opened from the outside. She returned to the tunnel and motioned for the girls to start bringing the go bags up the ladder. "Load the bags into the truck, and make sure you have enough gear on you in case there is a fire fight," Theresa said. She moved around to the east side of the barn, where she maintained a watchful eye on the house as the girls loaded the truck. She had selected an AR-15 with an ACOG four power scope. The ACOG was the choice of many military and police tactical teams because of its size and clarity. She watched the men walk back and forth in front of the windows for a while, until one man walked out onto the front porch scratching his head, looking around. He walked around the corner of the house and glanced back at the barn. Cocking his head sideways, he shouted, "Aadam, the barn doors are shut!" and started walking toward the barn.

Theresa heard movement in the house, slipped back through the back of the barn and said, "We have to move now! Get in the truck."

The men one by one stepped off of the back porch and slowly approached the barn as the leader tried the doors.

"They have locked the doors!" he shouted.

Theresa turned the key, and the engine roared to life with the signature rattle of the old Cummins powerhouse. Elise pulled the tarp off of the truck and rolled a grenade under the front door of the barn, giggling as she saw the shadows of the men under the door scramble. She jumped in the back of the truck, and Theresa floored the gas pedal. The grenade exploded, turning the door to splinters as the truck raced past the men who had dived behind the wood pile. Elise aimed her AR-15 as they tried to crawl out, peppering the logs with several rounds and making them scramble for more cover as the truck disappeared down the driveway. Theresa followed the road out onto Highway 412 and pointed the old dodge toward Tulsa.

"Where are we going?" asked Sara.

"Colorado!" Theresa replied.

CHAPTER 15

Sam and the rest of the deputies spent what was left of the evening at the club with Possum and his friends. They eventually made camp sleeping for just a couple of hours out by interstate I-35. Tired and worn from the long day, Sam fell asleep almost immediately and slept hard… Jennifer was there, not dancing this time. She was running, glancing over her shoulder, as if something were chasing her. She tripped and fell, twisting, landing on her back. She opened her mouth to scream, and Sam jumped startled from his bed roll. He blinked his eyes a few times shaking off the dream. The sun had yet to rise but was creating a thin blue line across the eastern horizon. He began to saddle Patton as the rest of the crew was getting up and around. Jam leaned on his horse staring at the sunrise and said,

"I would kill for an IHOP right now, or maybe a Waffle House, anything but jerky!"

April had come, and it seemed they were barely getting started. Their numbers had grown with Charlie and his crew joining the mission and they still had to meet Daniel and the Claytons somewhere close to Enid. Leather creaked against the strain of weight as each of the men climbed into the saddle and turned their horses away from the sunrise.

"We need to kick it in the butt guys. We need forty miles a day." Sam said. They rode hard and long for most of the morning making Enid by early afternoon. They located Daniel and the Claytons and stopped to water the horses at a pond in a small park in town. Enid had become like many smaller cities across Neverland with people who couldn't maintain living in seclusion or small groups. They would move into the larger, more populated areas seeking protection in numbers.

As they prepared to continue west, Sam turned and saw at least a dozen riders approaching from the east, following their back trail. As they drew near Sam recognized his old friend Matt Warner who was a Deputy from Wichita, Kansas. Matt waved, and Sam motioned him on in.

"You guys must have pushed hard to catch us this quick." Sam said.

"We were in Copan chasing an escapee when we got the message from the pony express rider. We cut straight across Osage County and tried to catch you at I-35 this morning, but you had already left. You made quite an impression on Joel."

"Joel?" Sam asked.

"Yes, Joel, you know the owner of the truck stop, you definitely have a new fan!" Matt said.

"Oh, Possum, I started calling him Possum because of his grin. I never thought to ask him his real name,"

Jam and Charlie approached with the other deputies as they had a few minutes of greetings and shaking hands. Once all the men were satisfied they were among good company they saddled up and headed west as they chased the sun.

Twenty-two Marshals strong, they were a formidable group but not near enough to face the army that waited in Salida. They spent the next few days riding with little rest, taking care of the horses and keeping them watered which was their biggest priority. Three days from Enid they crossed the Glass Mountains. Not real mountains by most standards, but they were beautiful high mesa's and buttes of red dirt, full of crystal and gypsum, carved from the winds of time. On a sunny day the hill sides will sparkle as the suns light reflects off of the selenite crystals. Early explorers referred to them as the Shining Mountains.

The group, covered with dust, looked more like a posse from an old western movie as they picked their way around the mesa's. They camped on the western side of the mountains finding a stream to water the horses. They were all running low on supplies so as morning broke Sam asked for two volunteers to move north and south of the highway by about half a mile paralleling the posse's progress hoping that they may take a deer or other game that was pushed in their direction. By noon both hunters had returned to the group one carrying a doe, and the other a large boar. Boars had originally been introduced into the wild for sporting purposes and being a very prolific and stubborn animal their numbers have multiplied beyond belief.

Sam stopped the procession and they built a large fire giving the horses a much needed rest. After skinning both the pig and the deer they put the pig on a spit and let it cook while cutting the venison into strips and smoking it over a smaller, smoldering fire. With the meat on the fire, Sam decided to go ahead and camp for the evening. They ate their fill of the pig saving the venison jerky for travel. With their bellies full, Sam went to his pack horse and grabbed a bottle of whiskey. He walked up to the fire and poured a shot into his cup and then passed the bottle around allowing each of the twenty-two men an opportunity for a shot. Sam raised his cup. "To our friends who are no longer with us, to the Constitution and Old Glory, long may she wave." Each deputy in unison raised their cup. Charlie added in song,

"We'll raise up our glasses against evil forces singing … Whiskey for my men, Beer for my horses." Jam pushed him over a log, and they all had a good laugh. Sleep came easy on a full belly. Fatigue easily overcame the incredible noise created by the sound of a large group of men snoring, and Sam soon became one of them.

They continued to ride for several days through Woodward, then Fort Supply. The rolling hills and lonely road lulled them all into a comfortable sense of complacency. Daniel had been doing a fine job working where he was needed while taking care of Sam's pack horse. Trust was still an issue, but the rest of the group seemed to like him well enough. Sam contemplated removing the restraints, but something told him to wait. Maybe it was just a paranoid old man being overly cautious.

As the men approached Guymon, Sam was again worried about supplies and by the way they were all smelling, locating a place for them to bathe was almost a necessity. Two weeks on the road and they were all rank. They were almost back on schedule, Sam thought, and he had to consider two things. One, the weather had gotten better as summer approached, and two, the days are getting longer. Traveling was getting easier so it was time to dust off, clean up, and maybe have a beer if one could be found.

It had been many years since he had traveled this far west. Guymon had always been Sam's halfway point on the road to his Colorado elk hunt. Sam, however had never made the trip on horseback. Charlie commented,

"Why don't we rest here for a couple of days. If this is halfway, then we can easily be there before July 4th."

"Charlie, we could if we went straight by the highway. That is something that we just can't chance. They will have the passes under surveillance. I'm hoping by early June the high country will have melted off so that we can pick up a trail that runs along the Continental Divide and follow it straight into Salida. The closer we get the more dangerous it will become and we will need to slow things down. Also we have to plan for unforeseeable circumstances. There is still the possibility for winter storms and heavy rain in June. Not to mention, rock slides, flash floods, and avalanches."

Sam glanced up watching the sky as he was talking about the weather. Ironically clouds had gathered in the southwest and the wind had picked up.

"It will be a good night to have shelter, It looks like we are about to get a storm."

A gust of wind almost removed Sam's hat as the leading edge of a storm brushed against them. "Pick it up fellas let's find a roof." They pulled their horses into an old vacant tire shop on the edge of town just as the storm hit. Hail pummeled the tin roof for several minutes making it difficult to hear the guy standing beside you. The building was solid made out of enormous steel beams. The concrete floor still smelled of motor oil and old rubber. There was an old bathroom in the back that was somewhat of a biohazard and the only thing left in the old building was a large commercial stainless steel sink that was covered with gunk washed from the hands of mechanics from times long passed.

Jenson found a twenty-five foot garden hose that was a little dry rotted, and his brother found a tarp in the corner of the front office. Jam took his gun belt off and walked out into the rain and found the water meter out by the highway. He turned the lever and waited. He cleaned the encrusted meter dial off with his finger and within seconds the numbers slowly started to turn. He returned to the building and walked over to the sink. Once he turned the lever on the sink a blast of stale air spat out of the nozzle then came some rank, muddy orange water, more air spitting, and then more water. After about a minute the water became clear in a steady stream. The commercial sink nozzle was fitted so that a hose could be screwed on to the end of it. Jensen brought the hose over and with a little ingenuity they built a shower stall out of some the old pipe and wire lying around the shop. Daniel had found a fifty gallon drum in the back storage room. He dragged the drum into the middle of the shop while several others were breaking apart the old office furniture for firewood. The shop was made like an old barn with a peak at the top and both ends open where exhaust fans used to be. Someone must have removed them years ago when tires and tire shops became useless.

Sam walked out the door in the back of the building and stood on a covered back dock. In the corner against the building was a stack of wood pallets that would make for more good fire wood. By sundown the storm was raging outside and the men were clean and cozy making camp inside the building with their horses, but still no steak or beer.

CHAPTER 16

Sunrise in Salida was always so beautiful. The sun's rays would peek over the eastern range, spilling its golden beams over the peaks like a tidal wave of joy. It made you feel alive, if only for a brief moment. Shining moments like these were what kept Jennifer going. Praying to God kept her dream alive that someday she would be reunited with her daughter. She smiled as she finished her cup of coffee and donned her burqa. She turned the corner of her office door and entered her classroom as Ali rounded the corner at the end of the hallway. He peered into the class with a mildly confused look on his face, and Jennifer smiled and said with a somewhat taunting tone, "May I help you?" Ali gave a look of confusion, then anger, and immediately retreated from the classroom door. Jennifer finished her class and directed them to a practical exercise in an adjoining building after lunch. They would see cadavers for the first time, and many would not make it through the day.

Ali was waiting in her office. He was sitting in her chair, leaning back, much too comfortable. *Not a good sign*, she thought. She approached her desk and remained standing opposite of Ali. Removing the burqa, she stood before him in her regular clothing, her beautiful hair flowing and eyes blazing as they made contact with his. She placed both hands on her desk and leaned toward him, intentionally maintaining a superior position elevated above him. He immediately felt uncomfortable, apparently threatened by a woman out of her place. He spun the chair to his right and stood up, moving laterally across the office. *Predictable, simpleminded fool*, she thought, retreating without a word. Just like any schoolyard bully, he tried to flex his muscle without using his mind. *So glad he never took my classes on kine-*

sics. Kinesics is the study of movement and response, the interpretation of body movements, gestures and facial expressions. Studying the nonverbal behavior of a person can reveal much about what they are really thinking. Implementing your own nonverbal movements can illicit predictable responses. She smiled as he stormed past her into the hallway. *He'll definitely be back*, she said to herself. He was persistent and seemed somewhat intent on her demise, but an average person challenging a genius to a battle of wits was not a wise decision, unless he had much more political muscle behind him than she realized.

The rest of the day passed without further incident. In fact, Ali was nowhere to be seen. After dinner and the evening call to prayer, Jennifer really started worrying. Ali was not the type to disappear during the day. He had spent the last six months making her life a living hell. Only today for the first time had she stood her ground and not let him win. She was proud, but now a little worried that he may have run to her superiors. *Even as a doctor, slavery sucks*, she thought. In the old world, by now she would have established her own practice somewhere with a larger-than-life home, heated pool, maybe on a beach, taking lavish vacations to the Mediterranean, Hawaii or Bora Bora....yeah that's it, Bora Bora. But, hell no, she had the wonderful opportunity to become a doctor in a society where she was a slave. Thank God she could escape to her one bedroom apartment. She thought, *Mental rant noted....it's time to leave this hell!* She opened the door to her apartment and turned on her light. Walking through the living room, she dropped her backpack onto the sofa and went into the bathroom, removing her clothes. She eased herself into a hot bath, sinking into a memory of days gone by. Warm water, sand, and a tall muscular man named Samson. *Only in a dream*, she thought.

At forty-nine, Jennifer had natural salt and pepper hair that cascaded casually around her shoulders, a dark, olive complexion that would indicate Mediterranean descent, and deep blue-green eyes – perhaps the most striking feature of all. Her life had changed drastically one night when she accepted a drink from a handsome stranger at a club in Biloxi, Mississippi. They danced for a few minutes and, suddenly feeling lightheaded, she knew she had been drugged. The rapid effects of the drink took control, and she woke the next day in a cell. Never being physically abused, she quickly realized that survival would require her to play along with whomever these sick people were. Standing in lineups with many other attractive girls, apparently being observed for one characteristic or another, then finally taking actual placement tests, Jennifer realized her net worth was being assessed. The mentally weak and the ignorant fell to the wayside, and eventually the groups of attractive young women had disappeared, leaving her standing alone in front of the one-way glass.

Soon afterward, she was transported to a facility in Florida where her captors implemented techniques used in behavior management. Behavior control is the exercise of manipulating human behavior – the modern term for brainwashing. Through various methods of positive and negative reinforcement, research indicates that human behavior can be manipulated and controlled. They would play a verse from the Quran in English, then in Arabic. "There is no god but God. Muhammad is the messenger of God." The next day it would be a different verse. On the third day she would recite both verses, alternating until they were memorized. She later learned that she was memorizing the Five Pillars of Islam. She was always under surveillance, even when sleeping. When in the presence of men, she was fully covered in a burqa.

She remained in the Florida facility for approximately six months before she was finally transported to South America. There, she attended her medical school. It was similar to most major universities in the United States, with the exception of two twenty foot fences containing razor wire at the top, completely surrounding it. There was a road between the fences maintained by five teams of men patrolling it to prevent escape. Some had tried and were immediately executed in the square at the center of the school in various barbaric ways. Some were merely decapitated. Others were brutally tortured, then allowed to slowly die as they were left to bleed out from their wounds. One man had both feet cut off and was left screaming in the square. His screams eventually turned to a whimper, then with his dying breath he cried, "Jesus, forgive me." With that, one of the nearby guards laughing and taunting him casually walked over to him. Squatting down, he crushed a cigarette butt into the young man's forehead. He then drew a large knife and severed his head.

Days turned into years, and upon graduating from the program, Jennifer was transported to the facility in the middle of the Buffalo National River Wilderness area. There were no graduation ceremonies or parties. She received no card from her parents, and as far as she knew, her parents assumed she was long dead. Soon after that, the pandemic struck. Coincidentally, the occupants of the base were already immune due to a series of vaccinations that were provided by the Sheikh's friends in Washington who coordinated the vaccine with the CDC. Sheikh Nu'man Mahannad was elusive, and mostly an introvert. He ruled his theocracy with an iron fist and no exceptions to the rules. Sharia law had been enforced since the creation of the compounds. The Supremacy Clause in Article Six of the Constitution basically says that the U. S. Constitution is the supreme law of the land. Sharia law eliminates any authority of the U. S. Constitution wherever it is allowed to be implemented. There is no tolerance. Sharia law is barbaric and brutal, with punishment often including the severing of limbs and mutilation of body parts. Women basically have no rights, and denying Allah was a capital offence requiring decapitation.

Jennifer woke early the next morning with the sound of someone beating on her door. She quickly slipped into her burqa and stood behind her door asking, "Who is it?"

Ali responded, "It is I Ms. Boudreaux, Ali. I have some news about your daughter. Please, let me in at once." Jennifer unlocked the door and opened it slightly. Ali was standing there alone with a worried look on his face.

"Come on in," Jennifer said hesitantly. "I have to be at prayer soon". Ali's worried expression quickly transformed into a more sinister smile and he responded in a less than worried tone.

"Maybe we can just stay here for a while, together, alone."

CHAPTER 17

Theresa leaned back and stretched her legs as she put the truck on cruise control. *This is so cool, push a button and the truck maintains the speed*, she thought. Teenagers after the Fall did not have the luxury or experience the anticipation of waiting to get a driver's license. For most kids then, it was a rite of passage, one more step in becoming an adult. She had spent about thirty minutes figuring out many of the controls on Sam's old truck, and tried to maintain about fifty to fifty-five miles per hour. In some places she had to slow down to a crawl, driving around potholes and through craters created by years of decay. In some cases, as they drew nearer to Tulsa, Theresa was slowly driving around old and rotting abandoned cars and trucks, left where they had died in the middle of the road with no one to tow them and no one who cared. The country's highway system had become more of a defensive driving obstacle course. The rattle of the old diesel engine had lulled Elise, Tiffany and Sara to sleep, and Theresa had the whole road to herself. On the west side of Tulsa, the cars and trucks thinned out, and she was able to resume a more comfortable speed. Theresa looked over at Sara – she was wide awake with a huge grin. Apparently, the anticipation and adventure of being free on the open road while running down a highway with the windows open on a clear spring day had them both feeling exhilarated.

The hours passed, the miles flew by, and Theresa realized they needed a plan for fuel. The truck had almost a full tank when they started, and the trip computer display still read 276 miles until empty, but if she could find fuel she would top off the tank at every opportunity. Hopefully she could catch up to Sam at some point, hoping he would stay on or near the highway. They passed the Cleveland, Oklahoma exit and continued driving on the Cimarron Turnpike that runs from Cleveland to I-35. It took only about an hour to reach the Stillwater exit. *Travel by motorized vehicle is amazing*, she thought. They could be in Salida in a day and a half. The girls were all awake now and enjoying the ride. It was not long before they topped a hill and could see the truck stop at the intersection of I-35 and 412 highways. Theresa released her foot from the accelerator. Elise looked at Theresa and said, "What are you going to do?"

Theresa laughed and said, "It's a gas station. I'm gonna get some gas." She turned into the station and pulled up next to a diesel pump as naturally as if it were twenty years ago. Four men leaning against their bikes were staring at the girls with their mouths hanging open, and another man almost fell off his horse as the horse turned abruptly reacting to the noisy truck pulling into the truck stop. Theresa nonchalantly stepped out of the old Dodge and walked around the truck toward the station, smiling at the men, leaving them speechless. One man stumbled, almost falling on his face as he reached forward to open the door for the beautiful young woman. *Well*, she thought, *this is going to take some getting used to.* Since she could remember, Theresa was treated like a slave with the exception of her mother, who treated her as a mother should. Women in the compounds were slaves unless their placement dictated otherwise, as in Theresa's mother's case. There was no chivalry. Men were taught to focus entirely on training and becoming soldiers. Chivalry was dead in the compounds. Romance was forbidden. The Imams maintained the perception that romance made men weak. Keeping the men satisfied was part of their brainwashing. Her mother had told her several years ago about life on the outside, and Theresa longed to dance on the beach herself one day.

She entered the building and approached the counter to the right. An older, heavier lady named Anna was behind the counter selling cigars, pipe tobacco, homemade pipes and other items that would interest the clientele of the club. Anna looked up from an old romance novel, somewhat surprised to see a pretty young lady, and asked, "What can I get for you?" Theresa replied,

"I need some diesel."

"What do you have to barter with?"

"I have some things in the truck I can trade," Theresa replied.

Ann shouted over the juke box playing in the corner, "Hey Joel! Gotta chick here that needs some diesel!"

The men standing outside had gotten past the initial shock of attractive women in old pickup trucks, and immediately became curious. All four approached the truck, and Elise, Tiffany and Sara became nervous. Not one to take chances, Sara and Elise picked up the handguns resting in their laps and pointed them in the direction of the four men. Elise shouted, "Stay where you are!" Sam was the first man who had ever treated them with respect, and they knew he was an exception. In this new world outside the compounds they did not know who to trust, and Elise was not going to take a chance with anyone. The man who had opened the door for Theresa took a step forward and said,

"Wait a minute, honey, we don't mean noth--" BOOM. Sara had shot the ground in front of him and shouted,

"Mister, I don't know you, and the odds are against you seeing the sunset if you take another step!"

Theresa burst through the door of the truck stop, running toward the truck and yelled, "Stop Sara, don't kill him!" The man looked back at Theresa with Joel following close behind and stuttered,

"I…I…I d-d-didn't mean no harm, ma'am, we'uns just l-l-lookin at yer truck." Visibly shaken, the man walked slowly into the truck stop, his friends laughing at him. Theresa looked at Sara sternly and said,

"Not everyone is bad outside the compound. We'll have to start trusting people again." Joel looked at Theresa with a curious expression,

"Compound?"

"It's a long story," Theresa said, avoiding the question. The wheels were obviously turning in this man's head, Theresa thought. "We need Diesel and can trade for it," she said. Joel looked at the truck, peering into the bed of it.

"Where in the hell did you girls come across an old truck like this?" he asked. "That is part of the same long story," Theresa replied. He was getting way to nosey, she thought, glad that he knew that the girls in the cab were all armed and not afraid to use a gun. He glanced over at Sara who was giving him the evil eye now.

"You're Sam's girls aren't cha?" Joel looked at Theresa, and it was her turn to look a little shocked.

"I'm not sure what you're talking about," Theresa replied, still wondering where this was going.

"Sam Crow, U.S. Marshal. Stopped here several nights ago and told me the whole story. Why are you following him?" Theresa paused for a minute, realizing she had to start taking her own advice and trust people out here in the real world.

"Bad men are still chasing us. They tried to kill us at his house," she said hesitantly.

"Ok," Joel said, "You girls put your guns away and come on in. Y'all will be safe here for the night and we'll lock your truck up in the shop. I believe you will enjoy someone cooking for you for a change." Joel took them to the back of the club into the kitchen and started grilling some hamburgers and fries. He poured them some sweet tea and said, "Now we have time for your story."

CHAPTER 18

The rain was fierce and the thunder rattled the metal roof for most of the night. Restful sleep was not to be had between the storm and the close quarters of the horses. Sam woke up long before dawn and started the fire from the remaining embers that still were glowing bright red. Most of the men were awake, but not yet ready to admit it. Jam was still cutting a snore that would make a grizzly jealous. That freight train of a man could make some noise. Sam found two cinder blocks and the remnants of an old metal chair for a platform to put a pot of coffee on to boil. As the darkness turned to grey and then to light, the storm subsided and moved on to antagonize someone else. As the sound of thunder grew more and more distant, the pot began to boil. Sam moved it to the side of the fire and poured a cup. He leaned back on his saddle and was beginning to enjoy the crack and hiss of the fire when he heard the shuffle of feet behind him on the concrete floor. He quickly stood and prepared for the worst. Reaching for his gun, he paused and looked into the eyes of an older man steadying himself with a cane. He stood there grinning for a second and then said, "You got an extra cup for an old friend?"

Sam paused and looked closely at the old fella who had obviously seen some wilder days. His old gray mustache curved down around his mouth almost to his chin, like a hairy horseshoe. He looked like he used to be tall, but life had taken him down a notch or two. He stood as best as he could with his Stetson Buffalo hat which had obviously seen better days. Sam looked into his eyes and saw something familiar, but wasn't quite sure. "Walt?" he grinned.

"I never thought I'd see a Marshal this far west ever again, much less a stubborn young punk like you," he laughed. "Son, the last time I saw you, you was at Judge McClintock's funeral, and you were still strutting around like a bull elk guarding his herd."

"Yeah, that's been a while," Sam said. Most of the guys were sitting up on their elbows, or leaning back on their saddles, grinning, watching the fireworks about to start.

Walt Conner had started his career with the U. S. Marshals in the early 1970s. His life of war began in a late 1960s tour in Vietnam as a Green Beret. He was hired by the Marshals and assisted in integration in the mid-1970s, facing riots, bigots and hard, ugly times caused by ignorance and evil. His attitude had always been pure cowboy. Saddle up when it's time and don't hesitate to do what's right. When Sam was hired in the early '90s, he was hanging up his gun. His only remaining mission was to make Sam a Deputy. Walt was the training officer, and was the meanest man Sam had ever met. He was taller then, by three inches, and had a grip that could bring a man to his knees. The first time Sam shook Walt's hand, he almost did just that. Walt squeezed, and Lord he squeezed hard. Sam returned the grip and squeezed as hard as he could. They stood there shaking hands for at least a minute. Sam remembered it well. He hurt me then, he thought, but I would never let him know it. They both released, and Walt looked at Sam, kind of how he was looking at him now and said, "You'll do."

Walt sat down, took his cup in both hands and swirled it like a glass of fine wine. He smelled the aroma of the dark, rich, black coffee and tilted his head up slightly, closing his eyes. He lifted his cup, "To the good old days," he said. They sat there quietly for a few minutes, seeming to embrace every memory of his past. After another sip from the cup, he paused and started talking. With his eyes still closed he said, "I saw many things then, things I never thought I would see in America. America…the name itself is enough to give a good man chills. The greatest Nation falls to the greatest of sins: greed and laziness. Socialism is a philosophy of sin that people grabbed hold of because they never, ever had to fight for anything in their life. Success was handed to them on the backs of others until the government ran out of success. The backs of those that made the greatest nation were broken and then the vultures came to feed."

Walt retired after Sam's third year, and he did not see him again until Judge McClintock's funeral. He often wondered about what became of Walt.

"Walt, what brought you this far west?" Sam asked.

"Well, we lived in East Tulsa for a bit, and then the illegals ran us out, stole almost everything I had. One day I looked at my wife and said, 'Let's go to my folk's home out west.' Their ranch was small, but I knew it was safe. It wasn't much, only forty-five acres that ran along the Beaver River. We had been here for almost ten years, so happy. I would never have thought I would find such peace in a place like this, with a woman like that, but I did. She led me to Jesus, and I found the joy I had been missing all those years. I had let my work lead me when God had been tapping on my shoulder all along. She died six months later when the pandemic came and took her home." Walt swirled the remaining bit of coffee in his cup and threw it into the fire with a hiss. "Thanks brother." Brother … it was the first time he had ever acknowledged Sam as an equal.

"Walt, I am sure you are here for a reason, if none other than to give more advice to your rookie. I need you to listen for a minute about what is happening right now. Whether you like it or not, one way or another, either because you were once a Deputy, or because you are an American, you are involved." Sam spent the next few minutes giving Walt the condensed version of the last few weeks of his life. Walt had taken two oaths in his life; both required protecting and supporting the U. S. Constitution. When Sam finished talking, Walt turned and started walking toward the door of the Tire Shop. Sam shouted, "Hey, where are you going?" Walt replied without turning his head or missing a step.

"I'll need my guns for this … and my horse." Sam shook his head, slightly amazed at first. He started to protest, but then thought *hell, in all reality I'm too old for this as well, and I was his student.*

Sam followed Walt outside and watched him step up into the saddle and swing his leg over. "I'll be back soon, don't leave without me, that is an order." He winked at Sam, and with an expression that seemed somewhat youthful, Walt urged his horse to a gallop. As he rode away, Sam realized there were people standing across the road in the yards, all the way down the highway. They were all walking toward Sam and his men. They were coming from every direction. Most of them looked like farmers or shop keepers. Men and women, black and white, with no weapons, no hate, and no one looked threatening. They all walked toward the heavily armed group together, obviously curious. Strangers traveling in large groups in this part of the country were not normal. In fact, usually this many men with this many guns was an immediate call for alarm, but the residents of Guymon sensed something different, if merely only by recognizing the fact that all the men were smiling. Most of the men were up and standing, horses saddled, ready for battle – or ready for breakfast, it didn't matter, but breakfast was always better.

A small group of residents approached the group of warriors as if they were delegates of the community, the leader being a young lady in her thirties. She reached out her hand to Sam and introduced herself. "Good morning, my name is Tala, Tala Johnson."

"Good morning, ma'am. My name is Samson Crow. I'm a Deputy U.S. Marshal, and these men are traveling with me on a mission. We appreciate the use of the old metal building during the storm."

"That's no problem," she said. "When we realized we had some new tenants, I sent for Walt so that he could check on things for us. We don't have a Sheriff or a Town Marshal, so we depend a lot on Walt for that sort of thing. I don't want to be persistently nosey, but it is a very strange day indeed when a group as large as yours shows up in the middle of nowhere Oklahoma on a top secret mission."

"Well right now, Ms. Johnson, there are too many eyes and ears, and news travels fast, even out here. I will say this. If we do not succeed, the future of communities like this looks bleak."

As the conversation came to an end, Walt was returning with his toys. He was very old school and would probably wear a denim three piece leisure suit if he could still find one. When he worked fugitives, he had always worn a pair of Smith and Wesson model 66's on either side, and in his day could shoot equally well with either hand. The Model 66 is a .357 magnum, and He preferred a 4-inch barrel. "Just because," he said, "it looks meaner." A small leather pouch was slung around his shoulder and hung loosely behind his left holster. It was just large enough to keep six speed loaders handy in case of a gun battle. In his scabbard was an old Winchester model 1892, also chambered in .357. Walt had always preferred quality over quantity. Even now, Sam would hate to tango with him. Being old in his case just meant that he had that many more years to get meaner.

Realizing there was no threat and there was little more to say, the crowd had started thinning, and people were returning to their homes. Ms. Johnson turned back to Walt and Sam and said, “I hope you and your men can stay one more evening with us. I think we can put together some pretty good home cooking, and it doesn’t look like you have been eating very well lately. Maybe we can find some supplies to get you through the next few days.”

“Yes ma’am. I don’t think my men would object to that at all.”

CHAPTER 19

Jennifer realized this was not going to be a good day, whatever the outcome. She was a woman and Sharia law inevitably leaves her at a disadvantage. This was primarily a damned if you do, damned if you don't choice she had to make. If she fought back and resisted Ali, she could be prosecuted for assaulting him and punished with a torturous death, usually by stoning. Most rape victims under Sharia law ultimately become the receivers of punishment due to the archaic requirement of evidence. There must be either a confession of the accused, or at least four Muslim adult male witnesses. According to the Penal Law of Islam, the evidence of women was inadmissible by Sharia Law on account of their weakness of understanding, want of memory, and incapacity of governing. Jennifer had seen too many young girls' lives destroyed to get in a situation in which the man was able to defend himself before the other Imams. It did not matter what the woman's evidence or testimony was, she would lose because of her gender. Her only alternative was to kill or be killed.

Ali entered the room and shut the door behind him, locking both the deadbolt and the knob. He turned around and scanned the room to find that Jennifer was not there. He walked through the living room and into the kitchen. The pantry door was open, but it was empty with the exception of canned goods and other assorted foods, a bag of potatoes and a large trash bag. He walked into the bedroom and the adjoining bath. Nothing … where did she go? Surely, he must have missed something. He knelt down to look under the bed skirt. *Shoes*, he thought. *Why do women need so many shoes?* He put his hand on the side of the bed to push himself up and was startled by a dull thud. As he tried to gather himself he heard it again, and this time something snapped … as he fell backward into darkness, the last thing he saw was Jennifer, standing over him with a cast iron skillet.

"Should have checked the trash," she said coolly. She knelt beside him to check for a pulse. Not finding one, she ran her finger along the flat spot on the side of his head where the skillet had crushed his skull. *I've wanted to do that for so long*, she thought. Ali had tormented her since the day she arrived. Most of the Imams at the Arkansas compound treated her well enough; politely, and with respect of her knowledge and profession. Ali had been different, resenting everything about her. He seemed threatened by an intelligent woman who had established a place for herself in a society of men, a society dominated by men, a society where women were slaves. She thrived as an exception, and his desire was to put her in her place. Her place as of now was standing over him with a skillet. *I wonder if he gets his 72 virgins now*, she thought.

Her mind racing, Jennifer knew she had to hurry. *Now, what do I do with the body?* she thought. *I need to go to prayer, be seen in public, and teach my class. I'll have to figure something out later.* Ali was not very tall, but he was fat and hairy. The thought of him in her bed made her stomach turn. She dragged him into her bathroom. The tile floor would be easier to clean if he started bleeding while she was gone. Bodies did strange things after death. Fluids followed the path of least resistance, and without a heart pumping the blood, gravity would allow it to settle. Blood lividity was used in crime scene investigation to determine how a body was positioned after death. It could tell investigators if a body was moved, and how long it had been since it was moved.

Jennifer made it to prayer on time, went through the motions and prayed to her God. She asked for forgiveness and guidance on how to deal with this, fearing that if she told anyone the truth, she would be stoned or decapitated. She finished her prayer and ran to class. By the time everyone was seated, she had written an extensive study guide on the board for a test on the following day, allowing everyone to have a group study for the next one and a half hours to prepare. There were thirty questions and thirty students.

"Each student must answer one of the questions in essay form, then share the answers with the rest of the class. This will not only determine your ability to research, but also your capacity for working as a team." She had made the whole thing up, but it was a good excuse to get away. Jennifer ran down to the lab, grabbed a powered bone saw that ran on a rechargeable battery and hid it under her burqa. *They've hidden bombs and tools of terror under their clothing for years. Now it's my turn.* She ran across the street and through the park to her condominium. It was used for many years for the skiing season, but no one skied anymore. Fumbling with the keys, she unlocked the door, ran to the kitchen, grabbed the trash bags and stripped down to her underwear. She picked up the bone saw and went into the bathroom, already regretting what she was about to do.

With only an hour left, Jennifer needed to hurry. He deserved to die, no doubt. *It was him or me*, she thought. And if she pursued the proper channels in this barbaric society, she soon would be nothing more than a memory. People who were stoned or slain as punishment were either buried in an unmarked grave, or cremated. There were no families here, only soldiers, leaders and slaves. *I am a glorified slave, she thought, being used for their benefit and when they are done, I will be discarded just as anyone else who isn't in their men's Muslim club.* She walked into the bathroom and the floor was empty.

She stood in shock for a moment and looked around, making sure her memory was correct on where she had placed the body. *He was dead, I know that he was. It is not possible for a man to survive a blow such as that, she thought. Have I lost my mind? I know I am not crazy.* She reconstructed the incident in her mind, going through every detail, yet had no explanation other than someone else removing the body…but who?

CHAPTER 20

Theresa began slowly at first, but as she continued to speak, the story flowed from her. As a bartender, Joel had learned how to be a good listener. It was a good trait for a bartender as it made for good tips, but he had made it an art. She told him everything about the girls, the kidnappings, the breeding of slaves, and the children being abused and discarded like old newspapers. By the time Theresa was finished, Joel had made a decision. He could not imagine being born into such a living hell. Speechless for the most part, he choked and said, "I am so sorry." He hung his head for a minute and started what seemed to be a confession. "I have taken advantage of people on this highway for a long time. I know me and my men have gotten away with some pretty rotten things. Sam changed that for me. He has good in him, and he seemed to remind me of a better time, when the reward was not a selfish one. He made me want to help. Now you and your friends are here, and I am convinced we are here for a reason…and it's not to become a Muslim!"

The night grew long for Theresa as she stayed up to talk more with Joel about the plans for Islam in America. Her eyes were tired and fighting to stay open, and Joel knew she needed sleep. He showed her and the girls to the storage room, and how to lock it from the inside so that they would not worry about being disturbed. The storage room contained two bunks for when they stayed late and preferred not to go home. Tonight, he was staying, he had much to do.

The next morning, the girls awoke to the smell of bacon, eggs, homemade biscuits and fresh coffee. They unlocked the storage room door and walked into the club. It was madness. Anna was cooking breakfast for everyone, and there seemed to be thirty or more men at the tables eating breakfast. Most were dressed in leather or jeans, wearing different colors of motorcycle gangs or motorcycle clubs from police or Christian backgrounds. One vest said "Regulators LEO's," and another said "Jesus Disciples.". Theresa walked through the club, stepping left and right to dodge the backs of chairs with men rushing about, getting ready for something. She saw Joel behind the counter, and he was helping Anna with breakfast. He saw Theresa and his eyes lit up. "Good morning, young lady. Hope you got enough sleep."

"Yes sir, I did," she replied. "What is all this … these people … these men? Are you planning something?"

"Well yes, I am. Have a seat, get some breakfast, and I'll come tell you all about it." Theresa and the girls sat down at one of the few remaining tables and waited on Joel. As the minutes passed, several of the men who had noticed them had walked by, tipped their hats, and in some form or another said thank you, whether it was a nod of the head or just a sympathetic smile.

Joel arrived at the table with an enormous platter of eggs, bacon, pancakes, and anything else you could imagine for breakfast. Elise, Tiffany and Sara were astounded and immediately dove in. It was a buffet of food like they had never seen. Theresa looked at Joel with a confused look on her face and asked, "What is going on here, Joel?"

He put the platter down on a table next to them and said, "This is all for you. It's for all those that have suffered like you. We are here to help. We are going to help Sam."

Theresa was dumbfounded. She looked at Joel and said, "Do you have any idea what you are going up against? There are thousands of soldiers in Salida. There are thousands in Arkansas, and several other areas of the country I am unsure about." Joel looked at her momentarily, then pointed out the window.

"Yeah, we figured that. But they don't have a flag!"

Theresa looked out the window, and Sam's truck was back at the pumps. It was loaded cab-high with crates of supplies tied down with cargo netting and ratchet straps. Attached to the tow receiver on the back bumper was a flag holder with a large American flag flowing majestically in the breeze.

She looked at Joel and asked, "Where in the world did you find all the supplies and the flag?"

Joel casually gestured to the room of people. "We have a lot of friends here, and many of the supplies are from my storage bunkers. I figure if Sam loses we won't need them anyhow. Now eat your breakfast, and when you're done meet me outside."

Theresa, Elise, Tiffany and Sara sat in awe of all the hustle and work that was being done in preparation. Men from all over had dropped everything in their lives to come to the aid of their country, not knowing the odds or if they would ever return home again. *What could stand against an army of men like this?* Theresa thought. They finished their breakfast and walked out to the truck. It was full, and several gas canisters were loaded in the bed with the other supplies against the tailgate. Joel met them at the truck and said, "You have enough diesel to get you to the Arizona coast if the need arises. We'll follow you on our bikes with several other SUVs, a couple of old Suburban's, and an Escalade with a 22,000 gallon tanker truck behind us so we will not run out of gas. We have about fifty people in all, with a multitude of weapons. We're not the military, but we're the next best thing!"

Theresa smiled and shook her head. "I don't know what to say. Thank you."

"Lady, you can thank me when we're done," Joel said with a chuckle. "I might not want to thank you once we get there."

Joel walked to the back of the caravan, checking with everyone to see if they were ready. He walked over to Anna who stood in the doorway of the truck stop, and kissed her goodbye. "Take care sweet lady. We'll be fine, and when I come home we'll take a ride down to the beach. Lie in the sand, feed the sea gulls, and have a cold beer."

She laughed and pushed him away. "Just get back here you stupid fool." He walked backward for a few steps and turned, blew her a kiss, walked to his bike, and then swung his leg over. He cranked his bike, and the rest of the crew cranked their bikes in unison. Tiffany and Sara jumped at the sound, surprised, as if it were a new threat they had yet to see. They turned to look, and it was just those little bikes making all that noise.

"Lord," Sara said. "That's worse than this diesel. Hope we don't have to sneak up on somebody." Theresa put the truck in drive, and they pulled out of the parking lot with Anna still standing in the door. She waved as they turned out on Highway 412, the American flag waving proudly on the back of Sam's old truck with half a hundred bikers and four girls on their way to war.

CHAPTER 21

President Bradshaw sat quietly in the oval office looking at the case that he had obtained from the National Archives Building containing the U. S. Constitution. As the rest of the world had succumbed to the pressure of Islam, he looked at the words of Ronald Reagan in the picture frame on his desk. "Freedom is never more than one generation away from extinction. We didn't pass it to our children in the bloodstream. It must be fought for, protected, and handed on for them to do the same, or one day we will spend our sunset years telling our children and our children's children what it was like in the United States when men were free." He put his face in his hands and wept. He would go down in history as the last president the greatest nation ever had. He would be the one that raised the white flag and said we don't want freedom anymore....take us, we are yours.

The United States was able to maintain for a while after the nukes, but an unforeseen foe rallied throughout the world. Islam had organized into one voice by one man, Sheikh Nu'man Mahannad. His name in Arabic meant "blood sword." The world had become mostly Muslim now because no one was strong enough to fight back. The ignorant were easily led, and those who rebelled were executed. The Sheikh had used money and intimidation to gain control of the United Nations, and they were well on their way to a New World Order with Sharia law being implemented in most countries. The only ally the United States had was Israel. Through all the international conflict and war, including nuclear missiles crossing back and forth across the globe, the tiny little country was still alive and kicking back.

Sheikh Mahannad had made it clear that if he did not surrender the Constitution on July Fourth, he would destroy New York City. Any attempt to block this action by law enforcement or evacuation would result in the immediate destruction of Manhattan. The president had a very small team of trusted individuals within the Secret Service searching for several things. They obviously had a mole in the White House, probably had The White House and Congress bugged. They could not trust anyone in the Department of Homeland Security, and the National Security Agency was being controlled by the United Nations at the request of Congress. Congress had basically sold their souls for twenty pieces of silver.

The Sheikh's plan was well on its way to being complete, and total world domination by theocracy was inevitable. Islam's ultimate goal was worldwide control enforced by Sharia law, and if the United States failed, freedom was lost. The Sheikh's people were communicating regularly by methods that had yet to be intercepted. Congress seemed to be helping the Sheikh indirectly by approving the funding bills for the United Nations that continued to support the destruction of the United States from within, ultimately at the direction of Sheikh Mahannad. The United States was paying for their own destruction with the United Nations holding the purse. The Sheikh alleged that he had a more than one hundred thousand man army scattered throughout the U.S. with military grade equipment to forcibly effect a takeover if this agreement was not reached peacefully. President Bradshaw knew that ultimately Neverland would never surrender, and blood would spill from sea to shining sea once the epic event took place on the Fourth of July. The Sheikh's plans were to video tape the ceremony of burning the U. S. Constitution and distribute the event throughout the world, proving that democracy and capitalism were failures, and that the only answer to world peace is Islam.

The agent supervising the President's Secret Service team arrived and knocked on the door of the Oval Office. The President got up from his desk, cleared his eyes and regained his composure. He opened the door for the agent and trusted friend of many years. "Kevin," he said. "How are you?" He shook the agent's hand and held his index finger over his lips, indicating not to talk.

Kevin said, "I am fine, and you?" Kevin Landrum had been around the Agency for years, and they had first met during a Congressional Subcommittee Meeting when Tom Bradshaw was a freshman Senator. The investigation involved the Counselor in the U. S. Department of State releasing top secret information in a press release that revealed the position of some operatives in hostile situations. Two of the men were killed and one was injured. They had continued to run into each other over the years as the President had continued to gain in popularity. Agent Landrum had become a very good asset to have, who also seemed to be a true patriot in spite of all the corruption that circulated through the ranks in Washington D.C.

The President rambled on about life in general and proceeded to escort the agent across the room to another door, leading him into the Rose Garden. He maintained his general comments well out of the snooping ears of anyone or any device that may betray their real purpose for visiting. "Well, Kevin. Have you found anything helpful?" He finally asked.

"Yes and no. I think we have identified their ability to communicate, but have yet to break the code. They appear to be using a series of antiquated analog cell towers. They are sending coded messages to each other using the towers and analog pagers from the 1990s, bouncing messages off of the towers just as they used to use the telegraph in the Old West. It is not a very efficient or secure method, but we have no way of intercepting their messages until we access the frequency of the pagers. I will keep you informed if anything else along those lines develops."

"Thank you, Kevin. Please do."

"One other thing," Kevin added. "A friend of mine from years ago was murdered last month in Oklahoma. Some believe he was executed for snooping around some of the wrong places we've been talking about. I reached out to another old friend who is an FBI Agent in Tulsa, and he confirmed the rumor. He also added that we may have some help out there soon. He wouldn't say what, but that we should just have faith in some old friends."

The President shook his head and said, "Thank you Kevin, it is always good to see you."

"Likewise, sir."

They shook hands and parted ways, the President returned to his office as Kevin walked toward the gate.

CHAPTER 22

The sound of the wind and the horse's hoofs were all that could be heard after leaving Guymon. The men hated leaving such wonderful hospitality after the peaceful evening of food and rest. Their bellies still full and the horses loaded with new supplies, Walt and Sam led the procession through the sweeping plain that was the Oklahoma Panhandle. The homegrown group of patriots had picked up six more men in Guymon, much to the dismay of their families and friends. Most realized that this, perhaps, was freedom's last stand. Grass and old broken down windmills lined the highway as far as they could see. Boise City was a ghost town. Nothing was left to indicate that anyone had been there in years other than to pilfer through the abandoned buildings and homes. Sam passed an old vacant restaurant that brought back some wonderful memories. His truck had broken down on the way to an elk hunt in Colorado, and he and Melissa had been stranded in the parking lot of this old restaurant. The people of Boise City had come to the couple's rescue by helping Sam repair his truck, keeping them on the road during their vacation. Every year afterward they would stop at the Rockin A Café to eat, regardless of the time of day. The building now was a mere shell with nothing more than a broken coffee cup on the counter to remind Sam of the past.

They arrived at the center of town where the Town Square and Courthouse is located. Boise City's claim to fame was being the only city in the United States ever bombed by a B-17 Flying Fortress Bomber. During a training run, a crew performing target practice mistook the lights from the town square as their target. Sam stopped at the square and realized he had a choice to make. For years he had traveled in this way by truck, and the fastest way by highway was southwest to Clayton New Mexico, then over to Raton climbing into the Rockies through Raton Pass. "I think we can save some time by traveling across country northwest from here. We can cross through the Black Mesa and into New Mexico at Kenton. I think we can make Trinidad in a week's time," he said to Walt as he nodded in agreement.

The days had grown warm and long, and traveling with the exception of occasional spring storms was good. Spring in the Oklahoma Panhandle is a game of craps. It can be eighty degrees, sunny and beautiful, and the next day twenty-five degrees with fifteen inches of snow on the ground. It can melt and be sunny again just as fast. Land around Boise City is flat, but its elevation was about 4,000 feet. A few miles northwest of Boise City is the beginning of some very beautiful and rugged country. At 5000 feet in elevation, the Black Mesa was a plateau that marks where the Rocky Mountains meet the shortgrass prairie.

They made camp at an old farm on the western edge of town which had a working well pumped by an old windmill. They had thirty-five horses now, and a good water supply was necessary. Knowing that from this point on the terrain was going to get more difficult, Sam thought it was a good idea to rest the horses for another day. Traveling in the high country for the next several weeks was going to be rough. Winter usually hangs around through the middle of June, and there is always a chance of violent storms, blizzards and avalanches. Walt walked over to where Sam was looking hard at a topo map.

"What's your plan, Honcho?"

"Well, the primary mission is just getting there. I would like to make camp close, within striking distance, and send in small groups for a week or two doing reconnaissance. We have to get some intel of what we are up against. That's where Daniel comes in. He has been there and is familiar with the layout and who is in charge. I have a real good idea, but it's going to take me trusting Daniel more than I do right now."

The next morning, the men rose at sunrise and prepared their horses and gear for travel. As everyone climbed into the saddle and situated themselves, Sam turned back to them all and spoke, "The way is about to get tough and hard, and I would understand if some of you are having second thoughts and would prefer to be home helping and protecting your families.

If we fail, we will all probably be executed. The odds are stacked heavily against us, and if you want to turn back, this is your opportunity." Sam waited a few seconds, sitting there leaning on his saddle horn, gazing at each of the men. Several of the horses nervously moved side to side, stomping their feet, anticipating the opportunity to go somewhere. Hesitantly, a voice from the back of the crowd coming from the youngest of the brothers from Stillwater said,

"Sir, we are all still here and ready for your orders." Sam nodded at the young man and silently turned Patton, pointing him northwest. He gave him a pat on the neck and urged him forward. Patton trotted through the gate as though he was excited to be on the trail again.

As they left the small abandoned farm, Sam took a moment to tie an orange strip of flagging tape to the gate they traveled through, hoping that others who had decided to help may follow. On the edge of the tape with a pen he drew a small star with a circle, easily identifying who had made this trail.

The weather in Boise City had been tolerable – warm in the sun when you are out of the north wind. At four thousand feet above sea level, the wind was still cool for April, but as they continued to gain in elevation, the temperature consistently dropped.

Sam was smiling. The beauty of the high country was always breathtaking, even though they were still just in the foothills of the high mesas. Those who embrace the moments in the wild welcome the chill of the clean air, and the peace of the wide open spaces. The thrills of seeing an eagle fly or the resonating trumpet and shrill whistle of the elk bugle bring a chill to those who live for these experiences. *Every time I return to the mountains, Sam thought, I have a deep rooted feeling that I am returning home, while every time I leave the mountains, I fear I may never see them again.*

They traveled for two days bushwhacking through the wild, not seeing any evidence of human traffic. As they rode slowly toward their goal, they were learning much about one another and becoming more like family, a band of brothers with a common cause. Sam was confident as they crossed into Colorado that they would have to be more and more discreet to avoid contact with settlements of people. There was no way for them to know who supported Islam. On day three from Boise City they topped a hill, and in the distance saw a small town. Sam backed off of the ridge for fear of being seen. "Sky-lining" is a term used to describe those ignorant of surviving in potentially hostile country by standing on a ridge above a potential enemy, easily revealing your position to them. The only advantage at this point was the element of surprise. A small team in secret can sometimes effect more damage than an entire regiment of infantry. The art of a covert war by a small team was to be a ghost of sorts. Sneak in under the cover of darkness, create fear and doubt with psychological warfare tactics, and wait for an opportunity. When it occurs, cut off the head of the snake.

Sam looked at the map and determined this was a small town just inside the southern Colorado state line called Trinchera. Sam and his riders retreated south for about a mile and avoided any contact with the residents, not wanting to call attention to their presence. Once they were comfortably south of the town, they continued west for another day and made camp along McBride Creek just east of Interstate 25. This interstate ran north and south through Colorado. Sam referred back to his map and determined they were about fifteen miles south of Trinidad, north of Raton Pass. Since they were traveling in a fairly large group, it was impossible to conceal signs of their passing. Walt suggested that they post a rear guard to maintain watch in case nosey people crossed their backtrail. Sam started the rotation the first night with two men rotating a position at least half a mile down the trail. There was no use in taking risks at this point. They had to maintain the integrity of the mission.

It was the beginning of May, and they were beginning to see what the mountains looked like to early explorers. The snow up high was starting to melt, and the streams and rivers were starting to swell. They had yet to see any of the extreme interior of the mountains, but Sam could not imagine the awe that Vasquez de Coronado or Zebulon Pike experienced during their adventures. Coronado spent several years seeking the mythical Seven Cities of Gold, but found the Great Plains of Kansas instead. Returning to Mexico a failure, he was almost prosecuted for war crimes and died of an infectious disease several years later. Pike attempted to climb a peak later named for him, and was captured by the Spanish after venturing into Spanish territory (southern Colorado) by mistake. He later died in the War of 1812. Both men were blessed to live their lives having seen the Rocky Mountains – something many people have never had the opportunity to do.

As Sam got closer to the mountains, he felt energized and youthful; not as tired as an old man should feel after weeks in the saddle. The Rocky Mountains was more than a view, it was an experience that affected a person not only physically, but emotionally and spiritually as well. Sam realized it was all part of him now: the clean, crisp smell of the high mountain air, the peaceful sound of the wind in the evergreens, the thrill of when a man stood on the edge of forever and looked across at the unbelievable to have watched a sunset that words could never describe. Sam truly believed he was home. He knew the mountains had created an addiction that could never be cured by anything less than more of the same.

CHAPTER 23

Jennifer sat quietly on the edge of her bed looking at the bathroom door, trying to wrap her head around the facts of this situation. Someone had to know something about what happened here earlier, someone who had access to this apartment and could get in and out quickly without any indication of forced entry, someone who had knowledge, experience and the strength to remove the body, a really fat body, cleaning the area as if nothing ever happened here. She glanced at the clock realizing she had fifteen minutes to get back to the class. She quickly pulled the burqa over her head. *Since I am probably being watched, I should wear this horrible nightmare of clothing twenty-four hours a day*, she thought as she walked out her door. Worrying at this point was useless. If the bad guys knew what happened, she would already be headless. Someone was watching her, maybe even helping her, and now she had to figure out why, and who.

The classroom was quiet as she entered. It was easy to hide her nervousness under the burqa. Heck, it was easy hiding a lot under one of these tents. She walked casually over to her desk and sat down. Her students were still finishing the quiz she gave them earlier. As each group placed their pencils on their desks, they all seemed to relax, breathing a little easier with one more burden of the day being lifted. Jennifer looked at the clock on the wall and said, "Time, please place your pencils on your desk and turn to face the front of the room." In unison, the classroom shifted until all desks were back in their original position, facing front toward her desk. "Now," she said regaining her composure after the confusion of the last hour, "without looking at the questions or the answers to this quiz, look at the person to your left. Okay, now look at the person to your right. How did you like depending on your partners for the answer? Are you sure they are correct? Do you trust the guy next to you?" Everyone sat quietly, unsure of how to respond. "Okay," she proceeded. "Open your minds and think outside the box. Help me out here. If you are in the field in an emergency situation, are you going to be able to open a book, or depend on the person to your left or your right? Odds are, your only resource is your mind. It is all on you! There are no group hugs in the field. There are no classroom discussions, and certainly no group projects. I am sure you initially thought today's lesson was cake, or easy, and you were getting off the hook, but think about this the next time you want to slack off on your homework or cheat on a test. This is about life and death, and you may have no other person to depend on when you're trying to save someone's life. Who wants to be lying in a puddle of blood, look up, and see the guy that depended on everyone else in class to save their life? Now pass your papers to the front for grading." She collected the papers and wrote the next day's assignment on the board. She turned to face the class of young men, each staring blankly at her, not used to being ridiculed or spoken to in such a fashion, but each of them realizing she spoke the truth.

Jennifer dismissed her students and turned, leaving the classroom. She walked briskly into the cold wind, crossing the street into the park separating the training building from the condo. As she walked through the park, she felt as if she were being watched. She huddled under the burqa, appreciating its one positive quality: warmth. Looking around, she saw no one there but an older Muslim man sitting on a park bench. At this point, being timid and afraid did not suit her, so she walked over and sat down. The man kindly asked, "How are you today?"

"I have had better days."

The older Muslim man stood slowly, pushing himself up with the arm rest of the park bench. He turned to face her, nodded humbly and said, "Do not let your heart be troubled, neither let it be afraid." He stepped past her and walked north toward the end of town as she sat quietly with her mouth open.

That was the book of John, she thought. He quoted the words of Christ. She stood shaking her head, and walked toward her condo confused, worried and somewhat at peace. *Apparently someone is looking out for me,* she thought as she unlocked her door.

She entered her apartment, walked back to the bathroom just to reassure herself that the body was really gone, then discarded the dreaded burqa and walked into the kitchen area. Reaching into the cupboard, she grabbed her favorite cup with palm trees and seagulls while warming some water on the stove. Once the little tea pot started to whistle, she poured the cup and dipped the tea bag, steeping it briefly before cradling the cup with both hands and collapsing into her recliner in front of the picture window facing the western ridge. Finishing her tea, she leaned back and cuddled into a blanket, falling asleep and dreaming of a younger better time when the sand was warm and the water crashed against the shoreline in a peaceful cascade, swirling around their bare feet as they walked hand in hand down a lonely beach.

Jennifer awoke to the sound of knocking at her door. Covering herself, she looked through her peep hole and saw Abdallah Kahlil. Abdallah was an Imam who, in spite of his young age, had gained the Sheikh's favor and handled much of the business at the hospital. Abdallah was always nice and gracious, one of the few who seemed to actually respect her for what she did. Without opening the door she said calmly, "Good afternoon, Abdallah. How can I help you today?"

"Dr. Boudreaux, I have been trying to locate Ali. I saw him early this morning and knew that he always liked to check on you and your class. Have you by chance seen him this morning?"

Jennifer responded, "No sir, he usually greets me at the door of my classroom after prayer, and this morning I did make a mental note that he failed to show."

"Well if you do see him, would you tell him that I am looking for him?" Abdallah walked away, and Jennifer knew she had to make a plan of survival. She needed a secluded place of safety she could retreat to if things started going badly here. Obviously there is someone or some group here that is working covertly against the Sheikh and his minions, someone that is surprisingly Christian.

She walked into her closet and grabbed a backpack that she used to carry her books in when she attended medical school. One of the things that she had learned about Combat Medic training was survival. The four keys to survival were shelter, water, fire and food. She put a small medical kit into the backpack which included surgical tools, quick clot, a tourniquet, a full pack of 4x4 gauze pads and medical scissors. She included four bottles of water and a large bag of trail mix consisting of dehydrated fruit and nuts which she had made herself. She folded a raincoat tightly, tucking it into its own pocket, compressing it into a little ball. She went into the bathroom and grabbed the extra shower curtain, thinking she could use it for a tarp if there was a need to construct a makeshift shelter. She opened a drawer in the kitchen, retrieving an old Leatherman tool, three lighters and a heavy bread knife with a serrated edge that she could use as a saw. She then collected string, zip ties, a small steak knife and a hammer. Looking in the cupboard, she threw in some canned beans and corn with a can opener. She lifted the bag checking the weight, and determined it was about as heavy as it needed to be for a hasty retreat. Satisfied that her go bag was complete, she went to her closet and set out an old pair of jeans, some hiking boots and a more suitable coat for a Colorado winter. The burqa wasn't going to cut it.

CHAPTER 24

The night sky was unbelievably clear. The moon was bright and high, creating almost daylight conditions as the sun started to mark its entry into the day. Sam already had a good fire going and a pot of coffee brewing as the men were loading up and saddling their horses. As the sky became lighter, the sound of a galloping horse was heard approaching. "Rider to the rear!" someone shouted.

"Secure a safe position, weapons ready!" Sam shouted to the men. One of the men standing rear guard was riding hard straight into camp.

"Hold your fire, hold your fire!" he shouted. He swung is leg over and dropped to the ground before his horse came to a complete stop using the momentum to maintain a jog over to where Walt, Daniel and Sam were standing. Grinning ear to ear and trying to catch his breath he stated, "A scout messenger trailing us approached and hailed us just minutes ago, requesting that we hold our positon for half a day and let his company of men catch up."

"Company?" Sam asked.

"Yessir, that's what he said."

"How do you know he's friendly?"

"He gave me this," he replied. "And he'll probably want it back."

The young deputy extended his hand, and within it was a badge that said "Deputy U. S. Marshal." Sam flipped it over, and sure enough there was a number indicating it was assigned to a commissioned Deputy. As the sun rose higher, a man rode into camp straight up our backtrail. He stopped for a moment looking around, finally making eye contact with Sam, and began to smile.

Sam laughed, "Get off your horse and have some coffee." Looking back at the messenger, Sam said, "Ride back out and grab your buddy, I don't think there is need for a rear guard at this point." Sam reached out his hand to greet the new arrival and said, "Long time brother, where have you been?"

"Texas, need I say more? Bad things are happening everywhere. Our Marshal got the message from your Chief, and we dropped everything. The word spread pretty quickly throughout Texas and by the time we hit Amarillo we had a small army and more kept coming, Marshals both active and retired, Texas Rangers, sheriffs, police, military, and heck just some good old cowboys lookin for a fight."

Sam returned the badge to the Deputy and said with a grin, "A business card would have done just fine." Years ago, back in the day, business cards were exchanged and collected to maintain contacts across country. Just like in any exclusive group of competitive people, it became a contest of who had the coolest business card. Then someone came along and invented smartphones with contact lists. Another tradition destroyed by technology.

Garrison Jones had been a deputy for five days longer than Sam. They had worked side by side on many assignments, and learned much about trust early on when dealing with some of the most dangerous people in the world. Garrison looked over at Jam, then at Walt, then around the circle of old friends. "Wow, what a crew. It's like getting on the bus the first day of school."

By noon the entire company of men rolled in, and it took them about thirty minutes to finally all arrive in camp and dismount. The man in front leading the procession proudly displayed a large American Flag. It was like a picture you would see somewhere in a library showing an artist's rendition of a Revolutionary War battle. Sam was amazed at the number of men and horses. There was an abundance of shaking hands and brotherly hugs. Most were loaded for war. There were four wagons carrying supplies, and one wagon carrying plastic drums of water.

Sam looked at Garrison and asked, "I know everything so far has been mostly by the seat of the pants, but we need to organize and separate this enormous group of troops into companies or platoons. How many men do you think you have?"

Garrison looked back down the long line of men relaxing after the long hard ride chasing Sam's posse and replied, "I quit counting at Amarillo. We had over two hundred then and I think we picked up at least that many by the time we entered New Mexico. They just kept riding in, and there may be more on the way. Thanks for the flagging in Boise City by the way. We were about to stay on the highway through Clayton when one of the scouts picked up the trail going off road."

"No problem, brother. We need an accurate count and a way to separate the men so that we can manage them as we develop a strategy."

Sam sent Jenson Clayton back down the line counting men. I looked at Garrison. "Do you know how many Marshals you have?"

"Eighty-two."

"And Rangers?"

"At least a hundred," he replied. "And a hundred more locals and cowboys combined."

Sam thought for a few minutes, looking down the ever growing line of men and said, "We have about three hundred and fifty soldiers combined. I think we should divide them into platoons of fifty, and select seven men to be their leaders."

"Who do you have in mind?" Garrison asked.

"I am not sure. But we have enough experience here to take out a small planet of terrorists. I have a plan for a small group of us to recon the town and get as much intel as possible. I am hoping that they have been untouchable for so long that they have grown lazy with their security. Maybe a team of us, with a little guidance from an asset we have developed in Daniel, can gain access to the Sheikh and maybe even intercept the President with the Constitution. If we start off with a show of force, the President will leave on Air Force One and we will have blown that opportunity. Let the insertion team covertly secure the package, then we can play Cowboys and Terrorists with all the wannabes wearing the dresses."

Daniel raised his hand, still attached to the other with a handcuff. I chuckled a bit. "Come over here." Daniel stepped over to where I was, somewhat embarrassed. "Show me your hands." He held out his hands and his poor wrists were rubbed almost raw from wearing his cuffs for several weeks. The kid never complained, and Sam obviously felt bad for letting it get that far, but he had just not reached the point where he could trust him with the security of this mission, until now. Sam pulled the key out of his pocket and removed the cuffs. "Daniel, I am entrusting you with intelligence of the highest priority. The security of what is left of this country lies in this small group of men and with our plan of action. I believe you have proven yourself worthy to be a part of this. If you prove me wrong I will hunt you down and skin you alive where you lie. Do you believe me?"

"Yessir," he replied quickly, nodding his head.

"Are you loyal to this country and our mission?"

Again he replied, "Yessir."

"Very well then, you'll do." Sam glanced at Walt, who winked back and grinned under that mean mustache of his.

"Now Daniel, what do you want to tell us?"

"Sir, there are a lot of troops there in Salida, but like me, many people are just trying to survive. They were kidnapped and sucked into this cult-like lifestyle where there is no freedom, and most think there is no escape. The minds of the people that were converted like me are basically brainwashed by the leaders or the Imams using propaganda. There is no information from the outside world. They probably don't have any idea that a chance for a true America still exists. If the word got out that America was making a comeback, I think there are many that would turn and fight for us."

"That may be a tool in our shed that we can use, and it is much appreciated. We just need to find a way to plant that seed and let it grow and spread without it being obvious," Sam replied.

Jenson returned and said, "Three hundred and sixty four."

Sam looked around the group of people closest to him and saw so much potential ability. Delegating who goes where is difficult when you have men of this caliber that can do all of the above. Sam looked at Garrison and said, "I need you to assign the leaders for the seven platoons. You know your men much better than I do, and heck you know most of mine. Also, there may be more men coming in from Kansas and possibly Missouri waiting for us at La Veta. The men I want on my insertion team are Charlie from OK City, Matt from Kansas, Jam, Daniel, Walt, you and myself. I think there is plenty of leadership talent that can follow orders and delegate our commands, but I need the most talent on the inside securing the President and the package."

Walt looked at me with a confused look on his face. "Are you sure you want this old man in your op?"

"Walt," Sam said with much conviction, "you, sir, are meaner and tougher than most men half your age. You'll be just fine!"

They loaded the wagons and pointed the wagon train northwest, climbing up onto I-25 by midday. They traveled hard all afternoon, seeing no one else on the highway. It was surreal traveling the country on vacant interstates by horseback. They reached Starkeville, Colorado in the late afternoon and turned west, avoiding Trinidad. Trinidad was sure to have a number of people who would take notice of a small army moving north through their state. They continued west beyond Trinidad lake until they intersected Highway 12 close to dark. Because of the proximity to Trinidad, they made a cold camp in a canyon east of Segundo. The following morning, they broke camp before sunrise and headed west. As they rode by one farm, children were out playing in the front yard and a man was splitting wood. The ground was still partially covered with snow, but it was warm enough for the man swinging an axe to wear a t-shirt. The kids were excited to see so many horses and people, and the man paused and watched as the procession passed. Sam waved to him, and he waved back with a puzzled look on his face. They made easy time on Highway 12 through Cuchara, and finally to La Veta. Then without warning, what Sam had feared the most happened.

CHAPTER 25

Agent Landrum quietly knocked on the second floor suite of the White House. President Bradshaw answered the door quietly and ushered Agent Landrum inside. The suite, referred to as the President's Bedroom is large, plush and comfortable enough to provide accommodations for both the President and the First Lady. Many past presidents did not sleep with their wives due to reasons including sleep apnea, stressed induced insomnia, the temperature of the room and promiscuity. Bradshaw on the contrary, preferred it. He commonly referred to their bedroom as his "Fortress of Solitude," claiming the First Lady was his peace of mind. William Howard Taft chose to sleep on the roof of the White House in a screened porch, probably due to the unbearable summer heat.

The First Lady, obviously still asleep with an abundance of hair in her face, leaned up on her elbow, looked at them without seeing, rolled over with her back to them and resumed her dreams. The President looked at Agent Landrum and with a nod of his head indicated that he should follow him into the next room. He closed the door quietly behind him, turned to Agent Landrum and whispered, "Is there any good news for a change?"

Kevin responded, "Yes and no, the good news is we have broken the code."

"And the bad?" asked the President.

"We believe it is their intent to execute you during the ceremony while burning the constitution."

President Bradshaw slowly took a seat in the high back recliner by the coffee table. He gestured to Kevin to have a seat across from him. "So now what?" he asked.

"Sir, we have one of our tech guys and several agents in New York working on locating the bomb or bombs. Agent Jonathan Stevens developed a small handheld dirty bomb detector from antiquated models that were developed after 9/11. The company that held the government contract has long since gone under, and no one currently makes replacements for the rechargeable batteries. Agent Stevens was somehow able to convert the power source to regular D cell batteries. The only problem now is that the detector burns the D cell battery up in just a matter of minutes. We either have to have some intel on the location of the bomb, or just get damn lucky."

"Keep trying," Bradshaw said. "I'm sure something will break. Any news from out west?"

"Nothing yet. Until we can get our own encoded towers back up we are limited to Pony Express. I'll keep you informed." Kevin rose and quietly exited the sitting room, letting himself out of the Suite. The First Lady still lay sleeping with one hand tucked underneath her chin, and an expression on her face that said she was thinking way too hard for it to be a dream. She grunted slightly and in one motion, lifted and turned to flop over to her other side.

President Bradshaw returned to the bed and sat on its edge. Quietly he stood, entered the enormous walk-in closet and dressed for work. He walked through the corridors greeting good morning to the agents who had the burden of standing post most of the night, every night. Surprised, each of them seemed somewhat grateful that he recognized their effort, and in turn they each returned the greeting, "Good morning, sir." President Bradshaw entered the Oval Office, picked up the phone and called the Vice President. After five rings, Vice President Moore answered and said "What?"

"Don't you miss the days of caller ID," President Bradshaw replied. Before the Vice President could say anything, President Bradshaw added, "I need you in the Oval Office immediately, see you in a few." Without giving him a chance to respond, he hung up and called the kitchen. A sleepy cook answered with, "Yes sir, what can I get you sir?"

The President replied, "A pot of hot black coffee please."

An hour later, the door opened to the Oval Office and Vice President Moore stormed in with blaring attitude. "This better be good," he stated shortly as he glared at the President.

"Get a cup of coffee, sit down and cut the attitude," the President said casually. He looked sternly at his choice for Vice President and said, "Richard, we have a choice to make right now. I think there are a few people that still love this country, and I am hoping that you are one. I read the names of our brothers in Congress, and I fear that most of them have been held hostage by money, fear or intimidation to lower their moral standards and betray this country. I have an idea that if what I fear comes to pass, the enemy will eventually kill us all. I need to know what side you are on."

"What do you mean what side am I on? Are you questioning my loyalty?"

The President stood, and poured a fresh cup of coffee and replied, "Richard, I have my sources, and much more at my disposal than you can imagine. I know what has been going on. I have information suggesting that you have been a part of this conspiracy, and for whatever reason it is not too late to turn from this madness and save this country." Richard's mouth dropped open. For the first time since he burst through the door, he was no longer the aggressor. He had fumbled the kickoff, and Bradshaw saw it in his eyes.

The President pushed him further. "I have been following the trails of money from the approvals Congress has been so willing to give the United Nations, and I am convinced that a majority of the members of Congress have committed treason and should hang for being traitors to this country and betraying their oath of office. Justify it how you will, but I think you know everything that is going on. I am giving you a chance to do the right thing."

Vice President Moore replied, "Are you out of your mind? They have guaranteed a place for all of us in their New World Order. We cannot back out now. They will nuke New York at the drop of a hat and if they hear of this conversation. They might do it anyway! You do not have any idea what they are capable of!"

President Bradshaw reached down and pushed a button on a panel next to his phone. Seconds later, three agents walked into the office as if they were looking for a fight. "No Richard, I had no idea what they are capable of, but I do now. And unfortunately I know what you are capable of. Agents, place this man in restraints." Without question, the agents handcuffed the Vice President and moved him to a chair, then stood guard on either side. One agent then took a post to stand outside the door of the Oval office.

President Bradshaw then reached into a drawer on his desk and pressed the stop button on an old battery-operated cassette recorder. He picked up the phone and dialed a number. On the other end of the line, Agent Kevin Landrum had just taken off his clothes and climbed into bed.

"Hello. I need you in my office. I've got a mouse in a trap and I don't know what to do with it."

CHAPTER 26

The diesel hummed and rattled down the highway, giving a rhythm to the roar of the motorcycles that followed. They rolled through Enid within an hour and knocked the dust off of the Glass Mountains two hours later. Joel had sent a bike ahead looking for signs of Sam's Posse. They arrived in Woodward just hours after they started. Theresa pulled the truck into an old truck stop and got out to stretch her legs. Elise, Tiffany and Sara all hit the ground running around to the back of the building looking for some privacy so they could use the restroom. Joel laughed with the other guys. "Just like old times," he said. As soon as the girls returned, they all took turns doing the same thing.

"I wish this place was still open," one man near the back of the line said. "They had the greasiest, most wonderful bacon burgers you ever sank your teeth in."

Everyone was ready to ride, and within minutes they were back on the open road. Two hours later they pulled through Guymon. Everyone in town heard the motors approaching and came out to wave as if it were a parade. The motorcade continued on to Boise City, and as they approached the town, the scout that Joel had sent out earlier was waiting by the side of the road. As they drew near, he pulled out in front and indicated for the group to follow him. He drove through town, around the Town Square with the Court House, and then proceeded west to the edge of town next to a farm, where he pulled over and stopped. Theresa pulled the truck over and Joel pulled in beside them. The scout got off his bike as they faced the setting sun and waited for the motorcade to come to a stop and kill their engines. Joel asked, "What'd ya find?"

The scout responded, "This is the only place that I have found consistent sign. They camped at this farm for a night. Then crossed the road over there and took everything through that gate. They flagged it with an orange piece of tape."

"How do you know it was Sam?" Joel asked.

"He drew a Marshal's star on it," the scout replied. "And that's not all. More horses came through and followed them a couple of days later."

"How many more?" Joel asked.

"A lot, I mean at least a hundred."

Joel looked at Theresa, who looked worried now.

"Tim, was the second group of horses running?"

"No sir and they had several wagons."

Joel turned to Theresa and said, "They are being followed by more Marshals. Bad guys would be moving fast, and they would not have left the trail marker." Joel turned to the rest of the group and shouted, "Let's camp here." Everyone dismounted and started making camp. The sun was setting, the land was flat and the sky was clear all the way to the horizon with the exception of a few high clouds. They had a campfire going before dark, and most were hungry and tired. The girls stretched out inside the truck, leaving the men to roll around on their hard bedrolls. Elise cracked the window on her side and started giggling. Theresa asked, "What?"

"Listen." Pretty soon they could hear just about every one of the men who had been riding bikes snoring. All the girls giggled.

The next morning was clear and cold, but everyone was up and ready to move. They broke out their insulated coveralls to try and stay warm as they rode. They traveled west through Clayton, New Mexico and on through Raton by noon. They climbed Raton Pass and entered Colorado the easy way. The further north they got the more snow they started to see, causing the bikes to slow down through some patches still lingering on the road. With the sun out, it quickly melted on pavement, but in the high country there were places in the shadow of the mountains all day. As they drew closer to Trinidad, they saw Tim the scout waiting at an exit. They all pulled in to stop, and Tim pointed over at a fence post on the west side of the road.

"Orange flagging with a star," he said to Joel. The motorcade turned at Starkville and cut over to Highway 12. *We are on the right trail at least for a little while, but at some point, Sam's going to have to take his army off road again*, Joel thought.

The motorcade pulled through Segundo and turned north at Stonewall. They rode past a farm with some children outside playing and a man in a t-shirt cutting wood. Joel waved to him and the man waved back, shaking his head. *The big diesel cruising by flying the American flag with an entourage of motorcycles had to be a good sign for people*, Joel thought. They picked their way through the mountains and made Cuchara by midafternoon. After a quick bathroom break, Joel approached the girls and said, "I think we can make La Veta easily before dark."

Theresa got out of the truck, grabbed one of the diesel canisters and started pouring it into the tank of the big Dodge. She looked across the bed of the truck at Joel and said, "We can camp at La Veta. But I would really like one of those hamburgers right now."

"Wouldn't we all," Joel laughed. Convenience was a thing of the past, and it would take years for the country to recover. Milk, eggs and anything that was related to mere survival was no longer easily accessible. Mere survival was now a luxury, and people were facing hardships that had not been faced in almost one hundred years. It was as if someone had pressed a reset button and took the world back to the early 1900s – the Great Depression.

CHAPTER 27

Sheikh Nu'man Mahannad sat quietly looking across the Arkansas River, sipping on a cup of coffee. He turned to the young man beside him and asked, "Are you sure our asset at the White House has been compromised?"

"We have had no word from him in three days now. We must assume the worst."

"Very well," said the Sheikh, "I think we need to reinforce their commitment to compliance. It appears that they may be underestimating my resolve."

"Is there a target in mind sir?" the young man asked.

"Always," the Sheikh replied with a smirk from his downturned lips. For almost two thousand years the people of Muhammad have waged a holy war against the infidel, against capitalism, against Christianity, against democracy, against anything and everything that is not Islam. Their barbaric laws and punishments were not accepted by Western civilization. The west had grown weak and sympathetic for the criminal, oftentimes turning its back on the victim, embracing a tolerance for those who perverted anything good and most of all, turning its back on its own God.

For the first 1400 years, Islam attacked relentlessly and would eventually be beaten back time and time again. But Sheikh Nu'man Mahannad had a revelation. Wait, be patient…. The West softens every day we do not attack. Give them time and they will destroy themselves by tolerating everything and enforcing nothing. Infiltrate by planting seeds and letting them grow. Plant them, develop them, let them influence transition. Patience will allow the conversion of a nation with minimal violence and bloodshed. The only roadblock was Neverland. The roots of the West grow deep in Neverland,

and here there will be war. *With the infrastructure and grid collapsed minimizing communication ability, it will be easy to hide the slaughter*, thought the Sheikh. *The people of Neverland will expect help from their government as always, but this time I own the government. I am the government. Interesting, I manipulated the United Nations, and then manipulated the U. S. Congress. They pay me to pay them to do my bidding. How simple it is to control the greedy. Find out what they want and dangle it in front of their face.* The Sheikh laughed to himself.

He looked to the young man waiting patiently for a reply. "Take out the Supreme Court. Tell the media to report it as "Christian Terrorism"...the agents of Neverland attacked the United States."

The young man replied, "Yes, Your grace." He then spun on his heel and retreated quickly from the room.

Sheikh Mahannad was raised in Iraq and was a member of the Imperial Guard during Desert Storm. After the collapse of Iraq, and with Saddam Hussein arrested then executed, Nu'man Mahannad dedicated his life to the destruction of the United States of America. He had been involved in the planning of the September 11th Trade Center bombing and had been present in the Assault of the U. S. Embassy in Libya. He had become passionate about spilling the blood of Americans. As his rise to power became evident, his ability to devise plans of destruction became his talent. A devious mind with sociopathic tendencies, the Sheikh quickly became the most dangerous enemy the United States had since World War II. Hitler failed because he started the fight at home and spread his evil with violence. The Sheikh had let Islam spread through the West on the backs of tolerant liberals who are more than willing to forget the violence of Islam while condemning Christians as fanatical domestic terrorists. Now with the United States so divided, it will be easy to destroy what is left of conservative Christians. The democrats were so willing to embrace Islam after George Bush's terms that they put Muslims in key positions, strengthening the influence of Islam and the mission of global theocracy.

The irony of cutting off your nose to spite your face, chuckled the Sheikh.

Salida was selected by the Sheikh for various reasons. Its beauty and mild summer weather is without question. The hot springs in the area were another attraction that the Sheikh adored. The most important reason, however, was the name of the mountain range that begins at Salida and runs south through New Mexico. The Sangre de Cristo, or the Blood of Christ Mountains. They are named this for two reasons: the reddish hue which is cast by the sun at sunrise and sunset, and also when the alpenglow occurs. Alpenglow occurs when a red glowing line appears on the horizon opposite of the sun. The Sheikh had decided that not only would he destroy the U. S. Constitution and the President of the United States, but he would rename the Sangre de Cristo Mountains in his honor, Nu'man Mahannad Mountains – the Blood Sword Mountains.

In the 1980s, Islam was not accepted at all in America. The only Muslim activity that occurred was totally covert. The forefathers of ISIS saw the need for safe havens where Muslims could hide and be protected within the United States. That is when they developed the idea for the compounds. They populated the compounds with young children who were kidnapped or homeless. Occasionally they would abduct young beautiful women for their own pleasure, and to breed soldiers. After the pandemic and the nuclear wars had concluded, the Sheikh determined that the time was right for the second phase of his plan. They would actively approach the United Nations and the American government with bribery and extortion until the whole world's leadership was corrupt and on the verge of collapse. Then Phase Three: burning the U.S. Constitution and executing the American President on television for the world to see, ushering in the New World Order and introducing The New World Leader.

CHAPTER 28

Vice President Richard Moore sat shackled to a chair in the Oval Office. Two Secret Service Agents stood guard at either side of him, and one stood guard outside the door. The room was quiet with no one talking. The only sound to be heard was the second hand on the nine foot tall grandfather clock facing the President as he sat quietly behind the Resolute Desk. A knock on the door broke the monotony. "Enter," said the President. Agent Landrum approached as the President stood to greet him. "Glad you could get back here so quickly."

"Duty calls."

"Kevin, your men searched him for weapons but nothing more thorough. I don't know if he has a bug or a pager or anything else small enough to be overlooked in a frisk."

Agent Landrum set his gaze on the Vice President. "Sir, let me make a few things very clear before you say anything at all. You have compromised the security of the United States. You have conspired to commit treason, and you, sir, are a traitor. What happens next will determine whether you will receive the death penalty or be prosecuted with the ability to negotiate your sentence with a United States Attorney. I am giving you the opportunity to cooperate, and the chance to pray for a reduction in sentencing." The Vice President glared back at Kevin, displaying his answer in the expression on his face. Kevin walked over to him and bent down as the other two agents held him. Kevin emptied the Vice President's pockets and then stripped the belt from his waist. In doing so, a pager fell from his belt to the floor. "Hmmm," Kevin said bending down picking up the pager. He flipped it open, noting several unopened messages. Looking back at the Vice President, Kevin said, "Are you sure you do not want to work with me on this?" Vice President Moore looked at Kevin coldly and said,

"Hell no!" Kevin walked back across the room to President Bradshaw and said,

"I'm getting this pager to my tech guy to see what we can find. I don't want to open the messages because it may have a coded kill switch in it. I also recommend that the VP be held in the isolation cell of the Underground West Wing Command Center."

President Bradshaw walked over to Vice President Moore. "At one time I looked to you as family. You were a trusted friend. It is a tragedy what you let greed do to you. Get him out of my sight." Agent Landrum helped the other agents escort the Vice President down to the cell in the basement. The cell was ten by ten and designed to hold someone for only a few hours. It was cold and painted clinical white with a solid stainless steel fixed bench that doubled as a cot, with no windows. The only connection with the outside was a security camera protected by a clear bulletproof box, watching every move. Agent Landrum pulled the door closed and motioned to the guard to electronically seal the cell block. A loud metallic clunk confirmed that the doors were secure. Kevin peered over the guard's shoulder as he watched the security camera and saw the Vice President sitting on the metal bench with his head in his hands, sobbing.

Kevin left the White House and immediately drove to his office. It was already six in the morning, and he needed more coffee to survive. He brewed a fresh pot and sat at his desk waiting on his fellow agents to arrive. At seven, Gene Stallings bounded in after a workout at the gym. Not your typical tech nerd, Gene was a large man that could bench press almost five hundred pounds. Gene threw his gym bag under his desk and waddled over to the coffee machine. He glanced at Kevin and winked saying, "Leg day." Kevin shook his head smiling and replied,

"Hey Gigantus, come here and take a look at this." Gene walked over to Kevin's desk, wide shoulders swaying like a silverback gorilla as he dodged the desks and chairs in the squad room. Kevin handed the pager to Gene, who looked amazed.

"Man, I haven't seen one of these since I was a kid. Two-way pagers could send and receive text messages as long as there was a functioning network. Since the collapse of our infrastructure, there has only been isolated use of line of sight Broadband technology mostly used for security and some larger corporations. Nothing that we know about has allowed anything past line of sight." Gene flipped the pager open and powered it on. The yellowish green screen lit up and several messages appeared. "Wow, hey this thing is really working!" Gene shouted in excitement.

"Can you tell if it has a kill switch coded in it?"

"No man," he laughed, "these didn't have that technology. Hey! And the messages aren't even coded." Kevin jumped around the desk to look over Gene's shoulder.

"Whose is this?" Gene asked.

Kevin replied, "Thor."

"What? *Thor?* You're friggin' kidding me! They're talking about killing Odin!" The Secret Service uses code names for Presidents, family members, and people in the administrations with a protective detail. This particular administration used Norse gods for their code names, the President being Odin, Thor the Vice President, and so on. "Can you find anything else?" asked Kevin.

Gene said, "They have sent several general messages that he hasn't responded to. This last message is asking him to respond, is everything okay?" "Shoot a message back. Everything is fine." Gene typed the words quickly and hit send.

Where have you been?

"Say I've been sick with the flu." Gene typed another message and set the pager on his desk.

"I hope they believe--" The pager started buzzing again. Gene picked it up and read,

We thought you were compromised. Stay away from the SCUS.

Kevin grabbed the pager and typed,

Why, what have you done?

The pager replied with the same words.

Stay away from the SCUS.

Gene said "What is the SCUS?"

"I can only imagine it is their way of saying 'Supreme Court of the United States.' SCOTUS," replied Kevin as he was moving toward the phone on his desk. He dialed the President. President Bradshaw answered and before he could say anything, Kevin said, "They're going to take out the Supreme Court."

"When?"

"I don't know, Probably today. They just said stay away from it." Kevin hung up on the President and called the Secret Service Headquarters. "This is Agent Kevin Landrum in D.C. Give me the S.A.C right now. It's an emergency." The Senior Agent in Charge picked up the phone and asked, "What's up Agent?"

"I have word that someone may be taking out the Supreme Court.

"What?"

"Yes, you heard right. I don't know how, but I intercepted a text on a pager that read the SCUS was at risk." At that moment the phone in Kevin's ear went dead.

"Damn!" he shouted as he slammed the phone down on the receiver. He picked it back up to dial the number, but there was no dial tone. Kevin grabbed the pager, then he and Gene ran down the stairs to the parking garage and drove to the White House.

CHAPTER 29

La Veta was empty, nothing more than a ghost town. The procession stopped not far from the north edge of town next to the high school, and began unloading the supplies to camp. As Sam got a fire going, he noticed the wind picking up more out of the west. He looked back over the western range and saw some very dark, menacing clouds flowing over the Continental Divide and sweeping down the slope toward the valley. Thunder and lightning seemed to be chasing them over the ridge. As the clouds moved closer, a cold, chilling wind wrapped itself around Sam and caused him to shiver. Within minutes, heavy rain mixed with large snowflakes put out the fire, which soon became nothing more than a pile of wet logs. The rain started to freeze as the temperature rapidly dropped. They quickly corralled the horses across the road at the football field which had seen much better days, and hauled the gear into the La Veta Redskins High School to seek shelter.

The multitude of men quickly filled the rooms, offices and hallways of the small town school. Sam grabbed Jam, Charlie, Matt, Walt and Garrison, and walked them through the halls to the Principal's Office. "You gonna give me some licks?" Jam asked.

"Not in your wildest dreams young man!" Sam laughed. "I thought this would be a great opportunity to sit down and talk about strategy. I think the insertion team needs to leave tomorrow and start recon and build intel on Salida. I think the rest of the men should wait here for a few days to see if we get any additional reinforcements from Kansas or anywhere else. Tomorrow is June the first. We have one month to build our intelligence and make a plan. I think in two weeks the platoons should split into two groups. One group should travel over to Alamosa and move north up Highway 285, and the other group should go straight north from here and move up Highway 69. Each group should take up positions on either side of Methodist Mountain. Each of us will carry a flare gun and will use it appropriately if the mission becomes compromised. If possible, we will maintain our covert op until we can hopefully intercept the Constitution, secure the President, and eliminate this threat once and for all. It is my opinion that at this point they are not expecting any resistance, and definitely no offensive aggression by Neverland. Now are there any suggestions or recommendations?"

Jam slowly raised his hand. "Ya got any food?"

"Okay," Sam said, ignoring Jam as Walt snickered. "I think that concludes this meeting. Do I hear a move to adjourn this meeting?"

"Aye," said Garrison.

"Very well," I said. "Let's eat."

Sam's small group moved back to their saddles and gear, and Sam reached into his pack and threw Jam a bag of trail mix. He laughed in his deep gravelly voice and said, "Thank you. I love you man!" Sam smiled to himself thinking that gentle giant was good to the bone. He made his bed and easily fell asleep on the cold tile floor, even with all the snoring. He woke up early, about four a.m., made his way through the sleeping men in the hallway out to one of the covered landings at the end of the hallways and walked outside. The storm had passed, and the sky above was full of a billion stars. No moon at this elevation meant that you got to see every star in the universe. This is what the high country is all about. Sam made a fire from some old wood picked up at a house three doors down and cooked a pot of coffee. Soon the whole insertion team was standing there waiting on the pot to boil. Water takes longer to boil in the high country, therefore coffee takes more time; one of the only things Sam did not like about the high country.

The morning broke, and Sam let the men sleep as long as they could. Most were up and about early due to habit. Garrison sent out a hunting party to acquire more food. The supplies were depleted, and they were in need of a small herd of buffalo. By noon the hunting party was back, and their pack horses were stacked with beef quarters. Garrison walked up to Sam and started to speak, but Sam cut him off and said, "I don't wanna know."

Several men in the camp set about processing the quarters and jerking the meat. Several others pilfered through the old town and finally designed a large cooking spit, then placed two of the quarters on it. After a few minutes, the beef being seared over an open wood fire began to smell like pure heaven. Beef over a wood flame was the best tasting meat on earth, without exception.

Afternoon became evening, and the sun climbed down the mountain, crawling behind the Continental Divide. Most had eaten and their bellies were full. Sam told the platoon leaders to keep sending hunting parties out daily. The insertion group began to prepare to leave in the morning. They would head up the valley paralleling Highway 69, and eventually would cut across to Highway 50 and try to stay out of sight. Sam thought they might make Methodist Mountain in a couple of days and establish a camp there. After that, the plan would have to depend on the intelligence they develop.

Sam asked Garrison to have a five man team to leave camp and follow the previous team each morning, and at noon in case they met resistance and needed backup. This would create a chain of support that could respond more quickly than having the entire crew two to three days behind. In five days, there should be several teams all within a few hours of each other. The first team travels light, functioning like a scout team. The second team brings a supply horse with food and extra ammunition. The third team brings two supply horses, with no team needing any more than three supply horses. By the end of the week, they should have twenty-five men with ample supplies camping within a close proximity to Methodist Mountain.

The fire had all but died under the spit, and Sam was hungry. He looked at two of the men who had cooked the previous quarter and asked, "Is there anything left to cook? I'm hungry, and I'm sure someone else is." Sam nodded at Jam, then the cooks looked at Jam, and he pretended to be embarrassed.

"As long as he is around, I would have something cookin'. I don't care if it's road kill. You haven't seen terrorism until you've seen this man hungry."

The men put two front shoulders on the spit, and Jam sat down next to the fire waiting on his next meal. Sam walked back through the ranks just to see the attitudes of the men. Considering the circumstances, most seemed to be in good spirits, and as Sam walked by the last of them, one turned and looked south.

"Ya hear that?" he asked. Sam paused for a second, but heard nothing.

Other guys around him heard it and one said, "Yeah, it sounds like a stinkin herd of motorcycles coming our way. Sam still didn't hear anything.

Getting old sucks, He thought. "Thank God I'm retiring after this." Finally, Sam started hearing the hum of motors, then a rattle. He looked at the young men to his right. "That, gentlemen, is a 1999 Dodge Ram 2500 Cummins Diesel. It is black in color and will have four gorgeous young women driving it. You will not touch anything, including the women." Sam turned, walked back to the spit, sat down on a log and waited by the fire. Moments later, the truck that Sam described and a group of motorcycles rounded the corner and pulled up to the Redskins High School to park. Four beautiful girls got out of the truck. The bikers all shut down their motors and swung their legs over their bikes, stretching and trying to relax after a hard day's ride. The men standing at the rear of the line looked back at Sam shaking their heads when the four girls walked past. Theresa broke into a jog, and as Sam rose from the log she wrapped her arms around his neck. He hugged each of the girls as they ran to greet him, and he realized then that they really had become a family.

The evening was a fine one. Everyone ate their fill, and Sam told the girls his plan. They explained the story of the assassins arriving and their escape through the tunnel to get to Sam's truck. He realized that they may be living on borrowed time. If those assassins had any amount of skill, it would not take long for them to figure out Sam's plan. Sam told the girls they were to remain in La Veta and stay with the main body of troops. Theresa objected of course, her priority being the safety of her mother. Sam pointed out that Theresa's concern for her mother would not matter if Theresa was dead, and she ultimately agreed.

After dinner, Sam made sure their new friends were taken care of with food and shelter. La Veta was no longer a ghost town. The homes around the school had filled with soldiers preparing for battle, and it was a shame that such a beautiful place had become a staging ground for a bloody war against an evil that many still refused to recognize.

The next morning, the insertion team met at dawn. The men checked their packs and supplies. Sam brought out his whole war bag for this one. He carried his .450 Marlin on the right side in a scabbard. The 300 SAUM (short action ultra mag) was on the left. He placed the AR-15 on a single point sling across his back with a Glock 23 on his right hip. It had a fifteen round magazine with extension, and there were two more magazines available for reload on his left hip. The vest he wore contained four more fifteen round Glock magazines and two thirty round magazines for the AR-15. If all of that fails, his Ruger GP100 was in a cross draw holster with four speed loaders in the pockets of his coat. The pack horse had no less than a thousand more rounds on him, in addition to the food and coffee. Bullets, food and coffee always make for a good day. Patton was just happy to be on the trail again.

CHAPTER 30

Jennifer sat quietly in front of her big picture window facing the eastern ridge, trying to escape into her book. She realized the reality of life was causing distractions, and daydreaming while holding an open book seemed wasteful. She closed her book realizing her mind was focused on something other than staying in her prison. She had no place to go, and the Sheikh's assassins would find her and kill her if she left, which she feared had happened to her daughter. She had heard about the accident and knew that the girls had fled, but they had no reports of her capture or death. She still maintained hope, but it was starting to dwindle. She walked into the kitchen and poured a cup of coffee feeling tense, depressed and desperate for change. She walked to her window and looked out into the park below her condo. The squirrels were playfully chasing each other at the base of the old large willow trees in the park while some birds were feeding on the crumbs an old man was throwing from a small brown sack. It was a cold and misty morning that kept most people indoors, and much too early on a Saturday morning for anyone to be out feeding the birds.

Without hesitation, and with total disregard for her burqa, Jennifer put on her heavy coat and pulled the hood up over her head as she quickly ran down the flight of stairs. She saw the man walking away at the end of the park and started to follow him. He traveled north, picking up his pace as he rounded a corner. Jennifer maintained a safe distance as they walked toward the hospital where she still occasionally worked when she was not teaching school. The man walked unusually fast, and Jennifer was having a hard time keeping up without having to break into a jog. He turned in front of the hospital, crossed the bridge over the Arkansas River and made his way into Smeltertown.

Smeltertown was named for an enormous smokestack and smelter that was built at the turn of the twentieth century in 1902. The site of the smokestack and the land around it later became designated as a Superfund Site by the Environmental Protection Agency due to the heavy metals and other types of toxic waste being dumped along the banks of the Arkansas River in the form of slag. The smokestack was placed on the National Register of Historic Places, and served as a monument to the history of Salida. The Stack itself was surrounded by a locked high fence with razor wire to prevent vandalism. The man stopped at the gate which was secured by a chain and a lock, and quickly looked around to see if anyone was looking. Jennifer had pulled up short, peering at him from around the corner of a warehouse. He slipped through the gate without securing the lock, leaving the chain hanging.

Jennifer stopped. *He knew she was here. He wants me to follow*, she thought. Jennifer brazenly stepped from behind the building, walked deliberately to the gate and entered the prohibited area. Tired of this secret squirrel nonsense, she was ready for a confrontation. She closed the gate behind her and secured the lock to purposely show the stranger her intent. She followed him through the facility and into an open door located at the base of the smokestack. Inside the vacant building was office furniture appearing to be a century old, with three men sitting at an old wooden desk. They were all seated comfortably and facing her. She pulled the hood from over her head and took a step forward.

"Ma'am, would you please close the door behind you?" She turned to face the men and walked over to the desk. Each of them stood to greet her and offered his hand as a welcoming gesture. She hesitantly reached out and shook each hand as the man in the middle spoke. "Ms. Boudreaux, thank you for coming. Please have a seat and make yourself as comfortable as possible. My name is Special Agent McCrory. This is Agent Smalls and Agent Smith. We are with the Secret Service. We believe you are on our side and have decided to see if you wanted to be of service to the United States of America." Jennifer sat back in her chair and looked at each agent, shaking her head in disbelief.

"Why me?" she asked.

"We have had this facility under surveillance for a while, and we think that you and several others have exhibited the characteristics of potential assets."

"Assets?"

"Yes, during our time here we observe people and determine who may be willing to help us. We know about the Sheikh's plan, and we think you could assist us in stopping him."

"Again, why do you think I am an asset?"

Agent Smith said one word, "Ali." There was a pause.

"Oh, so you admit to breaking into my apartment and hiding a dead body?"

Agent McCrory responded, "Yes, we did. We were going to make contact with you that day, but saw Ali go into the condo ahead of us. We paused outside the door in case you needed us. Once we confirmed that you were fine, we waited until you left and then cleaned the apartment. I figured you may have needed a few days to process everything before we made contact again. Nice job by the way."

"Thank you, I think. So how do you think I can help?"

"In a nutshell, we are at a point in this investigation where we are confident that the United States of America is at risk. We believe the Sheikh has intentions to destroy the U.S. Constitution, kill the President, and take control of the United States surrendering it to the United Nations. In light of your skill set as a medical doctor, we believe you may have the opportunity to get close to him, thereby opening the door for us to come in and do our job. All we need is for you to keep your eyes open and keep us informed."

"How do I contact you?" she asked.

"We have obtained some of their two-way pagers that send and receive text." Agent Smith handed Jennifer a pager. "Our numbers are programmed into the speed dial pagers as one, two and three. Try and be as concise and discreet, using a code if possible. I do not want anyone to suspect you are on the other side. Don't change your normal routine, and don't let anyone see you with the pager. Drawing attention at this point could be catastrophic to our mission. Any questions?"

Jennifer sat quietly taking in all the information. Then she said, "I'm still not sure that I'm quite clear on what you expect. I doubt that I will have the opportunity to use the frying pan. In fact, I only see him during his yearly physical or when he is not well."

"When is he due for his next physical?" Agent Smalls asked.

"Not until August," Jennifer replied.

"Is there a chance that you could come up with an excuse to move up his physical?"

"Maybe. I'll have to wait and see. I worked on and off in the lab at the hospital where we worked on the vaccine for the pandemic, but the CDC provided us with one quickly enough. We had the cure within the first two weeks. Those in control let the pandemic run rampant for a couple of months before presenting the cure to the public, pretending to be the world's savior. The agents looked at one another shaking their heads.

Agent McCrory said, "It's a shame you can't design a new strain for a one shot deal."

"Yes, I have heard of research on DNA bullets but fortunately I do not think that you can get that specific as to create a disease to kill or disable even a small group of people, much less singling out one specific person. As convenient as it seems in this circumstance, I could easily imagine how the science of a DNA bullet could be abused with greed choosing the target. The science behind biological warfare is problematic because by opening Pandora's Box, you unleash the wrath of evil on everyone. It doesn't matter who is good or bad, friend or foe. Unless there is a vaccine that immunizes those we want to survive prior to exposure."

"That's a thought," said Agent Smalls. "I think we are satisfied you will make the right decisions concerning our mission and goals. You probably should be getting back to your condo. Hopefully an opportunity will present itself soon. We are here if you need us."

"Thank you," Jennifer said. "I will make myself more available at the research department and the hospital…who knows, maybe we'll get lucky."

McCrory replied, "I don't believe in luck. Ms. Boudreaux. Let's create that opportunity." He smiled confidently.

Jennifer nodded, placed the pager in her coat pocket and made her way out of the smokestack and through the fence. The wind was picking up out of the north, and she looked back over her right shoulder to see the clouds gathering as they came rolling over Mount Antero northeast of town. She picked up her pace and hurried home, not liking the thought of being caught in a storm. She fumbled with her keys and quickly shut her door. Hanging her coat on the rack beside the door, she shrugged off the cold and embraced the warmth of her apartment. She walked into the kitchen and heated some water for tea. She turned facing the living room and looked directly into his sinister eyes.

CHAPTER 31

Agents Landrum and Stallings raced to the White House on foot, their primary concern being the President. Somewhat in a panic themselves, they had no way of knowing if their assignment, The President, had not been a target as well. The streets were in a panic with people running about. Those who had cars were stuck in a one-way gridlock. The agents worked their way through the crowded streets and badged their way through the front gate of the White House. The Uniformed Division Guards were obviously on high alert, but they recognized their own and let them pass. They made their way to the Oval Office where the doors were closed and agents stood guard. Agents Landrum and Stallings approached the door, and one of the men standing guard addressed Agent Landrum. "Sorry Kevin, it will be a few minutes before the President wants to see anyone." Gene sat down in a chair across the hallway from the door, catching his breath from the half-mile sprint and obstacle course they just ran. Kevin was too agitated to sit, so he tried to cool down by pacing up and down the hallway.

Minutes later the door opened. The President stuck his head out and said, "Kevin, come on in, glad you're here. It is worse than we thought. They leveled the Supreme Court. No Justices were inside, thank God, but there were civilian casualties. Then somehow they patched Mahannad through to my desk phone. Vice President Moore is not the only mole."

Kevin responded, "Yes sir, I know. I think we have to assume there are many more and must be extra careful now that the VP is secured and we have the pager. I should be getting a Pony Express message tomorrow."

"Are there any new messages on the pager?" President Bradshaw asked.

"None, but that doesn't surprise me. They apparently only send messages once a week for a routine com check, or when something important is happening. What did Mahannad say?"

"He questioned my ability to lead this country through it and emphasized his resolve to follow through with the transition regardless of my lack of loyalty to his cause. He stated that Neverland would be blamed for this bombing, and that if we didn't comply we would be next. Kevin, I don't need to tell you that I do not know how deep their moles have dug. I have no one in my cabinet or staff that I trust right now. You and your immediate support group is all we have. We must win, or America is lost forever."

"Thank you sir," Kevin responded.

"I have an idea," said Gene. "In light of this bombing we need to set up the old metal detectors. By scanning people as they enter the White House, we can determine who is wearing these pagers."

"Yes," the President said. "That is a good idea, and I need to develop a story as to where the VP is. Keeping him isolated in the basement at this point is kidnapping, but I'll face those charges later. If Mahannad is not taken out, kidnapping will be the least of our worries."

Turning to Gene, Kevin said, "Why don't you get the magnetometers and see if you can find the old metal detecting wands they use to pinpoint targets without anyone disrobing. Let's wait until late tonight to set everything up. That way, those wearing the pagers cannot leave them in their cars or at home. We should seize any and all pagers telling the employees they may pick them up once they are determined safe. I think now that the VP has had time to think about his situation, I would like to have a few minutes alone with him." Kevin walked quickly out of the office and made his way down to the basement cell block. He checked with the agent maintaining security of the cell block area and the electronic seal was disengaged, unlocking the door. Vice President Moore sat on the cot with his back against the cold grey wall, reading a book. Agent Landrum leaned against the wall and watched him for a moment.

He closed the book and set it on the cot. Looking at the wall, avoiding eye contact, he said, "Tell the President thank you for the Bible. I would go nuts in here without it."

Kevin replied, "I will. Have you thought about my offer of talking with me? Maybe putting our heads together and helping us with a plan to keep America intact?"

The Vice President continued to stare at the wall. "I made my bed. I became proud. I envied what someone else had and wanted it for myself. I think you and your people would be better off without me."

"What if you could go back and have another opportunity to make the right choice… would you?" Kevin asked.

"In retrospect, yes, but there is no way to undo the damage." Moore said.

"No, but we can minimize it," said Kevin.

"How?" asked Moore.

"I need a list of all those in the White House staff, the cabinet, anyone in Congress who is helping Mahannad. If you provide that, I'll help you stay out of prison. Think about it. If the President succeeds and you are instrumental in that success, then you may have an opportunity for pardon. If you do not help, you have failed in both efforts." Vice President Moore sat on the edge of the bed, now staring at the floor. Slowly rising, he turned to Kevin and stuck his hand out.

"I'll do whatever I can. Get me something to write with."

The Vice President spent the next hour creating a list of people he knew who were involved in this conspiracy to overthrow the United States. Once he was finished, he handed the list to Agent Landrum. Kevin stood there for a moment and said, "I don't see any names of Congress on here."

"There aren't any," Moore replied. "They haven't actively participated. None of them have a pager. They are told how to vote and they blindly obey. They've been voting this country away and they don't even know it."

"Look," Kevin said, "we all make mistakes, and sometimes when we are caught in a moment of weakness we fall. We have all been there. Think about this. Mahannad was going to get to this point with or without you. Your mistake has positioned us to identify the other conspirators. So in a way, your failure may have put us in a position to succeed. Your choice now shows your true character." Kevin gathered the list and exited the cell. He returned to the Oval Office and knocked on the door.

"Enter," said the President. "Did you have any luck with Richard?"

"Yes sir. I did," Kevin replied. He handed President Bradshaw the list of traitors, and with that the President inquired, "Do you think we still need the magnetometers at the entry ways?"

"Yes sir, I do," Kevin replied. "That way we can be sure the pagers are taken immediately, shutting off the ability for them to communicate. We need to create an event so that all those on the Vice President's list have to come through the doors of the White House, maybe an afternoon meeting tomorrow or a morning brunch the following day. If we can, we need to immediately assess where the repeater towers are and disable them "accidentally," so that the lack of communication seems somewhat normal due to technical difficulties."

"Would they be using some sort of central hub that stores and sends these messages?" asked the President.

"Yes," said Kevin, "they have to be using a processor of sorts, but I would bet the hub they have is somewhere close to their base of operations. They could not protect or service it if it were not close to one of the compounds."

"True," the President said. "Well get busy and keep me informed."

"Yes sir, will do," Kevin replied as he turned and left the office.

Kevin and Gene spent the evening setting up the metal detectors and briefing several agents on dealing with people while taking their pagers. Gene said, "Why don't we just arrest them on the spot for treason?"

"I would love to," Kevin said, "but if forty people got arrested on the spot the word would get out, and we'd be dealing with more bombs. By taking the pagers, they will not be able to communicate with anyone. The second you find their pager you cannot let them send one message. If they make a scene, designate one of you to rotate escorting them back to the office out of the public's eye. Explain to them the pagers have to be tested to make sure they cannot accidentally send a signal detonating an explosive device."

"Is that true?" asked one of the agents. "Technically yes, cell phones, pagers, walkie talkies all emit signals that can cause a detonation. But our purpose for this is to take the pager and clone each one so that we can intercept each message. It will only take a few minutes, and then the pagers will be returned before they leave the event.

The agents completed setting up the entry to the White House. Each person on the list provided by the Vice President was sent an invitation to an afternoon at the White House to discuss security and possible measures they can take to prevent another bombing. Almost entirely for show, tomorrow was looking to be a very busy day dealing with a lot of attitudes and political egos that would immediately be on the defensive about the pagers. Kevin left the White House and returned to his apartment, trying to shed the stress of the day he poured a small glass of Scotch – Glenmorangie eighteen year old, single malt. He pressed play on an antique RCA record player and leaned back in his old and worn recliner. As the needle hit the vinyl, he heard the initial crackle of the old record from a time long ago.

CHAPTER 32

Sam climbed onto Patton and shook the morning off with a shudder. The team had left La Veta two days before and was bushwhacking through the mountains, following old jeep and goat trails. Being careful to stay out of sight, it was slow going through country designed for hoofs. Game was plentiful with virtually no hunting pressure over the past ten years, but they could not risk the attention by firing shots at potential food. Sam kicked himself more than once for not bringing his bow. Most of the game so far had not even reacted to their presence in their home. The animals stood quietly watching as the men on horses slowly rode past.

Three days into the back country and it had rained for most of the ride. Creeks were already high from the spring thaw up on top. Rain aggravated already difficult stream and river crossings. Several times they had to work their way upstream looking for places to cross, and Patton would occasionally voice a protest with a heavy snort. When the sun climbed high on the morning of the third day, Sam looked down as they crossed an elk trail that intersected their path. The elk trail led up to higher ridges that paralleled the lower trail above, and in the trail were fresh horse tracks. Sam turned to Walt, called him up and asked the old cowboy, "What do you see?"

Walt observed the tracks for a minute. Looking left and right of the trail, walking up the trail for about ten yards then turning he replied, "Six horses, all carrying riders. No packs, they are traveling light and fast. They must have a camp down below."

"Charlie, you and the rest stay on the trail, be mindful of an ambush. I'm thinking we have found a little war party." The assassins who tried to take out the girls were traveling in the same manner, six riders, traveling light and moving fast. Sam had been afraid that those controlling Salida would have security patrols running the mountains, looking for groups such as theirs.

"We'll follow their tracks and see if we can determine the nature of their business without stirring the pot."

The four men slowly moved on down the trail as Walt and Sam started working their way up the trail, following the tracks of the unknown horsemen.

Walt and Sam followed the trail which extended about a mile up the mountain, winding around dead falls and washouts that guided the melting snow racing down toward the valley below. It then opened into a small field on a flat plateau that paralleled the ridge above and the trail below that Sam had just left. The tracks turned to the north, moving up the trail that would put the strangers into a position overlooking the rest of Sam's team. Walt and Sam picked up the pace, hoping to find the assassins before they ambushed the Sam's men on the lower trail. After several minutes, Walt raised his hand and motioned to slow down.

He pointed at the tracks and whispered, "They slowed down, almost to a walk." Sam pulled up on Patton and Walt was on the ground before him. Walt saw Sam looking at him with a curious look and whispered, "I guess all this fun has my leg feeling better." The duo made their weapons ready and moved quietly through the forest. The Aspens and evergreens were thick and beautiful, but dangerous in this situation. A thick forest could make it easy to walk right by the men if they were all being quiet. Walt and Sam were off the trail, but still following it.

Walt motioned with hand signals to hold, that he had eyes on target. He moved back to Sam and quietly whispered, "The horses are there, but no riders. I think they have moved over the edge of the plateau to move down on top of our men." They cautiously moved to the edge, staying away from the assassins' horses. A good horse will sound an alarm when a stranger comes near. Walt slipped over the ridge and Sam followed looking for targets, keeping low. The rain and wet ground made it easy to slip noiselessly through the forest. Walt halted their progress, indicating that once more he had eyes on target.

All six assassins were spread out and positioned behind several deadfalls that were about fifty yards above the trail Sam's men were gradually approaching. Sam motioned to Walt that he should flank the left side, and he would take the right. Walt eased back up the hill and kept a small ridge between him and the assassins as he moved into position above them. Sam maintained his position about fifty yards above and to the right of Walt. He signaled thumbs up and Sam returned the gesture. Sam did not want his own men to move any further into harm's way, so he shouted to the men below. "U. S. Marshals, you are surrounded, show me your hands!" Apparently shocked by realizing they were now the prey and not the predators, they initially froze, not moving. "Show me your hands I said!" One man on the end closest to Sam started raising his hands. The man next to him followed suit. The man in the middle was squirrely though, and it was obvious he was trying to determine where Sam was hiding. Walt was covering his side of the deadfall and before Sam could shout another warning, Squirrel was turning and leveling his rifle in Sam's general direction. Walt's Winchester barked twice as he rapidly worked the lever, and Squirrel was now rolling into a pile at the base of the deadfall.

"Anyone else wanna fight?" Sam yelled. Two of the men closest to Walt were lying face down on the ground while the other three were still being ornery. "Walt, hold your position. Don't leave cover."

"Jam," I yelled, "you, Charlie and Garrison move up and cover these fools from your side." One of the three still acting ornery had yet to show his hands. Sam waited until Jam was in position.

"Jam, you got these boys in your field of fire?"

"Yes sir!" Jam reported. Loud and confident communication in this particular situation let the fools on the ground know who was in control.

"Now then," Sam said as he addressed the ornery ones. "Just so you know there are two more of us that you do not know about covering you with an AR-15 and a shotgun loaded with double naught magnums that you are all well within range of. Do we have to kill any more of you?" The two on the end were out of the fight. One was crying and one had probably peed in his pants. The three in the middle had yet to show hands and they were all looking for a way out. Walt held his position as Sam moved over and closer, taking up a position behind a tree with only twenty-five yards between us.

"Gentlemen," Sam said, "just a few minutes ago you were willing to wage war on innocent people. You were willing to kill them because you had every advantage. Your ability to cower and hide behind one another now says much about your lack of character. Now we have the advantage. You can either surrender or die.... It's your move." One of the men looking to surrender raised his hands in the air and stood walking toward Sam. The men behind him had other plans as he blocked Sam's view. They raised their weapons at Sam and he quickly stepped behind the tree he was using for cover. The bullets landed softly in the wood on the other side of the tree making a dull thud. Jam, Walt, Matt and Garrison all lit them up simultaneously. In a matter of seconds it was over and the only remaining sound was two young men whimpering in their wet pants, lying face down on the ground. The man surrendering was shot in the back several times by his partners in their last stand of defiance.

"What a way to wake up the neighborhood," Charlie said.

"We need to secure these men and move on quickly. That fire fight could be heard for miles in these mountains and I don't want any more surprises today." Sam said. "Matt, you and Jam hook 'em up and get 'em on a horse and run them back to the second team. You shouldn't have any trouble catching us. We will move up the mountain on that next ridge and follow that trail, making camp in about five miles so you will have time to catch up." Matt and Jam searched the young men and placed them in restraints. The team parted ways as they turned back south and disappeared quickly from sight.

Sam pointed Patton's nose north and started climbing to the next trail. It was early afternoon and the riders made good time on the plateau. They stopped to water the horses at a creek and Sam took the opportunity to look at his map. He rode Patton up the ridge about a mile above the tree line to get a bearing. From what he could tell, it appeared they were almost directly west of Howard, and about another half a day's ride to Methodist Mountain. Sam rode back down into the trees, returning to the group. The wind was surprisingly still for an afternoon in the Rockies, and the sun was just behind the ridge, meaning they still had a couple of hours of daylight left.

"Let's camp here and give Matt and Jam a chance to catch up," Sam said. They would be able to move much faster than without the pack horses, and once they got back up on the plateau it would be an easy trail. It was not long after sunset during that prime time of the day that Jam and Matt rode into camp. They watered their horses and slipped their saddles off, giving them a rest.

"I'm assuming you found Team 2?" Sam asked.

"Yes we did." Jam then squatted in front of Sam with a grin on his face. "They took our prisoners and immediately relayed them on down the trail to Team 3. No one wants those whiny kids in their camp during the night, and guess what?" Sam looked up. Jam was still squatting there in front of him with an enormous grin.

"What?" Sam said, slightly agitated.

"Kansas showed up…..and brought Missouri and Nebraska with them!" Jam paused, teasing Sam a little. "Aaand that is not all. More people have ridden in from Texas, and some of them brought in a fairly large herd of cattle. There are over fifteen hundred men ready to fight in La Veta." Sam stared at him blankly, not knowing what to say. Jam added in a pitiful deep voice, "I just wish I had one of them cows."

CHAPTER 33

Jennifer jumped, startled as the man dressed in black silently stared at her. "Where have you been?" the assassin snarled. Jennifer stood silently, shocked that he was in her apartment. She knew that her face had guilty written all over it. "Well?" He pressed, taking a step toward her. Jennifer retreated two steps.

"I was out for a jog," she replied. "How, how did you get into my condo?"

"That is unimportant. I have reason to believe that your daughter has contacted you."

"What?" she asked.

My daughter is alive? Her mind was racing. She thought at first this was about Ali, or going across the bridge to Smeltertown. Relief immediately spread through her as she realized that this was a fishing expedition, and that he had confirmed that her daughter was alive.

"No, no, she has not contacted me, and I doubt very seriously she would come here if she were still alive."

"Oh, we are certain she is alive. And we are fairly confident that she is traveling here to be with you. I can promise you it will not fare well for either of you if we catch you two together."

He turned abruptly and left the room, letting himself out. She shook nervously knowing that she had no privacy, and the assassins were now watching her.

The next morning, Jennifer walked down to the Palace Hotel to locate Abdallah Kahlil. She arrived at the hotel that had been transformed several years ago into a lavish home for Sheikh Mahannad. The hotel had originally been built in 1909 and had only three floors. It was a beautiful yet quaint historical building nestled in the Rocky Mountains, resting beside the Arkansas River. Many years ago, Sheikh Mahannad had recognized the beauty of the location with the convenience and comfort of the summer weather. The Sheikh had already begun to build in the area using government land, which is plentiful in Colorado, and bringing in military equipment to build on this land. The airport was converted and expanded to handle the largest of jets. It also became the most convenient place to maintain the military armament that they had been collecting since the late 1990s. The base housed five thousand soldiers, with many of the support personnel living in town. The Sheikh then sought a location to make worthy of his home. He saw the little hotel and soon made it his own. Within weeks, he had begun transforming it into a true palace which consumed the entire block. The Sheikh allowed Imams and members of his entourage to maintain residence in the lower floors of the hotel while his suite took up the entire third floor. Jennifer pressed the button for Abdallah's room, and within seconds his voice replied back over a speaker.

"Yes, can I help you?"

"Abdallah, this is Dr. Boudreaux. I would like to discuss something I think is of great importance to all of us. Do you have a minute?" Jennifer asked.

Abdallah said politely, "Yes, doctor. I will be right down." Within minutes, Abdallah appeared on the stairs, descending them quickly. "What is on your mind, doctor?"

"I have been involved in many different facets of medicine over the years, and I feel my talents are being wasted teaching students combat medic techniques. I see the necessity for that, but I think someone else could be doing that now. My transition here was difficult at first, and I understand the concern with my daughter being missing, but I am at my wit's end now because I would rather be contributing in a more proactive way."

"And how will you do that?"

"I have been thinking about the pandemic and how the CDC supplied us with the cure soon enough to save most everyone, but waited to present it to the world. It was obviously a tactical maneuver on their part benefiting our mission. I was thinking, what if we fell out of favor with the powers that control the CDC, somehow another illness occurred and they elected to protect everyone else but us? Wouldn't it be wise to have a research laboratory already preparing for other biological attacks?"

Abdallah looked at Jennifer excitedly and shook his head affirmatively. "Yes, Yes, that makes sense."

Jennifer continued, "I would like to open a research lab at the hospital, maybe in the north wing that is reserved for emergencies and disasters for a triage. I could start tomorrow moving supplies and equipment back in from storage. It would take me but a few days to set up the lab, and I would not use much of the hospital's resources."

Abdallah again was shaking his head. "Dr. Boudreaux, I think that is a very good idea. Let me present this wonderful idea to his Grace, and I will get back with you as soon as possible. Thank you for your interest in volunteering your time." Jennifer bid farewell, Abdallah bowed graciously as always, and Jennifer returned to her condo, slipping out of the burqa.

Oh my gosh, to be back in a lab coat behind walls where I wouldn't have to wear this dreaded thing, She thought.

CHAPTER 34

Abdallah immediately walked up the stairs to the top floor. Sheikh Mahannad was the only person allowed to use the elevator. As he approached the enormous doors to the Sheikh's suite, the guards outside the door blocked his way. Abdallah bowed his head and stated, "I would respectfully like to request a moment of the Sheikh's time concerning a subject of utmost importance." The guard on the right side of the door turned and pressed a button on an intercom, then spoke softly into the speaker. He turned back a moment later, gestured for Abdallah to be seated and said,

"Sheikh Nu'man Mahannad will meet with you shortly." Abdallah sat down on the edge of the sofa and waited patiently fidgeting awkwardly while the guards stared, analyzing his potential to be a threat. Minutes passed, and finally the Sheikh's boy servants opened the doors and held them open as the Sheikh entered the room. Another boy servant followed and placed a tray with a tea pot and cups before him. Abdallah stood and bowed as the Sheikh approached the coffee table, then sat down opposite him in an enormous high back chair that resembled a throne. Abdallah took his seat and waited for the Sheikh to start the conversation. The Sheikh took a moment as a servant poured a cup of tea. "Chamomile," he said. "Soothing and relaxing, while good for digestion."

"No thank you, sir," Abdallah said.

"What can I help you with this afternoon?" the Sheikh asked.

"Thank you for seeing me, your Grace. I was approached earlier today by Dr. Jennifer Boudreaux about a concern of hers. First of all, she is a very talented doctor who has a PhD in medical research and bioscience. Her reason for approaching me was that she wants to be more productive with our mission. She recognizes the risk of trusting our current friends, who may be our future enemies. Her position is that, with the current climate of political volatility within this country we now seek to overthrow, she feels that being dependent on the Center for Disease Control for help in the event of another pandemic is somewhat risky. They assisted us this last time, but what if the winds of politics blow in another direction? We currently have no research facility to combat new or mutated strains of disease. She has offered her talents and skills to set up a research facility in a small portion of the hospital. In return, she would like to relinquish her teaching responsibilities in the Combat Medic Program. I have checked, and we have two instructors at this time that could fill her position in the classroom." The Sheikh slowly sipped his tea and placed the cup on the saucer, handing it to his servant. He leaned back in the large chair and let out a heavy sigh as he started to speak.

"Abdallah, I know of the good doctor. She has been with us almost from the beginning. But I am concerned about her loyalty in light of the current status of her daughter. Have we received any word from Arkansas on their location?"

"Nothing recent, sir. We completely lost contact with the first team sent to take care of them, and the second team returned with a story of the girls defending themselves with military style weapons and escaping in an old truck. One of our men contacted the doctor earlier and believes she has had no contact with her daughter, and was in fact surprised to learn that she was still alive. Dr. Boudreaux addressed her concern for her daughter, but emphasized that it would in no way interfere with her work or her loyalty to us."

"Very well," replied the Sheikh. "She makes a very good point about preparing for the worst. Let her do as she pleases, but keep a close eye on her. You may want to assign an assistant to her that is without question loyal to our cause."

"Yes, your Grace, I will do so. Thank you for your time. I will tell her immediately so that she may get started setting up the lab."

The Sheikh started to get up, staggered a bit, and both servants rushed to take his hand and help him from the chair. Abdallah rose and bowed as the Sheikh returned to his suite, the doors closing behind him.

With that, Abdallah spun on his heel and quickly exited the room. After leaving the hotel, he made his way to Doctor Boudreaux's condominium. She was walking out the door as he arrived. "Good afternoon, Abdallah," she said. "I was just on my way over to the hospital to see if there was anything I could help with."

"Well, Dr. Boudreaux, I have some good news. The Sheikh thinks very highly of your idea and has given me the permission to grant your wish about the research facility. You may start as soon as possible."

"Thank you, Abdallah. Would you walk with me to the hospital so that I may show you the space I had in mind?"

CHAPTER 35

Kevin's eyes popped open and he sat up quickly, rolling out of his recliner and looking around disoriented. He looked at his watch to see how late he was. Realizing he had only been asleep for two hours, he relaxed a bit, took a deep breath, then walked back to the bathroom. Three in the morning and wide awake. Sleep was a rare occurrence these days, usually coming in restless naps. Two to three hours of a dreamless coma, waking up shaking, sweating and tired. Working long hours with basically no schedule for seven days a week regularly batters a person to the point of insanity, causing depression, alcoholism, obesity, drug abuse and divorce. *Some reward for saving the world,* he thought. He sat on the sofa, ran his fingers through his hair and sat there contemplating the possibility of two more hours of sleep. *Not a chance*, he thought. *Mind's working ninety miles an hour now.* He rose, put on his shorts and decided to dress for work.

Arriving at the White House at five a.m. was not out of the ordinary for the Senior Agent on The Presidents Team. The job for the most part demanded it. Kevin double and triple checked the X-ray machines, magnetometers and the metal detecting wands. This had to go without a hitch. Gene walked through the door and said, "Couldn't sleep either I see."

"Nope, don't like it, or at least that is what my body tells me. I prefer no sleep, walking around like a stinkin' zombie all day, yeah that's me … friggin' zombie agent!" Gene laughed and started checking a machine.

"I have already checked them several times. Why don't you go and make sure the equipment is ready to clone the pagers?" Gene left, and Kevin made the rounds checking the posts and greeting the morning shift.

After making sure everything was in order, Kevin walked around to the Oval Office and knocked on the door. President Bradshaw responded with,

"Enter please." Kevin walked over to the desk and stopped briefly, looking at the President who had his eyes down as if he were intently reading something.

Kevin realized there was nothing there for him to read and asked, "Sir, are you okay?"

"Yes, unfortunately I am fine. I wish I could find some excuse why I should not have to deal with this any longer. It would be so easy just to walk away, to just go along with everything Mahannad wants. The world wants it, and most of the people in America do not care."

"Excuse me, sir, but there are enough of us that do care. Neverland cares. The only people that don't really care will realize they should have been concerned after it is way too late. Freedom is a responsibility that we have to pass on to our children. If we miss this opportunity to propel freedom into the next generation, it will be lost forever."

President Bradshaw looked up from his desk, rubbed his eyes and said, "When this is over, remind me to put you on my speech writing team."

"Sir, fatigue is an animal that we are all fighting right now. The business of the day demands it. You have an hour to freshen up and gather yourself until guests start arriving. We will be seating everyone in the Press Briefing Room. If all show, we should have about eighty people. That should make it believable to the forty on the list."

President Bradshaw stood, walked toward Agent Landrum and said, "Kevin, I appreciate all that you and your squad is doing. I will hit the head and throw some water in my face. I want to greet everyone as they arrive. It's time for me to be more presidential."

The President greeted everyone passing through the metal detectors and diffused several confrontations with some who seemed overly concerned about the temporary loss of their pagers. While the guests were being ushered to the Press Briefing Room, Agent Stallings rounded the corner and grabbed Kevin's arm.

"Come with me," he said with urgency. They turned another corner in the hallway. Kevin stopped Gene and said,

"Hold on. I don't want to get too far from the President right now." Gene pulled something from his pocket and pressed it into Kevin's hand.

"A pager?"

"It's yours. Our friends out west sent it to you. They have three and now you have one, so by using Mahannad's own comm system we can communicate without the Pony Express!"

"This maybe the break we needed. Thanks, Gene. I better get back to the President."

Agent Landrum walked to the Press Briefing Room and slipped into the door just as the President started speaking. "Ladies and gentlemen, I have no intentions of keeping you long. I wanted to address my concerns in light of recent events. We are very concerned that someone has decided to put the United States at risk. Some have questioned my patriotism, and I want to emphasize now more than ever that I will fight for this country and what it stands for until I am dead. Some may think that this may be an empty promise, but no one knows what tomorrow may bring, and I can tell you that a tomorrow without freedom is closer than you may think. And also the enemy I speak of is like the devil who may come to you as an angel of light.

The enemy can promise riches, luxury and a lavish lifestyle, but ultimately the enemy will bring destruction. The enemy we have is an enemy that is currently hiding like a coward and attacking at will, with no regard for innocent life. In a free society, we cannot tolerate the cowardice of such an evil, and we must take a stand against this enemy or forever lose the freedom we now experience and enjoy. There is no one left in this world to protect the weak, to ensure that there is a safe haven where freedom not only exists, but flourishes. I ask each of you to stand with me against this evil, and any evil that threatens our freedom. You are the core of this administration, and without you we are nothing. Now I will be making a press release later, and I hope that I can have everyone's support. Are there any questions I can answer?"

Gene slipped through the door behind Kevin and whispered, "All the pagers are cloned." The President looked around the room waiting for a question. One man slowly raised his hand.

"Yes Jonathan, what is your question?"

"Sir, who is this enemy you speak of?"

"Jonathan, I am not at liberty to go public with the enemy's name just yet. There is an ongoing investigation, and I fear if the public becomes aware that we know the enemy's plan then we may jeopardize the investigation and put the agents involved at risk."

"Well, sir, I guess my question is how do you know they are enemies? I mean, no disrespect sir, but what if their intentions are honorable and in the best interests of this country?"

"Jonathan, I am only at liberty to reveal certain information. The agents involved have intercepted transmissions and are monitoring them now. In these transmissions were basically contracts to assassins. I can only tell you this: the enemy I speak of has not only put a price on my head, but every person in this room."

Well, that'll get a response, Agent Landrum thought. People started moving nervously, reaching for the empty space on their belts or in their purses where their pagers were normally found. The President looked over at Kevin, and he gave him the thumbs up. The President turned back to the podium and the microphone and said, "If there are not any more questions, I think we have accomplished a great deal today. I want you all to think heavily about the future. Think about the future of this country and what it has meant to so many people. If we fall, there will no longer be peace efforts in needy countries, or someone to defend the poor and the weak. There will be no one to fight evil because evil will be ruling the world.

We are the only power left in this world that can stand between good and evil. Now, I was elected to stand before this country as a servant. I was elected to swear an oath. I placed my hand on a Bible and promised God that I would protect this country and the Constitution on which we ultimately depend. If you want to destroy all of that then leave right now. I am not kidding. Get out of your chair and walk out that door. If you want to work with me and restore this country to what it once was and what I believe it can be then we need to get to work."

Agents Landry and Stallings were in shock. The President was calling all of them out right now in front of God and everybody. Many were looking at the exits, eyes darting about. Some were looking down at the floor, not willing to make any eye contact. The President continued, "I don't see anyone leaving so I guess I am to assume that all of you are still with me."

After a moment of extremely awkward silence, a young man in the back raised his hand. The President recognized him. "Yes?"

"Sir, I never left."

President Bradshaw, still standing at the podium, shook his head.

"Thank you. Thank you for staying. All of you, Thank you for staying. I would like to meet with each of you individually in the near future to discuss your current role in this administration and see how we can improve on working together."

President Bradshaw moved away from the podium and started to leave. A young lady on the front row quickly waved him down and said,

"Mr. President, what are we to do about the potential threat on us and our families?" President Bradshaw turned and responded.

"I'm sorry, I should have addressed that. If you want a security detail as you leave and retrieve your pagers, give your name, home address and work address to the agents manning the desk at the security post exit. We will have a team respond to your needs as soon as possible. If you do not want a detail with you at all times, don't worry about leaving any information."

Agents Landrum and Stallings were still in shock with what just took place. Agent Landrum was wondering where he would get the manpower for all of these details. The President left the room and returned to the Oval Office. Agent Landrum followed closely. President Bradshaw turned, sat down on the sofa and placed his feet on the coffee table. Leaning back he let out a heavy sigh.

"Sir, that was a great speech, but you showed your hand a little early don't you think?"

The President took another deep breath and said, "Yes, I did. Sometimes you have to go with your instincts, and this morning I went with mine. The time seemed right and the opportunity was there. I would like to know at this point who has picked up their pager."

Gene tapped on the door and leaned in,

"Mr. President. No one has left, and they are asking if you would return to the Press Room."

Kevin looked at the President and he stood, straightened his suit and returned to the crowd of people still gathered in the Press Room. All of them were standing. All of them were looking intently at him. Jonathan stepped forward and said, "Sir, I think some of us have made a horrible mistake and would like to make it known that our patriotism is not in question. We were, however, led to believe that yours was. Those of us that arrived today with pagers were led to believe that you were selling what is left of this country to the United Nations. We were given the pagers by a person representing himself as an agent of Homeland Security and told to report anything that we observed that may seem out of the ordinary. Sir, I know that sounds somewhat ridiculous, but I saw the man's credentials and he was very convincing."

The President stood quietly before the crowd and humbly said, "I failed you for a period of time. I have never questioned my patriotism, but I faltered in my mission. The responsibility to maintain freedom has a great cost, and I let down my guard for a while. However, we must now accept that responsibility and move forward. Do not worry about the past, but focus on the future. I think we will need to have a debriefing tomorrow, so if all of you could return, I will have enough agents here to talk to you about the man who spoke with you and hopefully we can get everything back on track. Now, I need you all to keep this to yourselves. Please do not tell anyone of the talk we have had here today. The security of this nation depends on it." Everyone was nodding, and soon everyone broke into applause. The President spent the next few minutes shaking hands and reestablishing the connection he had lost with his people. President Bradshaw looked at Kevin and winked. *Well played, Mr. President, well played,* Kevin thought.

CHAPTER 36

Morning broke, and it was perfect for the first of June. The wind was blowing just enough to provide the soft sound that only occurs in evergreen trees. Sam grew up in the South, and played underneath the pines. He noticed at an early age that when the wind blew through the needles they created a unique, wonderful and peaceful sound that he would always enjoy.

They were on a ridge facing east and could see the sun coming up over the Front Range. Instead of getting up as usual and busting rump to move on, Sam sat on the ridge quietly waiting and watched the sunrise. A small herd of elk moved across the plateau below, grazing as they walked. The bulls remained in the thicker forest while the cows talked amongst themselves. The calves darted and played butting heads, pretending to be daddy. Every now and then moments happen like this that you cannot explain or control, and all you can do is simply watch in gratitude as the world unfolds. The other men had awakened and looked to Sam to see if he was getting ready to leave. They were content to roll over and get another few blinks. A couple of them joined Sam in this spectacular moment of morning. A pair of golden eagles soared on the gentle breeze as they decided to put on a show, chasing each other for a minute and soon flying out of sight. Sam smiled, looked over at Walt and said, "A shining moment indeed."

"Yessir, it was."

"And now we must deal with real life, or soon lose it. Roll 'em up, boys. Let's get packin'."

The men loaded their horses, and Patton gave Sam a nudge. He reached in his pack and gave him a lump of sugar from a bag he kept hidden. Patton sometimes reminded Sam that he could get a lot more mileage with the occasional lump of sugar. He swung into the saddle and headed west. He believed they were looking at Methodist Mountain to the northwest, and he had intentions of using an old hunting cabin he found once years ago at the headwaters of San Luis Creek. It was well hidden on the southwest side of the mountain on a bluff overlooking a vast valley in front of it. It could not be approached from any direction without being seen. Whether it was still standing or not did not really matter. The location held a tactical advantage that would be an outstanding position for a base of operation. They moved across the valley from the ridge they had followed, and started up Methodist Mountain.

The valley behind them formed a bowl and looked to be a place that may provide good hunting if this campaign unexpectedly turned into a long one. Elk and mule deer were everywhere, and food hopefully would not be a problem. By noon they had made it to the bluff that ran around the southern side of the mountain, and Sam was looking for the creek. To the south and west you could see for miles. The mountain itself protected their backside, and it was not long before they came to San Luis Creek.

They followed the creek upstream until it leveled off, crossing a field full of beautiful flowers already blooming in spite of the still cool temperatures. Patches of red paintbrush and purple sage were scattered all over the meadow, and Sam could see the outline of the cabin well inside the woods across the field. As they approached the cabin, it appeared to be in better condition than Sam imagined, and as they got closer he noticed some fresh wood cut, split and stacked to the left of the front door. He raised his hand indicating for the group behind him to stop, and then motioned for them to dismount and move left into the woods around the cabin, setting up a perimeter. He saw no reason for concern, but they had no reason to get lazy and take chances at this point. Sam dismounted and walked closer to the cabin stopping just inside the trees. It was obvious now that the cabin, was occupied and had been for some time. As he stood beside a tree to use as cover, he called to the cabin saying,

"Ho cabin, anyone home?"

The woods were quiet, and there was no sound or movement from inside. Sam slowly moved forward, approached the front door and knocked.

"Hello, is there anyone home?"

He knocked again, with no response. He pushed the latch open, gave the door a shove and it slowly creaked open. Sam looked inside using the door as cover, and saw a man lying there on a bed who appeared to be unconscious, with a young boy and girl back into a corner beyond him. The boy had a small revolver with him and was pointing it in Sam's direction.

"Good afternoon, I can see your dad is in a little trouble. Is this your dad?" The young girl nodded.

The children were about nine or ten, and Sam could see that the man was breathing, but could hear a raspy sound every time he exhaled. He appeared chilled even though he was covered with sweat. Sam looked at the young boy still holding the revolver and said,

"Young man, I would like to help your dad, but I really do not want that gun to go off. I promise not to hurt you or anyone here. Can I look at your dad?" Slowly he nodded and lowered the revolver, keeping a white knuckle grip on it just in case. "I have to go outside and get some medicine. I will knock before I come back in so I don't scare you. Okay?" The young boy again nodded slowly. Sam walked outside and went to his pack behind Patton's saddle.

There he kept a first aid kit that contained a bottle of anti-inflammatories and several other medicines, including a round of amoxicillin antibiotics. He retrieved the anti-inflammatories from the pack along with the amoxicillin and then motioned to the men to move on, that all was secured. He then turned back toward the house and knocked on the door. Sam approached the man lying on the bed and showed the young boy his medicine bottles. "I have to give your dad some medicine or he will get worse. Do you mind if I do that?" He again gave Sam permission to help his dad.

Sam looked at the young girl and asked if she could get a cup of water. She ran to the table by the window, dipped a cup of water out of a bucket and walked back, carefully handing it to Sam. He smiled and asked, "What is your name?"

She returned the smile and said, "Samantha."

"Really? Well my name is Sam and I am going to try and do everything I can to help your dad." The young boy still sat in the corner holding the revolver.

"Now I need to see if we can wake your dad and get him up to swallow this medicine. What is his name?"

"Ronald," said the girl.

"Okay Samantha, I want you to talk to him and see if you can wake him up." Again she nodded.

"Daddy, Daddy, wake up. Someone is here to help you."

Sam shook him gently a few times and his eyes fluttered open. He tried to speak, but was very weak so I started talking.

"Ronald, I am a United States Marshal and I have some medicine that can help you. I need you to swallow these pills Samantha is going to give you. Can you hold out your hand?"

His hand shook a little, but he was still too weak to lift it.

"Ronald I am going to put this water to your lips and let you drink a bit before you take the pills." Sam held the cup as he took a bit of water in his mouth. He choked a bit, but got it down. Sam placed the pills in his mouth and again lifted the cup to his lips allowing him to drink the water and swallow the medicine.

"Now, I will be giving you this every several hours, and hopefully soon you will be feeling better. Samantha, I need another pillow or something for him to lean on to elevate his head so that he can rest in an upright position. Try and get some rest. I will have my men make some venison stew so that you can get some food in you." Samantha ran over to her cot, got her blanket, rolled it up and gently positioned her dad to where he could rest comfortably without the added stress on his lungs.

Sam walked outside, told the men what was happening and asked Matt and Garrison to see if they could find a mule deer or elk for supper. They needed to get some good fresh food in this man to help him fight his illness. These kids needed him. Matt and Garrison jumped at the chance for a little hunting in the high lonesome. They were galloping across the meadow within seconds.

"Guys we are going to be here awhile, and I would like to make this place a little more accommodating. Soon more and more of our little army will be arriving, and we have to take into consideration where we will need to expand the camp. Daniel, I want you to ride with me this afternoon. I want to cross over and see what we can see with my spotting scope on the other side of the mountain."

"Yessir," Daniel said sounding eager to be busy with something other than being the tagalong. Jam grabbed an axe, throwing it over his shoulder and headed for the woods like Paul Bunyan. Sam turned Patton north and Daniel followed as they started the recon of Salida.

"Keep in mind, Daniel, of where you are at all times until you start doing it subconsciously. Situations like these can change in a second, and you cannot be disoriented or you will get yourself lost. Getting lost can be fatal at this altitude." They crested a ridge and rode through a saddle on the southeast side of Methodist Mountain. They worked their way north until they climbed up onto a bluff overlooking the vast valley that Salida makes home. Still somewhat cool on the shady side of the mountain, they tethered the horses and walked over to the ledge with Sam's spotting scope. They sat on the ledge, and Daniel started explaining the layout of Salida since the Sheikh had begun his renovation.

"The tunnel that the compound was in prior to the Fall was on the eastern side of the valley over there. They still use it for storage and maintain it as a shelter in case of natural disaster or nuclear blast. It has enough supplies for two thousand people to live comfortably for six months, longer if they ration the food. The front of the tunnel is twenty-five feet tall and forty feet wide, and is protected by four foot thick blast doors that can withstand a direct hit in Salida from a small nuclear bomb."

"What is that tall smokestack?"

"That's Smeltertown; it's probably a ghost town now. The ground was poisoned by all the mining. The soldiers mostly live west of the smokestack at the airport. That's where they keep all the military hardware. They had just finished building the base there when I was here several years ago. The last time I was here, they didn't have a lot of the heavy guns, just a couple of tanks and a recon airplane. Getting fuel here was a big problem then."

"What about the living quarters? Where would the Sheikh stay?"

"From where the smokestack is, follow the river down to about the middle of town. There is an old hotel there called the Palace. That is one of the major renovations they have made. You can't miss it. It is right off of the river, and it is the biggest building in town. Most of the Sheikh's more trusted personnel stay there in the lower floors while he lives on the top floor in a suite that covers the entire building. It's as big as a city block."

"Any idea where others are staying?"

"Oh, you mean like your doctor friend?" Daniel grinned as Sam gave him the look. The one from underneath the brim of his hat that said *be careful and tread lightly.*

"Yessir, She is a concern of mine."

"The wonderful thing about Salida is that it is not too big. You can walk anywhere. Transportation is like most places either by foot, bike or horse. I would imagine they would have a doctor being housed close to the hospital. There are some condos and apartments close by. I would probably start there. But you will have trouble finding any female."

"Why is that?"

"All women wear burqas in public. The men wear the dishdasha, but not when it is very cold. They will dress normally, as does the military. What's good for the goose is not for the gander."

"Obviously," Sam said. "Let's head back. I don't want to be in unfamiliar woods come dark."

CHAPTER 37

Jennifer rolled out of bed thirty minutes before her alarm, excited that she had a new challenge before her. She dressed quickly and left the condo without breakfast or coffee, not really knowing what to expect as she walked to the hospital. She carried an old black tote with her containing a pair of scrubs and a lab coat. The sun was just starting to rise, but she couldn't wait to get started. The clouds were low this morning, and fog had settled across the upper Arkansas Valley around Salida. It was less than a mile from the condo to the hospital, and she did not mind the walk especially this early in the morning as the world started waking. A rabbit darted out of the bushes to her left, startling her as it ran across the trail toward the river. As she watched the rabbit something suddenly caught her eye moving among the trees across the road from her. *I must be seeing things in the fog*, she thought. It looked like a cowboy from an old western movie. Horse, hat, saddlebags, he turned and moved back into the trees, disappearing as the fog embraced him and leaving nothing but her memory of what she thought was impossible. She looked back for a moment hoping he would return, but he was gone. She turned and made her way to the hospital, very confused. *I am not out of my mind*, she thought. Soldiers occasionally rode into town on *horseback,* but no one was allowed to ride a horse in town. The Sheikh thought an abundance of horses in town would provide opportunities for potential escapes. Outside of their necessity for the battlefield and their use to deliver messages, he did not want them anywhere around the town. *A cowboy in Salida, she thought. What are the odds?*

Jennifer entered the hospital and met with the administrator on duty to confirm her space for research had been approved. She obtained a key and made her way to the north wing of the hospital. Entering the vacant office area seemed almost hauntingly familiar. The empty space echoed her footsteps, reminding her of an old movie. She shuddered at the thought of a nut with a hockey mask chasing her through an empty hospital. The space had everything she needed with the exception of the research equipment.

The hospital maintained a constant source of electricity from a combination of platforms. Solar panels covered the roof and part of the field behind the building; they powered lights and other standard electrical needs. Back-up tri-fuel generators were always on standby with an enormous amount fuel that could enable the hospital to run for weeks without the sun.

Jennifer compiled a list of equipment she would need to bring the research office up to speed. She also needed to approach Abdallah to ask permission for her to wear a hijab while she was working instead of the burqa. The hijab is basically a head covering that wraps around the head and neck, also covering the chest area. The burqa is a head to toe dress that covers everything including the face. Sheikh Mahannad demands the burqa at all times, but maybe he would make an exception for a laboratory setting. The binding and constricting dress of the burqa could be an occupational safety hazard when doing research.

After arranging the furniture and assessing the needs of the lab, Jennifer took her list to the hospital administrator. Zaid Mahmoud was in his office meeting with Abdallah when Jennifer rounded the corner and lightly knocked on the door. Zaid said, "Come in, doctor."

Both men stood and turned to greet Jennifer as she walked into the administrator's office.

"So glad you came back by. This is perfect timing. Abdallah and I were just discussing trying to locate a good lab assistant for you."

"Yes," Abdallah added, "Someone with experience. No one should have to address this task alone."

Somewhat caught off guard Jennifer said, "Thank you, sir. I'm perfectly fine working alone, but I will gladly welcome the help. I just dropped by to see if any of this equipment on this list was available here in the hospital."

She handed the list to Zaid. He glanced at it for a moment and responded,

"I see several items we can spare, but not all. There may be others in storage where we moved the last lab to, but we will have to check that another day. I will have someone move what we do have to your lab by tomorrow."

Jennifer then turned to Abdallah and said, "Sir, I have one other request. I know the Sheikh's position on the burqa, and I have no problem with it. However, it's very confining and inhibits movement while performing lab work. Could there be an exception while I am performing in the lab to wear scrubs and a lab coat with a hijab during the time I am working research instead of the burqa?"

Both men looked at one another and Zaid said, "Most of the nurses and doctors here would agree with you and I have no problem with it as long as you maintain a professional appearance."

"I agree," Abdallah said. "That is only for when you are in public. I think you will be fine following the current policy of the hospital."

The next morning, Jennifer again left her condo thirty minutes early, this time excited that she was no longer wearing a burqa. She opened her survival backpack. Then she placed the laptop and flash drives from her previous research carefully into the main pocket of the pack and quickly followed the path that paralleled the Arkansas River. She was startled by another rabbit as it hurried across the road into the tall grass along the river. This time she looked intently around, searching for the cowboy she had seen the day before, but nothing was there. She crossed the old empty parking lot approaching the emergency room entrance to the hospital when she heard what she thought was a horse nicker. She turned and smiled. *I know you're there,* she thought.

CHAPTER 38

Sam stood there for a moment in the trees while she turned and walked into the hospital. They had been watching the town for almost a week now, and it was poorly defended. No security except for the guards at the hospital and the Palace Hotel. Occasionally soldiers would pass on patrol, but they were easily avoided as they remained close to the main trails. Sam was sure it was Jennifer. Even in a burqa the day before, there was no mistaking her graceful walk, and then today he saw her face as she turned and reacted to Patton's nicker. No doubt in his mind that Sam was finally getting extremely close to his dream.

Sam and Patton made their way back upriver, staying hidden in the woods. They crossed the Arkansas River as the sun started to rise, and Patton climbed the north bank. They stayed just below the line of sight, working their way west on the Smeltertown side. They stopped for a moment and Sam looked up and down the river, making sure they stayed out of sight when he heard someone clear his throat.

Startled, his first reaction was clearing the Glock 23 from its holster. Sam spun to his four o'clock to see a man in jeans, sitting on a log, smoking a cigar. He said, "Brother, I don't know what has you distracted, but you're lucky I'm on your side." Sam holstered his Glock, and climbed down off of Patton and walked over to the man on the log. Smoke." He offered the cigar.

"No thanks, I have to go north of the barracks, and they would smell it for miles."

"Yeah, these are Dominican too. I don't have many left. They are very hard to come by these days. I sneak down to the river bottoms early in the morning just to get some peace of mind in all of this madness."

"Who are you with?"

"Secret Service, Agent McCrory."

"What is your mission here?"

He grinned, looked at Sam slyly and said, "I don't know … what is YOUR mission here?"

"Well, I guess there is no need in wasting time, my name is Sam and I am a Deputy U. S. Marshal. We are here to save the Constitution and eradicate the evil that threatens it."

"We?"

"Yeah, me and my men. Now, my turn. Are you alone, and what do you know about the President's visit?"

"The President is basically being held hostage. The Sheikh has bombs planted throughout Manhattan and D.C. and claims that if he doesn't hand over the U. S. Constitution along with all authority and power to the United Nations on July Fourth, he will detonate the bombs. Our mission is intel only. We currently do not have much of an army at our disposal."

"I do," Sam said smiling.

The agent was done with his cigar, and he smashed the remaining butt into the log.

"Well we picked you up on one of our cameras yesterday, and I immediately figured you for some sort of old time law enforcement from the style of vest and small arsenal you carry. No one around here has guns anymore. The only citizens here surviving the Sheikh's wrath have had to relinquish guns and accept Islam. Those poor souls that refused are dead."

"Well, hopefully we will soon put a hornet up his dress," Sam replied.

McCrory Laughed, "You certainly have a way with words. How many men do you have?"

"I'm not sure. We started with two, and then it grew to five, then twenty-two, and so forth until we crossed into Colorado with almost a thousand men. When we stopped at La Veta we were joined by a group of bikers and recent word from our messengers said that help is still coming in on a daily basis. Now we are up to about two thousand."

"Holy cow, two thousand? Who are they, and where in the hell did you find that many willing to fight?"

"I didn't, they came when the word got out about the Sheikh's plan. At first it was mostly Marshals, then Texas Rangers, then a mix of local sheriffs, former military, police, firefighters, bikers, farmers, ranchers, you name it. They all want to help."

"How did you hear about the Sheikh's plan?" he asked.

"I ran across a group of girls in Arkansas that had been slaves to their soldiers. There are at least three more compounds of thousands more girls and young boys just like them. It's as much a slave trade as it is the destruction of our way of life. One of the girls has a mother here. She is a doctor that has been a slave since she was kidnapped thirty years ago."

"That would be Dr. Boudreaux."

"Yes," I said. "How did you know?"

"She is working with us, as an asset. We met a couple of weeks ago when she killed a dude with a frying pan." Sam held his mouth open a little too long after that because Agent McCrory was laughing at him.

"Yeah a guy named Ali wanted more than she was willing to give so she took a skillet to his head. We disposed of the body for her, then developed her into a good asset."

"How do you fit in over there?"

"We have disguises we've borrowed from some of the less fortunate of the Sheikh's men that wandered into Smeltertown. Smeltertown is bad juju to them now. There have been many legends or myths about the ground here being poison from back when the smokestack was working. Many people died over the years and supposedly haunt the town, but we all know it's just us agents."

"How do you talk to Jennifer?"

"She has a two-way pager. We have some of the pagers from the men that were unfortunate enough to wander into our side of town, plus the man that Jennifer pounded. Somehow they have set up an old analog system that we have been able to tap into. I am sure it is based on towers only. We can actually text D.C., but we only do that for an emergency. We don't want to push our luck. I will be checking in with them today and tell them what you have said."

"Could you give Jennifer a message for me?"

"Give it to her yourself," he replied. "Let's go to my office and I will give you your own pager."

They walked over to the smokestack with Sam leading Patton to get his pager. Sam was able to meet Agents Smith and Smalls. They talked for a while and then Sam had to leave. "I had better get back to camp. I'm already a couple of hours overdue."

"Where is your camp?" Smalls asked.

Sam looked over the top of one of the buildings and pointed to a mountain. "I have a spike camp at the base of Mount Shavano. The main camp is behind Methodist Mountain. I am going to report over there tomorrow. We have to start making a plan to stop this. When is the President arriving?"

"Not until the day of, wheels down at oh-nine-hundred," Smith responded.

"One thing to keep in mind," Sam added.

"What's that?" McCrory asked.

"The Constitution and national security is the priority. If this goes to crap in a hurry, all of us, including the President are expendable when it comes to losing this country. If we lose, there is no country."

McCrory shook his head. "Yeah, I know…" Sam turned Patton and headed for camp.

CHAPTER 39

Kevin and Gene decided to relax for a couple of hours and walked down Pennsylvania Avenue to grab a bite to eat.

"Pizza is always good food to eat when you're living on the edge," Gene said.

Kevin shook his head. "No, Gene. Pizza is always good, period. I never met a pizza I didn't like."

They ate and sat back enjoying their meal for a change, relaxing and watching the people as they walked by the Spies Like Us Pizza Place. Laughing and joking, they decompressed from the events of the day. Kevin finally got up and payed the bill.

Gene shaking his head said, "Thanks, man." As they returned to the White House, they began to refocus on the business at hand.

Kevin and Gene walked through the West Wing and knocked on the door of the Oval Office. President Bradshaw opened the door and returned to where he was sitting at the desk looking over a map. Kevin and Gene approached the desk, and President Bradshaw asked, "Where would be the least obvious place for Islamic terrorists to put a bomb in New York City?"

Gene immediately responded, "A Christian church?"

The President said, "That's a possibility, or maybe in mosques. There are a million places they could be hiding bombs. Mahannad said the minute he finds out we are looking for the bombs he will press the button. If he suspects we are trying to thwart his plan, it's over."

Kevin replied, "I think the issue now is who is the enemy in New York City and who is this agent from Homeland Security handing out the pagers? We still have enemies here, and we should be very careful about the next few days. I'll call our office in New York and tell them our current situation. If we can figure out a way to eliminate the good guys off of the list, we can start focusing on potential enemies and their targets." Kevin walked over to the desk and was looking at the map of Manhattan when his pager vibrated for the first time. He awkwardly jerked his hand to his belt, took the pager from its holster and flipped it open. "President Bradshaw, you should hear this."

"You have my attention, Kevin."

"Our Agents out west have sent me a message that they have made contact with a Deputy U. S. Marshal that is assisting them with intel in the area. He claims to have at least two thousand men positioned and ready to strike in order protect the Constitution and the United States." President Bradshaw paused looking at the map and slowly sat down in his chair. Before he could say anything, his phone started ringing. He answered it and raised the receiver to his ear.

"Good morning, Mr. President. I hope you are well today." The President looked at Kevin and Gene and scribbled on a notepad, "The Sheikh."

"Yes, Sheikh Mahannad, I am fine. Thank you."

"The reason I am calling you today is that I am concerned that you still may be having second thoughts about our arrangement."

"I can hardly call this an arrangement. You are holding our country hostage by threats of violence and intimidation. If we comply with your wishes we still lose everything."

"No," the Sheikh replied. "You get to keep your life. In fact it is very simple. Everything stays the same except you are no longer president, and I will allow Manhattan to live."

The President responded angrily, "How do I trust you? How do I know that you will not destroy New York City anyway?"

"Because I have not destroyed you … yet," Mahannad said coldly. He added, "Mr. President, do not underestimate my resources. You will be here July Fourth, on your Independence Day, to surrender your independence," he said laughing. "If you continue to play this cat and mouse game, you cannot imagine the war I can bring to your land. Do I make myself clear? Just so you will know that I am through with these games, I am going to destroy the Washington Monument. You have until three o'clock to try and stop this tragedy. I do not mind if you evacuate the area. This is to prove to you that you are powerless. Have a good day, Mr. President."

Kevin immediately opened the door to the Oval Office and picked up the telephone in the hallway. He called his office and informed them of the looming catastrophe. "Inform the Capitol Police and clear the area from Constitution to Independence and from 12th Street to 17th. Have someone meet me at the base with a bomb dog in ten minutes. We have two hours to locate the bomb if we can." Kevin and Gene ran out of the White House and crossed Pennsylvania Avenue. They jogged through the Ellipse and across Constitution Avenue as Police were putting up barricades and blocking the roads into the park surrounding the Washington Monument.

As Gene and Kevin arrived at the monument out of breath, the Capital Police EOD team was arriving with a K-9. Kevin approached the Team Leader and gave him a briefing about the information on the bomb set to go off at three o'clock. Kevin looked around for Gene, who was no longer behind him. He walked around the monument and found Gene preparing to enjoy his pizza again. The EOD team spent the next hour using every method possible to locate a bomb. The dog, a Belgian Malinois, seemed confused at times but never alerted to anything.

Finally, with fifteen minutes left, the team leader approached Kevin and said, "I am sorry, sir, we cannot find anything to indicate a bomb here."

"Well let's clear out. We do not have very long to find out if they were bluffing," Kevin replied.

Everyone moved back beyond the barricades and waited. Kevin checked his watch, one minute 'til. He watched the second hand on his atomic watch roll past the nine, then the ten. Then the countdown in his head, five, four three, two, one, and then what sounded like a deep resonant thump, followed by a large explosion that caused the Monument to look like it had been momentarily displaced at the base of the structure. It tilted sideways and fell, landing with an enormous crash. The ground trembled with the impact. There were some who actually cheered. *Be careful what you wish for you fool.* Kevin thought.

Kevin walked over to the EOD Team Leader and said, "This is now a crime scene. Do not let anyone near it. I have a special forensic investigator that I am calling to examine the scene."

The team leader said "Yes sir, I am sorry we didn't find it."

"No worries, I am willing to bet there is nothing you have that would have located that bomb," Kevin replied.

"Well I'll establish a perimeter and have dispatch make a rotation schedule in case this takes longer than expected," the Team Leader said.

Kevin and Gene returned to the White House where the President was waiting on the South Lawn. President Bradshaw looked hopefully at both men.

Kevin said, "We didn't find anything, but I have an idea. I have called an old friend who recently retired from Alcohol Tobacco Firearms and Explosives, and I'll have him look at what is left of the monument. President Bradshaw, while I am waiting for his arrival I would like you to join me in another talk with your Vice President."

The President and Kevin walked through the corridors of the White House, then down to the sub levels. They arrived at the Security Command Center, and Kevin retrieved the lock to the Vice President's cell. As they entered the room, Vice President Richard Moore raised his head from his reading. Obviously emotionally worn, he had lost weight in the last few days and had dark circles under his eyes. He closed the Bible he was reading and placed it on the side of the bed.

"What can I do for you today gentlemen?" he asked.

"Since you've been in this cell, we have lost the Supreme Court Building, and now the Washington Monument. I thought you may have decided to help by giving up that list, but I'm starting to think that maybe that was just a distraction or a decoy. What are you not telling us?"

"Why would I keep anything from you?"

"Let me put it this way," Kevin said. "When we initially put you in this cell, you were full of hate. You talked to us as if you were willing to slit our throats. Then you had a change of heart and I bought it. You gave us a list, but I think you haven't told us everything. The people on the list are not actual co-conspirators. They were deceived by DHS into thinking they were helping take down a corrupt President. I think you know more than you revealed then, and I am curious how deep your connections go into this conspiracy."

Kevin walked over to the bed the Vice President was sitting on, picked up the Bible and opened it. He walked over to the President and showed him the book. Inside the cover was a cleverly concealed Quran. "Where did you get this?" Kevin demanded.

"I brought it to him." The President said. "I picked it up off of his desk in the West Wing thinking it was his Bible."

President Bradshaw was visibly shaken. He took the book with both hands and held it for a moment, processing the weight of this situation. He looked at the Vice President and said, "How long have you been Muslim?"

The Vice President responded, "That is not important."

Kevin asked, "Why did you give us the list?"

"Those pawns were no longer needed," he replied.

The President said, "Richard, I have known you for many years and I have always thought that you were Christian. I always thought that you were a patriot."

"I am a patriot," he said. "A patriot of Islam."

"Have you thought this through? What if your side fails?" the President asked.

"They will not fail," he said with confidence. "And, even as I have failed in my mission, my failure was in an effort to please Allah. I will soon be in Paradise."

Kevin was shaking his head.

"Sir, how could you let yourself be so mislead? Islam only exists because of ignorance, fear and intimidation. The only thing you will soon be in is serving life at a United States Prison!"

The Vice President held his gaze with Kevin glaring at him. Kevin laughed and said. "So this is how you are willing to be remembered, as a treasonous, backstabbing snake betraying your country for seventy-two virgins. Are you kidding me? What does your Allah think about the lying and deception that you have had to perpetrate through this entire fiasco? Does 'Allah' not condemn sin, or the supporting of murderous terrorists?"

The anger in the Vice President's eyes were intense as he said, "Islam allows such things in order to further Islam. It is called Taquiyya. Taquiyya basically is the blessing and forgiveness of sin committed in the furtherance of Islam."

"So Islam gives you permission to lie, deceive and kill?" Kevin asked.

"If it furthers the mission of Allah," the Vice President replied.

The President had kept quiet through this exchange, but then quietly added, "It sounds like Allah and Satan have a lot in common." President Bradshaw motioned for Kevin to leave the room. He waited until the door was closed, then sat down beside his choice for Vice President.

Holding the Quran he said, "This is a lie and you know it. If you are right, I hope you enjoy your paradise. If you are wrong, then Hell is a bad place in any religion."

The President rose and walked toward the door, then turned and said, "I will not be back. You will be held for treason and tried as a traitor. You may very soon find out if you are wrong."

President Bradshaw turned and left the cell. He met shortly with Kevin and said, "I know you probably don't want to do this, but you will have to write a report on this conversation and present it for prosecution. I will be a witness. At this point there is no question to his treachery. I thought, at one time, he was a friend." The President turned and walked away. Kevin let him go alone. *Sometimes alone is where you need to be*, he thought.

CHAPTER 40

Sam led Patton up the Arkansas, staying well hidden in the trees along the banks and turning west about a mile north of Smeltertown. They followed a small tributary, avoiding the scouts and patrols of the Sheikh's army that did not seem very interested in solid security. Their patrols maintained a predictable pattern which allowed Sam to easily slip in and out of Salida without being detected. The creek took Sam several miles into the wilderness where he had set camp with Walt, Matt and Daniel. Sam took a chance slipping into town for a couple of days with Daniel and Walt, using the spotting scope from a vantage point high on the mountain to watch the troop movements. Five separate patrols had a scheduled rotation of movement that was difficult to avoid around town. Walt recognized the first day that each patrol would take a shortcut south of the hospital, allowing anyone to stay undetected along the river on the north side of Salida close to Smeltertown. The problem was that if a threat was observed by one patrol, it would only take minutes for all five patrols to converge, providing support for one another. They seemed to be tactically savvy, and were definitely not your typical security guards just making rounds. The biggest concern was the individual scouts that had no predictable route or schedule. Walt had identified three different scouts at one time from the vantage point, but Sam had yet to see one on the ground in Salida.

Patton picked his way through the brush as the slope began to rise and the valley gave way to the mountain. The valley was for the most part high mountain desert with various types of pine trees. A battle with pine beetles for many years had decimated the old growth forests of the Rocky Mountains, and as the old pines died and fell, they created major deadfalls which lit like a striking match one hot summer several years before the Fall. The Rockies have a way of taking a bad thing and creating something beautiful from it, so now the forests were not as cluttered with deadfalls, and new growth had sprouted making the trees young, bushy and perfect cover for reconnaissance.

Patton was the perfect personality as horses go. After many years of trail riding, he and Sam had grown close and somehow learned to read each other's instincts. Patton's senses kept Sam in line, and Sam had learned to watch Patton's ears for anything to alert him to danger. As Patton walked upstream, he paused for a second as both ears went forward. They stopped together as one and listened. Sam heard nothing, but Patton was obviously not happy with what he was hearing.

Sam dismounted and proceeded on foot, leaving Patton behind. He moved off the path to the north and proceeded forward quietly. As he continued up the mountain, he began to hear distant voices during breaks in the wind. There, it sounded like laughing toward the spike camp. Sam continued to move right and uphill as he circled the area, pinpointing the source of voices. As he got to the point where they were directly south of him, he moved closer. Sam rotated the AR-15 to his primary weapon position and kept moving.

Silence … He held his breath for a minute and still no sound. Sam started moving again, still right and closer until he was almost directly west of the camp. Sam had initially approached them from the east, yet was now approaching from the west and flanking the target using the advantage of higher ground. The object was to never take a straight line into the target. Still, his senses were telling him nothing. He gradually crept closer, realizing that the voices he sought were no longer there.

Sam stood and walked into his camp, looking into the hollowed holes of what used to be the eyes of Matt Warner. Matt was standing and stripped naked. His face looked forward, frozen in a moment of pain. Matt had been nailed by both arms and legs to an old tree stump that had survived the fires. It was broken off at about six feet tall and had a few broken limbs that they had been hanging their gear on. His hands and feet had been severed and taken. His eyes had been gouged out with the end of a fiery stick. Sam looked on in shock and disbelief as he realized they had taken their time with him. His torment had been a great struggle. The tracks do not lie. His death was slow, and they savored every second that he had suffered until he died.

Sam took Matt in his arms and removed him from the tree. With tears in his eyes, he laid him on the ground and prayed. He prayed a selfish prayer. He prayed a prayer that God does not want to hear. He prayed that God allow him the opportunity to be the instrument of vengeance. He prayed for the retribution of those who tortured his friend, and prayed that they could experience a mere moment of his wrath. The rage in Sam rose until it could rise no more, and then he sat there with his friend and wept.

Matt had been tortured in the manner that Muhammed personally directed during his reign of terror. The assassins had come and gone, leaving much of their gear. Undoubtedly, Matt had not revealed the mission, or they would have waited in ambush. They had left our badges and anything connecting them to the Marshals in their gear at base camp, so Sam was not really concerned that they had any suspicion of a greater plan at work. As darkness approached, Walt and Daniel returned from the vantage point on the mountain. Not really sure how to react, Daniel sat down for a moment staring at Matt's lifeless, mutilated body.

Sam looked at Walt who was still a little shaken at the brutality of Matt's murder and said, "We need to pack up and get out of here and leave as little sign doing it. I am certain they will be back to see if they can find the rest of us."

They left the spike camp at sunset with Matt's body in tow, wrapped in a tarp, hanging across his horse. They followed the trail up the mountain to the vantage point, hoping to lose anyone tracking them in the rocks up high. Then the group traveled around to the back side of Mount Shavano and down to McCoy creek where they made camp. The camp was cold, dark and quiet. No one spoke, and no one slept for more than a few minutes, if any.

As darkness became light, Sam retrieved a folding shovel and started digging a grave. Daniel and Walt brought rocks from the creek to cover the grave. Once it was completely covered, they all stood in silence bidding farewell to their brother, each of them praying silently. Sam placed Matt's hat on the pile of rocks and said, "See you later, brother."

The group arrived in camp later that day. Jam immediately knew something was wrong as Sam led Matt's horse into camp with an empty saddle. Base camp had grown to over a hundred men, and every one of them paused as they saw the empty saddle and understood the reality of war.

Ronald exited the cabin and saw Sam, walked over and said, "Thank you, for the medicine. I would not be here if you had not come along."

"You're welcome, sir." *Interesting*, Sam thought, shaking his head. *The Lord saves one and yet takes another.*

Sam pulled the pager from his belt and typed a brief message of the incident to Agent McCrory. He looked at the pager for a moment seeing Jennifer's number, and for some reason he typed,

Hello.

He pressed send.

CHAPTER 41

Morning is a label of time, nothing more. Usually it comes abruptly with an alarm clock startling a person out of a dream. However, sometimes your body wakes after a full night of sleep, and the morning itself is a complete surprise. Lying in bed, waking up naturally without anything more than your body telling you to rise is a wonderful thing. Jennifer pulled the covers around her, creating a tight comforter cocoon as she lie on her bed in her condo. She peered out her window at the Rocky Mountain sunrise.

Tossing the covers aside, she placed both feet on the floor and walked into the kitchen to start a pot of coffee. She glanced at her backpack lying on the coffee table that had the pager clipped onto the strap. The little green light was flashing. *Oh my, she thought, I have a message.* With the excitement of a teenager she rushed to the pager to see what super-secret spy business she would be getting into today. She flipped open the pager and the screen merely said,

Hello.

Hello? Really? I have a pager that is exclusively for saving the world and my first text message is "Hello"? The more she thought about it, the more irritated she became and realized she needed to put the pager away and relax. The message might be a wrong number and not even concern her. She took a shower, treated herself to a cup of hot coffee and tried to think about something positive.

Jennifer spent the rest of the day being lazy, curling up in a ball and reading her book, but time after time she caught herself daydreaming and remembering nothing of what she had been reading. *What is wrong with me?* she thought. She placed her book on the table and thought of the pager and the message. *The only people I know that have pagers are the Secret Service and some of the Sheikh's assistants. It couldn't be the cowboy in the bushes. How would he get the number?*

She had to let go of this romantic notion that someday she will turn a corner and bump into someone who will sweep her off her feet and take her away from this nightmare. Who knows, she may not be able to function socially outside this prison. She could not let herself be fooled into thinking that a life in this community of insanity can experience romance. There was no love in this place. There was no room for love. Love challenges everything this false religion stands for. The evil in this place had ripped her from the only true love she ever had. It had ripped her from her family and changed her life forever. She asked herself many times why must she continue this charade, isn't there anything else for her out there?

In reality, she knew why she was here. God had selected her to bring comfort to those here who had nothing, helping those who had become trapped like her, becoming nothing more than a new shiny toy that was callously discarded, or sometimes tortured then killed. She had on so many occasions tried to save the innocent lives of those who were maimed or dismembered for mere accusations or amusement. Islamic theocracy with their sharia law is barbaric and evil to its core, and the thought of it being allowed to exist is testimony to the gradual decline of America's moral compass. *Ignorance is as evil as hate*, she thought. Choosing blindness to an obvious lie for the convenience it provides is as evil as the lie itself.

Jennifer looked carefully at the number and realized it was not one of the three numbers the Secret Service Agents had already programed into her pager. Who else would have this number? Frustrated, she took the pager, opened the screen and typed a message to Agent McCrory. She typed the number from the text and said,

I received a message from this number today. Who does it belong to?

She then put on her clothes, dropped the pager into her pocket and went for a walk to clear her head. She turned toward the hospital out of habit, but continued walking past it toward the sun as it was dropping past the peaks of the western range behind Monarch Pass. She walked to release the stress, and her mind started to wander beyond the worries of the day. It was so easy to lose yourself walking in this beautiful place where the mountains meet the sky. It was also easy to lose track of time.

Jennifer's hands went to her pockets as the late afternoon air caused her to chill. She felt the pager and was still uneasy about the message. She continued to walk and soon realized that the sun was setting and it was rapidly getting dark. In the twilight of the evening, shapes are distorted and light plays tricks on the mind. To see something clearly, you must not look directly at it. Looking to the left or right tricks the brain into seeing it more clearly. She looked ahead on the trail and saw a man on a horse. *Okay, she thought, I am done with this elementary school playground crap.* She faced him and deliberately started walking directly at him, and as she approached he turned and faced her. She was within ten yards now and could almost see his face under the hat.

"Who are you and why are you stalking me?" she demanded.

The man lit a cigar, his face reflecting the flash of the match, showing his weathered features. He took a long draw from the cigar and replied with a rough Middle Eastern accent while exhaling the bitter smoke of cheap tobacco through yellow stained teeth. "If I had been stalking you, you would have been taught some manners before I took you to my tent!" The man turned his horse and moved even closer to Jennifer until his horse was standing right beside her. He was not very well kept, but had a look about him that seemed dangerous. His eyes were empty and uncaring. His face was unshaven and his hair unruly, indicating that he was used to living outside the convenience of civilization, more comfortable in the wild. She saw the guns on his belt and the rifle in the scabbard, then she saw the saddle horn. Tied on a string wrapped around the saddle horn were the hands and feet of a man. She could see the wedding band still resting on the left ring finger with dried streaks of blood running the length of the hand down to the tips of the fingers. She looked at the man on the horse and a menacing smile grew on his face. His eyes grew cold. He swung his leg over his horse, dismounting and stepping closer to Jennifer who took a step back to dodge his outstretched hand.

She stumbled, fighting for her balance, then turned and ran. She could hear him laughing, taunting her as she ran. His laughter reminded her of a demon in a haunted house she had visited once as a small child. She ran until her legs were struggling, pumped full of blood and her lungs burned from the cool mountain air. Finally, up ahead she could see the familiar streets that would lead her to home and safety. Realizing he had not pursued her, she slowed to a brisk walk, and as she got to her condo, she could still feel her heart pounding, and her hands were shaking in reaction to the obvious danger she had just eluded. She fumbled with her keys and opened the door to her condo. Locking the door and securing the deadbolt gave her a small feeling of comfort, but she doubted she could sleep after seeing the assassin with his trophies.

She peeled off her clothes and left them where they fell. A hot tub bath was a perfect solution when wine was not available. She spent the next twenty minutes soaking in a wonderful, steamy, hot bath. She toweled off and walked through the house just to satisfy her paranoia. Eyeing the pager, she realized the light was blinking again. She picked it up and flipped it open to see Agent McCrory's one word message:

Sam.

CHAPTER 42

Kevin walked back to his office trying to make sense of the day. He realized that this enemy was something like they had never seen. Mahannad was not the typical terrorist that came to protest and kill indiscriminately trying to prove a point. His mission was one of ultimate and complete destruction. The key to the success of his mission was to remove the only obstacle in his way. *It's funny*, Kevin thought, *how blindly people ignore the importance of freedom until they are no longer free.*

Mahannad was one step ahead of them on all counts. Just when they thought the odds had turned in their favor, the Sheikh found a way to cause doubt in their minds, having planted seeds of fear and paranoia. Kevin knew through his years of training that Mahannad had waged a very effective mental war with the President, and it had almost worked. Mental war was an art which terrorists have exploited for years with efficiency. In times past, war was war. It was horrible and bloody and the destruction was purely physical with the dominant participant raising his hand as the victor.

Terrorism was the art of horrific surprise, creating the fear and paranoia of destruction that, if not eliminated, can cause society's foundation to crumble. The Preamble of the U. S. Constitution revealed the common desire of every society: establish justice, ensure domestic tranquility, provide for the common defense, promote general welfare and secure the blessings of liberty. Mahannad's mission was obviously to destroy nothing less than the very core of everything for which the Constitution stands.

Kevin arrived at home and soon fell into his dull routine of Scotch and his recliner. The turntable began to spin, bringing to life America's Lonely People. *What is left?* he thought. *I'm exhausted, so tired of the insanity of day to day crisis situations.* Taking a sip of the scotch and rolling the ice in the glass, he stared at the drink then set it down on the end table beside his chair. He leaned back and closed his eyes, trying to relax and hoping for a moment or two of sleep. Just as he started to drift off, he heard a tapping on his door.

What in the world? Can I not have a minute of peace? He jerked the door open and an old familiar face was grinning at him through a thick grey beard.

"Can I borrow a couch for a night or two?" he asked. Kevin took a step back shaking his head, and with a sigh and a chuckle opened the door wide so that Jericho Smith could enter his home. Jerry had spent thirty years of his life as a forensic investigator with the Bureau of Alcohol Tobacco Firearms and Explosives, spending the last five years in retirement as an instructor at the Academy. There was no one better to examine a crime scene than Jerry.

Kevin gave Jerry a bear hug and said, "So good to see you. I didn't expect you here until tomorrow though."

"I wanted to see if you were still listening to those lame seventies albums I gave you years ago."

Kevin and Jerry spent the evening sharing a bottle of scotch and reminiscing about good times and old friends that had become vague memories over the years. The conversation slowed as old age and scotch took their respective toll on the two friends, and just after midnight Kevin ended the evening by falling asleep in his chair. Jerry made himself comfortable on the couch, and both were soon fast asleep.

Morning came abruptly with the screech of an alarm clock in the bedroom. Kevin rolled out of his chair and tripped over Jerry's bag as he ran to turn it off. Jerry stretched and moaned a complaint-filled yawn as he swung his legs into a sitting position. Both men dressed. Kevin in his standard issue Secret Service suit and tie, Jerry looking more like Jerry Garcia in faded jeans, a T-shirt and ball cap. They grabbed a bagel and a cup of coffee at a deli on H Street and took turns talking in between bites as they walked toward what was left of the Washington Monument.

The Monument had disintegrated only at the base, causing the displaced tower to fall like a tree that had been cut down. Jerry and Kevin stepped under the crime scene tape and approached the rubble with badges drawn, identifying themselves to the security team protecting the crime scene. Kevin explained to Jerry how the event took place. The explosion seemed internal and synchronized with his watch to the second, indicating that it may have been triggered by a clock that was set by the Atomic Clock at the U. S. Naval Observatory here in Washington D. C..

The base of the monument appeared to have been severed about eight feet above the ground. Jerry walked around the remaining structure to make sure there would be no accidents while he focused on his work. The integrity of structures is usually compromised even after surviving a blast. They may crumble and fall without warning days later. Once Jerry was confident that the area was safe to search, he began laying out a grid pattern. Once evidence is collected, it is photographed, secured and labeled as to its location on the grid pattern.

Jerry walked around the outside of the foundation examining every rock and crevice along the smooth concrete. He then moved inside the base of the structure. He pulled out a magnifying glass and looked at the edges of the base all the way around the structure. On occasion he would take a small brush from his pocket and sweep the residue into small evidence containers, labeling each container with the location description. Totally focused on the task at hand, he seemed somewhat obsessed, neither speaking nor taking a break as he worked silently through the lunch hour. Kevin got tired of checking his watch and finally just sat down on a park bench nearby. At three o'clock Jerry stopped and noticed a young boy playing in the grass beyond the crime scene tape.

The boy was looking down in the grass, then stooped to pick something up. Jerry immediately yelled, "Stop!" The boy straightened and looked back in Jerry's direction. Jerry started running toward the boy. He jumped the crime scene tape and sprinted to where the boy stood looking at him like he was crazy. Jerry looked down at the ground, and there was a tiny electronic device attached to what appeared to be a detonator. Jerry looked at the boy and said, "Go find your Mom, now! It isn't safe to be here." The boy ran off looking more confused than scared.

Jerry stooped to look at the device in the grass. Kevin trotted over to see what he had discovered, and as he got closer he could hear a tiny high pitched whistle or ring, almost inaudible for his old ears. Jerry looked at

Kevin and said, “Stay back! It could still be active.” Jerry immediately reached for a tool on his belt and went to work looking at the device from every angle and finally decided to act. The device was very small, and the time piece was an atomic clock that could be programmed with a remote. A tiny copper wire served as an antenna receiving the signal from the Atomic Clock, as well as receiving information on setting the alarm with a remote control. Jerry separated the time piece from the detonator, moved back and waited for a few minutes. Breathing easier, Jerry lay back in the grass and looked at the clouds.

“I am waaay too old for this,” he said still catching his breath. Kevin’s face appeared between Jerry and the clouds, and Kevin said,

“You alright, Bud?”

Jerry rose to a sitting position and said, “No, I am not.” He pulled a small flask from his jacket and took a deep drink, feeling the bourbon scorch the back of his throat. He wiped his mouth with his sleeve and said, “I am not the man I used to be, and it really hurts when I try to be.”

Kevin laughed and said, “You could be a rapper.”

Jerry looked at Kevin and took another quick swig of bourbon. Returning the flask to his pocket he said, “If you are done with the comedy routine, I will tell you about your bomb.” He motioned for Kevin to sit in the grass. Kevin hesitated and realized protesting would help nothing. As the crime scene security watched from the base of the monument, a guy that looked like Jerry Garcia was sitting in the grass passing a flask with the Supervisory Agent in Charge of the President’s Secret Service detail. The security team supervisor shook his head and moved toward the perimeter barrier to tell his agents to watch the east side of the monument. All was secure here.

Kevin and Jerry sat in the grass discussing matters of national security that could determine the course of world history as nonchalantly as a couple on a picnic discussing what puppy would be best for their lifestyle. Jerry was still shaking off the device in the grass that could have killed the child when he turned squarely to Kevin and said, “You, we, all of us, have a huge conspiracy to overthrow the United States here. I cannot tell you in any clearer way than by saying that this plan has been in play since the last time this monument was restored. I’m guessing around 2013.”

“How sure are you of this, and can you prove it?”

Jerry confidently said, “One hundred percent, and yes!”

Kevin got to his feet, held out his hand to Jerry and said, “Let’s go see the President.”

CHAPTER 43

Base camp had changed dramatically since Sam and his crew had been at spike camp. The mission of the insertion team had confirmed that the enemy was legitimate and capable. They were cold blooded and willing to kill. They held many potential hostages who had no idea how quickly the cowardly enemy would easily turn against them and use them as human shields. They held a tactical advantage of three million people in New York City as ransom, and as far as anyone knew the entire leadership of this country was hostile to the U. S. Constitution. Sam feared their days were numbered, but with the continued reports of volunteers, regulators, minutemen, or patriots if you will, arriving in La Veta on a daily basis, he realized there was still hope.

Jensen Clayton was one of the first volunteers from Stillwater, Oklahoma. He was still working as hard as he could, running messages to La Veta and returning by guiding trains of pack horses with supplies for the ever growing numbers. Jensen reported on his last trip that there were at least five thousand men ready and willing to defend the Constitution and fight for the United States. After the last few years, it was hard to imagine there were five thousand men left in this entire country who cared.

At the peak of the cabin rooftop someone had planted a beautiful American flag, and she waved proudly in the gentle mountain breeze. Sam walked to the cabin and checked on the family. Ronald met him at the door and seemed to be doing very well in spite of almost dying a week ago. His children were coloring on the table. Jensen had brought them back crayons and a coloring book from La Veta. Sam sent Daniel to find Jam, Walt, Charlie and Garrison. They needed to have a meeting and discuss strategy.

Minutes later, the group came together and knelt down like kids on a football field drawing the play in the dirt with their fingers. Sam picked up a stick and drew the mountains surrounding the area of Salida, then drew a wavy line through the middle indicating it was the Arkansas River. He then drew the creek Sam had followed north of town that led down from the Spike camp at the base of Mount Shavano. Next, he drew the airport landing strip west of town and the multiple apartments that had been built to house most of the Sheikh's assassins. Finally, he drew lines indicating the main roads in and out of town, and across the road at each end of town.

"Okay," Sam said, "these are check points here and here, and they are pretty much the only stationary security. There are guards at the Palace Hotel for obvious reasons, but the majority of their security is always mobile. They consist of five teams of five to six men rotating at random throughout the valley in and around Salida. If one group encounters resistance, one shot fired brings the other four teams running. The rest of the troops are on standby in what I think is general rotation in twelve hour shifts. I never saw any of them called out, but there is always a fairly strong contingency at the ready. I imagine as we get closer to the Fourth they will turn up the intensity of their security throughout the valley. We have a little over a week to establish a plan and begin our own troop movement. I think we need to send a message back down to La Veta and have them start moving this way. We established that our platoons would each have fifty men in them. At this point, we will have one hundred platoons. I think we need to split the force and have a division march straight up Highway 50. I am sure they will have scouts react and hopefully assume that is all we can muster. The second division will cut across and move up highway 285, flanking Salida through Poncha Springs."

"What about the rest of us?" Charlie asked. "There is at least a hundred of us right here."

"We are going to be the element of surprise. I would like to take the remaining men here and move them north of town coming in from Smeltertown along the Arkansas River. I would like to lead a small team into town in the early morning hours and plant some surprises I brought from home. We need to eliminate the potential for their army to get organized and on horseback. They will be formidable if all of their assassins mobilize. If we time this right, the main element of troops will be reacting to the first division, which will allow us to secure the airport for the President. The first division will be the distraction. Hopefully the bombs I plant will keep the soldiers on foot."

Daniel looked at Sam sadly, and Sam knew what he was thinking.

"No, Daniel, I am not going to blow up their horses. I just want to blow the fence and send them all running for the hills. Does anyone have any other plans that would benefit this mission? Walt, what are you thinking?"

"I would think we should have a small team take up a point of observation from now until the Fourth to make sure we are not missing anything. I would hate for this plan to be implemented and realize they had moved the show."

"Good point Walt. We'll make it happen." Sam rose slowly, feeling his age, and walked over to his pack to retrieve a notepad and pen. He began writing the plan down. Sam made three copies, one copy for each division and one for him. He walked over to where Jensen was preparing for the ride back to La Veta and handed him the orders folded in a leather pouch.

"Jensen, I need these delivered to the names on the envelopes. They are now the Division Commanders, and these envelopes contain their orders. I want you to move as fast and safely as possible. I need the messages delivered today. I think you should have no problem making the trip by sundown. Eat and get some rest overnight and return immediately in the morning. If you do not return tomorrow I will have to assume the mission is now compromised."

Jensen stiffened and immediately realized the importance of his ride today. Saluting Marshal Crow he said enthusiastically, "Yes sir!" He shoved the pouch into an interior pocket on his coat and leapt to his saddle. He turned his horse and trotted through camp down the trail to La Veta. Sam returned to his meeting and looked at Walt.

"Find Jensen's brothers and have them begin the rotation on surveillance of Salida. We should run no more than five hour shifts. I don't want anyone falling asleep and missing anything. We also need lookouts on each side of Methodist Mountain, preventing an approach from either side."

The day passed quickly as people prepared to mobilize for battle. Soldiers were checking and rechecking their weapons. If all went as planned, the one hundred here would move across Monarch Pass and establish a position north of Salida. As Sam prepared his own gear, he felt the pager vibrate on his belt. He took it from its clip and flipped it open.

Agent McCrory had sent a text.

Hope all is well, just checking on your new hobby.

Sam responded,

The porridge is just right and there should be about 5000 bowls ready in a couple of days. Hope Papa Bear likes the surprise. I'll swing by for a visit in three.

He should get a kick out of that, Sam thought. The reply read,

Wow, thanks. See you soon.

Sam returned the pager to the clip and walked back to where they had been meeting. Jam had walked over to the cook tent looking for something to eat. Walt was whittling on a chunk of aspen wood. He took a walk out to the edge of the trees and sat down on the ground. He leaned back against a tree and watched the remaining light fade from the sky painting a spectacular display of various shades of orange and yellow that gradually faded to gray, then darkness.

CHAPTER 44

Kevin and Jerry walked across the White House lawn, making their way up the stairs and through the corridors to the office of the President. Once outside the door, Kevin started to knock, and one of the guards in the hall said, "I'd give him a minute. There are several Congress members inside. From the looks on their faces when they entered the room, now would not be a good time to interrupt."

"Thank you, Agent." Kevin and Jerry walked down the hall to a set of chairs and a coffee table so they would not be observed when the congressmen left. Several minutes went by, and eventually the congressmen filed out of the President's office in single file, all with a stoic expression and not even acknowledging the presence of the agents. Kevin waited a few minutes. Reaching down, he retrieved his pager from his belt and realized he had received a message at some point that he had missed. *Probably while running to save the world again*, he thought. He flipped the pager open, and he had received a message from the team out west.

Five thousand strong now will be in position at wheels down.
We'll meet with head honcho in three days.

Kevin shook his head in disbelief. "I cannot believe it. These Marshals are off the chart crazy. How do you find resources for five thousand men in the middle of nowhere?" Kevin stood and lightly knocked at the President's door. The President opened the door quickly as if he were standing there waiting for him to knock. Almost laughing, he led Agent Landrum and his new friend into the office.

Shaking Jerry's hand, the President introduced himself. "You must be the ATF Forensic Bomb investigator Kevin told me about." Jerry nodded, shaking the President's hand.

"Yes sir, Kevin and I go way back."

Kevin interrupted and said, "First thing sir, I have an update from out west. The Marshals seem to have been able to increase the size of their army and now stand at five thousand men. They will be in position to secure the airfield when we arrive."

The President smiled and said, "That is fantastic. I'll tell you why I am smiling. Those five senators who just left tried to come in my office and bully me into maintaining the deal with Mahannad, and I basically put a boot in the middle of their butt. I told them that I had a handle on things and would be taking care of it all at a level that they had no business dealing with. They threatened me with impeachment, and I laughed. I said hell, you're all trying to kill me right now anyway. What will it accomplish to impeach a dead president? Then I ushered them out and told them to go back to whoever has bought them off and tell them to pound sand. This is still America for a little while!"

Kevin had never seen the President so animated before. Watching the years pass during a term of a president was always taxing. Being president is like living in dog years. Aging seven years to everyone else's one, and President Bradshaw was dealing with things never before seen in the history of the office. However, now he was getting back to his fighting weight as his confidence was growing and his attitude was getting much brighter.

He said, "Five thousand men! That is just incredible. All true heroes no doubt!"

Kevin added, "Sir, Jerry also has some information that's pretty important. Jerry would you tell the President what you have discovered?"

"Mr. President, the nature of the explosion was a very typical localized time bomb that had a couple of very unique qualities. The bomb was detonated inside the structure itself by a remote controlled alarm clock, probably solar powered. We found one of the devices still intact with the detonator attached. They have been made safe, but you have to understand the type of explosive, clock or remote is not as important as the fact of where the bomb was located."

The President looked somewhat confused. "You've told me it was inside the monument right? What is so unique about that?"

"I'm sorry Mr. President my description wasn't as specific as it needed to be. Holes were drilled inside the walls of the monument and the devices were placed inside these holes, then sealed there until the opportunity arrived to use them. I'm guessing the last time the monument was refurbished, probably in or about 2013."

The President sat down and had a blank expression of shock on his face realizing that the country was being betrayed for almost two decades. Jerry continued, "Mr. President, it's probably worse than we thought because many federal buildings were renovated during that time, and there is no telling how many buildings are just waiting for someone to press a button."

Kevin walked over to the door, stuck his head out into the corridor and spoke briefly to one of the agents. "Find Gene and have him come up here immediately."

"Yes sir," the agent said turning and walking briskly down the hallway.

The President then said, "The enemy has hated Western civilization and our success since they realized what we could do with our freedom, and they have tried to destroy us at every turn."

Kevin responded, "They changed, sir. Instead of the constant onslaught of terror they pretended to be nice, forgiving, working their way into our society by using the tool in their religion called Taquiyya. Taquiyya allows them to lie, cheat and deceive to further the mission of Islam, and they did so until their population numbers started putting people in office and elections were won. It became an accepted practice of some of our leaders to have Islamic advisers creating an enemy in the camp atmosphere. Islam invented the pandemic, then tried to bomb us while we were weak. They have destroyed their own land and now they want to take ours. How many of their own did they kill to put Mahannad in this position to assume leadership of the free world? You said it best the other day, sir. Sounds more like the mission of Satan."

A light knock at the door and Gene stuck his head in. "Come on in," The President said. Gene's wide body moved awkwardly through the door and he had a look on his face like a kid that just got caught with his hand in the cookie jar.

"You are not in trouble, Gene," Kevin said grinning. Breathing a sigh of relief, Gene relaxed a bit.

"Jerry, show Gene the remote alarm clock." Jerry held out his hand, showing Gene the tiny device.

"Gene, this is what they used to detonate the monument with. The bomb lies dormant for years inside a building and the alarm clock has a very high end heavy metal battery, or a tiny solar panel mounted obscurely somewhere on the building. They get within range of the clock and activate the alarm with a remote never having to lay hands on the explosive. They probably do not even know who placed or set the explosive."

Gene took the clock and turned it back and forth in his hand looking for any clue to its origin or function. "These were individually custom made for this purpose only. This one still functions, so it must have an internal lithium or nickel cadmium battery. These types of batteries could easily last a decade and then some without charging, running nothing more than a small alarm clock. I've seen watch batteries last well over ten years and that's running stop watches and other extra items on a watch."

Jerry looked at Gene and said, "Can we remotely kill the power to the clocks?"

"That is easy," Gene replied. "Set off an EMP." It will interrupt most electrical devices, and this one that is a designed frequency receiver is a perfect conductor for the pulse.

"But won't the pulse set off the explosion?" the President asked.

"Not likely, the alarm will not be able to go off after the circuit itself is destroyed. The pulse will end at the circuit. Once the bombs are rendered useless, we can locate them later by finding the records in the building manager's office of where renovations occurred."

The President looked at Gene and said, "I would like a little more assurance than not likely. You said these are custom designed for this specific purpose, who knows, maybe they put a failsafe in these to prevent us from doing this very thing."

"Very true," Gene said. "Can I take the clock to our technical lab to examine it further and maybe give you some stronger assurances after that?" Everyone in the room agreed that was a plan.

The President stopped everyone before leaving the room. "Men, we have less than a week to find a way."

CHAPTER 45

Jensen returned to camp by noon the next day, reporting that all was well with the multitude of soldiers in La Veta, and they were preparing to leave immediately. Sam gathered his goods and packed everything he could carry on Patton. They had no room or time for pack horses on this campaign. Sam called everyone around, and a little more than a hundred men stood in the trees around the cabin. He stepped up onto a stump and started speaking.

"Gentlemen, none of us thought this day would ever come, but once again we are going to war fighting for the very survival of freedom. In four days, we will determine the course of history for the rest of the world forever. A horrible evil that has been brooding and planning our demise for centuries has risen to power again, and it is up to us to stop them. Like once before many years ago, the knights of old assembled and waged war in the Holy Crusades against this very evil. If it is left unchecked, it will consume the very soul of freedom, America will be no more. If in the end we must make the ultimate sacrifice, then let us die well as free men rather than living a lie in the chains of cowardice. If any of you are having second thoughts, it is time to address them. There is no shame in the fear of battle. There is no shame in fighting for this country, and there is certainly no shame in being willing to die for this country. But our mission is not to die. In the immortal words of General George S. Patton, our mission is to make the other bastard die."

They broke down the camp and took only what each soldier could carry. Sam made sure he had each of his guns and an abundance of ammunition. He hesitantly sacrificed the 450 Marlin, leaving it and several boxes of ammo with Ronald. Giving up the rifle and the weight of the enormous bullets allowed him to pack several hundred more rounds in magazines of .223. If he were unable to return to pick up his rifle, Ronald may need it to survive and defend his home. The long line of soldiers on horseback crossed the highway a mile west of Mayesville and made a beeline for the dark timber.

Following a game trail, Sam saw various tracks of goats, deer and elk. Luckily, the day was somewhat cloudy, and they had climbed high enough to hide in the clouds. The trail they were following was about a half mile higher up the mountain than where Matt was killed. Sam rode Patton higher with the intention of staying on the trail just below the tree line.

They eventually intersected the trail that had led them behind Mount Shavano the day of Matt's murder. Sam pulled on Patton's reigns, stopping him for a moment as he looked down the trail to where Matt was buried at the bottom of the mountain. He urged Patton on and remained quiet for most of the day. He continued to use the terrain to their advantage and kept the mountain between his troops and Salida for as long as possible. By the end of the day, they had arrived at the base of Mount Antero. Exhausted and weary, they removed their saddles and watered their horses in a nearby stream that ran out of the mountains between Mount Antero and Mount White. Sam looked at his map and determined camp to be about seven or eight miles north of Salida. They camped without a fire and kept noise to a minimum, staying several hundred yards inside the tree line. Most were trail weary so they took care of their horses, ate some jerked elk and called it a night.

As Sam lay on his bedroll, he felt his pager vibrate. He flipped it open and read the screen.

Hello Sam, I hope you are close. Please come get me soon. Jennifer.

Sam closed the pager, put it on his gun belt and tried to sleep with her on his mind. Some things immediately ruin a night's sleep for most. For one, the anticipation of battle can deprive a man from even a moment of sleep. A woman is probably the second most common reason for sleep loss in men, and tonight Sam was dealing with a double shot.

The night was clear and cold, and somewhere in the high country a chorus of coyotes would howl just about every time Sam started to drift off. He woke the next morning cold, tired and sore from sleeping with no fire. He was cold to the bone and ready to fight for a hot cup of coffee, but started gathering his things and waking the camp so that they could move across the valley under the cover of darkness. They crossed the valley on the north end and followed Browns Creek down to where it runs into the Arkansas River.

Sam and his company crossed the river and continued west as the day was breaking. By the time it was light, they had moved into a small valley just below Aspen Ridge. They made an early camp so everyone could relax for a full day. Sam took the opportunity to slip into Smeltertown and meet with his friends from the smokestack. He came down out of the mountains maintaining cover as much as possible. Slipping through the vegetation was easy, but there were fields that left him vulnerable in the open, so he kept low to minimize his outline and hurried across as quickly as possible.

Sam trotted Patton across one more field, down the road to the smokestack and past the trees along the river bank. He tied Patton to a small tree and walked back up the bank, across the open lot to the chained gate of the main building. He squeezed through the opening in the gate and opened the door to the office. It looked vacant. He walked to the back of the building and saw the room where Agent McCrory had sat at the table two weeks earlier.

He began to worry that something was not right and turned to leave. Immediately drawing his Glock on instinct, he kept it at the ready fearing his friend's position had been compromised. He checked two other rooms and still nothing. Where the hell were they? McCrory knew he was coming today. He slipped back through the gate, quickly jogged to the river and got out of sight, feeling more secure with trees around him and with Patton close enough to escape upstream. He moved downriver to see if he could see anything in town. Suddenly he heard something buzzing, vibrating like a pager, but it was not the one on his belt. He started moving closer to the river and walking through some very thick underbrush, suddenly realizing he was standing on a hand.

Sam bent down, moving vines and leaves away from the body and saw that it was Agent McCrory. He checked for a pulse and could feel the beat strong and steady, but McCrory was unconscious. He cleared a spot in the underbrush and moved him back underneath a large cottonwood, leaning him back against the tree. The agent had a large knot on his head in addition to being bruised and cut from running through the brush. He had been there for at least several hours.

Realizing he was hurt pretty badly but going to survive, Sam walked back to Patton and got his medicine bag. He returned to McCrory, opened some small alcohol towels and started cleaning some of the lacerations and abrasions. His pager was still going off, so Sam removed it and opened it to preserve the battery. The current message was from Agent Landrum who merely wanted to check in and confirm all was still good. Sam took the liberty of replying.

Marshal Crow here, McCrory injured, down but not out. Other agent's location unknown. My men are present and accounted for continue as planned for now.

He pressed send and prayed all was not lost. Occasionally, the agent would jerk or twitch as if he were dreaming. Sam finally patted him on the cheek to see if he would wake. A couple of times his eyes fluttered, and Sam thought he would respond, but he fell back into his unconscious state. Sam pulled his pager from its holster and opened it to read Jennifer's message again. He typed,

Where are you?

Almost immediately, as if she were waiting for the message she replied,

In the condos southeast of the Hospital.
Can you get across the river without being seen? Sam replied.
Give me twenty minutes.
Patrols have been increased and being outside is dangerous.

CHAPTER 46

Jennifer jumped from the couch put on some old jeans and regular clothes with hiking boots, grabbed her go bag and then put on her burqa over her regular clothes. She slung her backpack over her shoulder and slipped out the door hoping she would never have to return. There was nothing for her here. She watched one of the mounted patrols ride down 1st Street that parallels the river and waited, letting them pass before she moved quietly out from behind the stairwell of the apartment next door. She walked toward the hospital and across the parking lot hoping for a chance to make it across the bridge before she was seen. Not seeing any horses or men, she crossed 1st Street and started across the bridge. She walked with purpose, but did not want to attract attention by running. More than halfway over the bridge she heard the sound of hoofs behind her and turned to see a man on a horse coming toward her. She turned and waited, confident she could not outrun a horse.

The man approached her cautiously and asked, "Where are you going?" Jennifer recognized the horrible voice and started shaking. She looked at the saddle horn, and the hands and feet were still dangling from them. Smelling rancid with flies fighting for a spot on them, the assassin's trophies were still proudly displayed. Trying to play the game again, she lowered her head in submission and said, "I was just going for a walk and have never been across the bridge. I am Dr. Jennifer Boudreaux from the hospital."

"Well, I don't care who you are and you are not where you are supposed to be, Doctor. Funny, your voice sounds somewhat familiar to me. Have we met before, perhaps on a trail late one afternoon?"

“No sir,” she replied, visibly shaking and now certain he could see it. “I work in the lab at the hospital until dark every day. I rarely walk. I just needed some fresh air today.”

The assassin replied, “I think you are lying.” Suddenly the assassin stopped and looked past Jennifer across the bridge down the road to where it forks. Standing in the fork of the road was a man on horseback wearing a cowboy hat. He paused there for a moment and turned his horse toward the bridge, urging him forward and walking slowly. The assassin looked confused at first, then his expression turned to one of hatred. He leaned forward in the saddle and urged his horse to a trot and then a gallop until he brought him to an abrupt stop right in front of the cowboy who sat there casually waiting for him with his hands crossed and resting on his saddle horn.

CHAPTER 47

Sam looked at the assassin with a smile on his face and said, "Good afternoon." The assassin looked as if he could not decide whether to be confused or mad.

"What are you doing here?" he spat, still trying to pretend he was in charge.

"Oh, I am just out on a Sunday afternoon ride with my trusty old horse. What are you doing here?" Sam deliberately looked over the assassin's shoulder, reminding him of the woman.

The assassin glanced back at the bridge and realized the woman in the burqa had disappeared. He turned his horse momentarily back toward the bridge having lost all focus on his true threat, eyes darting to the river bank on either side of the bridge. He had lost the woman. As he spun his horse back toward Sam, he found himself looking down the barrel of his Ruger GP100.

Still smiling Sam said, "Lose somethin'?" He paused for effect, letting him embrace the gravity of his dilemma. The big hole in the end of the barrel also gets bigger the longer someone looks at it. "Now, sir," Sam said as politely as possible. "Now that I have your undivided attention, I want you to slowly, with your left hand, unbuckle your gun belt and let it fall to the street." He moved slowly and did as Sam asked. His belt hit the street and Sam said, "Now please sir, open your coat and with your left hand place your thumb and your forefinger on the butt only of the gun you have hidden in the shoulder rig under your coat." He did so and that gun hit the ground as well.

"Okay now let's ride around the corner of that trailer over there and we will have a little talk." Keeping the gun on his new friend, Sam let him lead the way to the other side of the trailer. He wanted to get out of sight as quickly as possible. He dismounted and indicated for the assassin to do the same. He looked and saw the hands and feet of his friend hanging from the assassin's saddle horn. He forced the criminal against the trailer and frisked him for additional weapons, finding a small .22 hidden in his belt and two knives.

Sam removed the man's coat and vest and handcuffed him behind his back. Sam then opened the door of the trailer with his boot, led the assassin in and sat him down on the floor. Jennifer, moments later, walked through the door wearing some old faded jeans and a flannel shirt which somehow, in spite of its rough logger, look still made her the most beautiful woman he had ever seen. Her hair no longer coal black, was a salt and pepper mix of gray falling about her shoulders.

She caught Sam staring at her. "I haven't been outside without a head cover in years," she said smiling. "This feels extremely awkward."

The assassin spat at her, "You whore. You are a worthless piece of dirt that will be tormented in hell forever."

Sam patted him on the cheek and said, "Look sunshine, in America we treat women with respect. We do not talk to them that way."

He spat on the ground at Sam's feet and said, "You are weak! You are nothing more than an infidel, a parasite that will easily be defeated! I will gladly die for my belief."

Sam squatted down in front of him and said, "Dyin' is the easy part. You'll be surprised at what you can live through. Keep that in mind next time you want to run your mouth." Sam lifted him to his feet, took the cuffs off. "You are accustomed to hiding in a group and attacking the weak. You think that you are strong when the only opposition you have ever faced was someone you knew you could easily defeat. Sam walked him across the room and turned the assassin, standing toe to toe with him. "You are a weak, empty, foolish shell of a coward that can only exist by intimidating women and children. It took a whole group of you to take out one of my men and he was unarmed. You are pathetic and not worthy of your false god."

The assassins eyes filled with rage and he swung, landing a punch on Sam's cheek turning his head. Sam looked back at him casually and smiled. The assassin swung again and Sam took another punch and paused. Sam tilted his head, side to side, stretching his neck, smiled and said, "C'mon sunshine, is that all you got?" The third swing Sam blocked with his forearm and he jabbed the assassin square in the nose. Sam continued to punch rocking the assassins head backward as the man in black finally fell to the floor covering his face with his hands. Sam stood him up and said, "Did you give my man a chance like this or did you hide in your pack of cowards still clinging to the delusion of how tough you are, tormenting him without honor, finding joy in his pain?"

The assassin looked at Sam through the blood with hatred in his eyes, standing there with his fists clinched. He took a step forward and Sam jabbed him again. His nose exploded into a bloody mess. Sam finished him with a right hook collapsing him into an unconscious ball. He taped his feet and legs together, then put a piece of tape over his mouth. Sam took his guns and put them on his horse. He then took the hands and the feet of his friend and wrapped them in a towel, carefully placing them in his pack.

"It's really good to see you, Jen."

She smiled and grabbed the reigns of the assassin's horse.

"What are you going to do with those?" she asked.

"I am going to return them to their rightful owner. He was a friend of mine."

Sam led Jennifer over to the river bank where Agent McCrory was lying unconscious. She took off her backpack and removed an ammonia inhalant from a pocket on the side of the pack and broke the capsule open holding it under the agent's nose for a second. He jerked awake and blinked a few times, then drifted back to sleep. She waved the capsule under his nose again and his eyes immediately opened. He became somewhat alert, though he was in obvious pain from head to toe.

"Agent, do you remember me?"

He mumbled, "Hello Sam."

"Do you think you can ride a horse out of here?"

"I'll try," he said. They climbed up the river bank, and Sam helped Agent McCrory into the saddle. The sun was setting, and it was getting dark, which was good because we could not travel fast. Jennifer rode behind Sam on Patton with her arms wrapped around him, occasionally squeezing him a little tighter. It was a really good squeeze.

CHAPTER 48

Gene spent the evening in the technical lab at Secret Service headquarters analyzing the mechanism inside the small alarm clock. Jerry watched the process as Gene dismantled the clock, and Kevin sat quietly making sure the coffee cups never ran empty. Every now and then, Gene would sigh and say "hmmm." Finally losing what little patience he had left, he said, "Okay Gene, what are you seeing? Let's talk this out and maybe together we can open a different door in that amazing mind of yours."

Gene finished his cup and held it out to Kevin, mocking him as he poured his fifth cup. Gene said, "The circuitry is easy enough. It's just a clock. The remote turns the alarm on and off. That's all. It's the alarm circuit to the detonator that is unique. The alarm circuit is controlled by a Micro Nano Controller. The remote station involves a coded RF transmitter-encoder that is in turn controlled by a manual pushbutton switch for energizing the transmitter. The pushbutton switch unit is provided with an indicator lamp, which is controlled by an indicator timing circuit that is activated by the pushbutton switch. The timing circuit then provides timed energization of the indicator lamp when this push button switch is closed. The transmitter is energized by the closure of that switch and transmits an RF coded signal to the receiver, which decodes this RF signal and delivers an output signal to the timing control unit, which in turn interrupts the operation of the oscillator unit activating the alarm and detonating the device at the predesignated time."

Kevin and Jerry just stared at Gene shaking their heads. Kevin said, "Just a simple alarm clock. Okay, this time in English. Dumb it down a bit, will you?"

"Basically any interruption in the oscillator will detonate the device once the alarm has been initiated. An EMP will activate the oscillator but then collapse the energized system, in turn stopping the oscillator and detonating the bomb."

"So, EMP bad … that's all you had to say … EMP bad!"

"Yes, and what is so amazing is that this device and its eventual detonation was planned and placed almost two decades ago, which ironically coincides with an administration that maintained an abundance of Muslim advisors on its staff."

"Okay, back on topic," Kevin said, "or I'm cutting the coffee off. How do we stop this bomb?"

"The only other way to get at this bomb is to attack it at its signal. We can assume that the RF signal is universal. If we can power this clock up and figure out the signal to turn it off or deactivate the alarm, we can render the bomb useless. We can use a powerful transmitter with the off signal and transmit it throughout New York and Washington, and pulse that signal periodically to make sure it stays off. There is only one problem."

"What's that?" Kevin asked.

"The only way we will know if it works is if the bombs do not go off."

Kevin sat in silence for a moment looking for answers when Jerry said, "That means there is no way the terrorists can know if their radio frequency actually activates the alarm detonating the bomb until it goes off."

"Correct," Gene replied. "It is a two way street."

Jerry then said, "Hasn't the military been using RF jammers for decades blocking radio frequencies?"

"Yes," Kevin said, "they have. We have used them on occasion when the President traveled into foreign countries. We keep portable ones in each of the limos and on all of the aircraft including Air Force One. We will need larger ones for the buildings in New York City. Okay Gene, find the frequency to turn off the alarm. If we can turn off the alarm then use the RF jammers to block the remote frequency I think we have our answer." Kevin walked through the squad room into his office and picked up his phone. Kevin advised President Bradshaw of the current situation and the need for Large stationary RF jammers in Washington and New York City.

"How confident are you that Gene is on the right track?" the President asked Kevin.

"One hundred percent, sir. His tech skills are top notch. My only concern now is being able to apply the technology in both cities successfully. We aren't even sure there is another bomb in D.C. but I do not want to take that chance."

Kevin returned to the lab and brewed a fresh pot of coffee. Always impressed by Gene's ability to work with technology, it did not take him long to power up the clock and determine its frequency by using the circuits and controls in a universal television remote control. Once the T.V. remote could turn the alarm on and off, he determined the frequency the remote was transmitting by an RF Electronic Frequency Detector. Kevin returned to his office and called a friend who was now in charge of the F.B.I Anti-Terrorism Task Force. After ten minutes of navigating through the automated answering service Kevin finally spoke to a human.

"Chad Wilkins, please."

"May I tell him who is calling?"

"Absolutely, Kevin Landrum, Secret Service." Only a minute on hold and the receiver picked up.

"Kevin, how in the world are you doing? Looks like you have your hands full."

"We all do. Chad, I need some help on this one. I need to meet with you in person, in private, as soon as possible."

"Meet me in Judiciary Square in twenty minutes," Chad said.

"See you soon," Kevin replied.

Kevin walked the five blocks much more quickly than the twenty minutes Chad had given him and sat on a park bench watching the people. Chad finally arrived and sat down beside him.

"Wow. Kevin, you really need some rest. You look as if you haven't slept in a week."

"I haven't. Look I do not have a lot of time. We haven't contacted your agency because the President ordered me to handle this internally, but I need some equipment yesterday that my agency cannot provide, and it would take too long to get it from the military."

"I'll try to help, brother," Chad replied. "What do you need?"

Kevin said. “Stationary RF jammers in every federal building in D.C. and New York City.”

“What the hell? Why?”

Kevin provided Chad with a brief synopsis of the situation leading to their meeting. “On the morning of the Fourth, three days from now, Mahannad will set off bombs we believe to be placed in New York and possibly Washington. We have the transmitter frequency to disable them and we need the RF jammers to keep them from re-activating them.”

Chad responded, “Some federal buildings already are equipped with RF jammers. The Pentagon, most law enforcement agency headquarters, the White House. The problem is that unless we know when and where the attack is, the RF jammer is turned off so that people can have the convenience of remote control, and now that cell phones are making a comeback there are more and more of them around. Especially with the only ones who can afford them. That is what happened at the Supreme Court building. Their RF jammer was turned off and boom.”

“I am betting we can have an AWAC circle the area transmitting the RF signal, disabling the device so that we can activate the RF jammers,” Kevin said.

“Sounds like a plan. We have twelve spare jammers in storage if you need any more. I will have some of my analysts determine what buildings do not have the jammers and let you know as soon as possible….Kevin, you should probably have someone you trust activate and stand guard on the jammers in each building.”

CHAPTER 49

Agent McCrory was in bad shape, and it was difficult keeping him awake on the five miles back to camp. Sam and Jennifer managed to get there about an hour after dark. They arrived in camp and Jam, Walt and Daniel were getting their bed rolls ready for another night of restless sleep.

Walt looked over and said, "Well damn just like him to bring in a couple of strays." Sam dismounted, helped McCrory out of the saddle and leaned him back against a tree. Now that several hours had passed, there was not a place on his body that was not black, blue or cut. It was going to be a cool night, so Sam took the bed roll from the assassin's pack and tried to make the agent as comfortable as possible.

Jennifer saw to his cuts and lacerations and said, "These cuts are from a knife. I've seen them before, usually on dead bodies. I've never seen anyone survive the torture. They must have been interrupted because when they are done with the slow cutting of the victim on the exposed parts of the body, they cut off the sex organs, on both women and men." The men around them got quiet as they listened to her speak of the torture and some of the horrors she had seen for the last thirty years.

McCrory raised his head and leaned up on his elbow. Daniel caught him and helped him back up, leaning him against the tree. It was obvious he wanted to say something.

He looked at Jennifer and Sam and said, "Thank you. I certainly would not have survived the night on the river bank. They caught all three of us. They tied us to some trees along the river and beat us relentlessly. Then they started the cutting, first with Smalls, then Smith, and then with me. She is right. I watched them cut my men to pieces. First it was small cuts, just enough to bleed a little, then they seemed to get worked up into a frenzy about the cutting, excited about it. They began cutting bigger and bigger pieces out of their arms and legs.

"They made me watch, and once both my men were dead they started on me. But then the strangest thing happened. They stopped for a second. We all heard it and they turned and looked just in time to see a Harley Davidson motorcycle flying by at about sixty. I haven't seen one running in years. I thought I was hallucinating at first, but they saw it too and tried to chase him. I guess they didn't think I was going anywhere. They didn't search me good, and I had a folding blade hidden behind his belt. I was able to work it loose, cut myself free and climb down into the river to hide my tracks. I was too weak to make it very far, and the water was so cold. I knew I would die of hypothermia in a matter of minutes. Next thing I knew you were waking me up. I guess I lost my pager. I moved it underneath my belt when I saw we were going to get caught. Smith and Smalls threw theirs into the woods somewhere."

Sam reached down, pulled the pager out of his pocket and handed it to McCrory. He flipped it open and saw that Sam had responded for him and thanked him again. He took a minute to type another message then closed his pager, leaned back and almost immediately fell asleep.

The next morning, Sam took Patton across the valley and worked his way south, finally reaching the base of Mount Shavano. Patton slowly worked his way up the trail to the old spike camp. The old tree where Sam had found Matt still had blood stains on it, dark and dry but still there. It looked like a bear had come through smelling the blood and destroyed just about everything the crew had abandoned. Sam followed the trail up and over the back side of the mountain and down into the valley where Matt was buried.

The river rocks were protecting him perfectly. Sam removed each rock and carefully dug away the layer of dirt and sand that covered Matt. he moved the tarp aside and retrieved Matt's hands and feet from his pack. Sam put them where they belonged and covered him once more with the tarp, then the sand, then the river rock. It was a beautiful little valley overlooking a small meadow full of flowers that filled the air with the smell of spring. Sam knelt and prayed. He stayed with Matt for a while remembering the past. Finally he rose rose to his feet, dusted off his pants and said, "See you soon, brother."

Sam followed the trails on his way back to camp and decided to visit some of the old homes and trailers he had passed, thinking he could salvage a blanket or two to make McCrory and Jennifer more comfortable. Sam had given Jennifer his bed roll and froze on the ground with no protection from the elements. Even in early July, it can get down in the thirties at this altitude. Sam arrived at the trailer closest to the tree line and opened the door. He walked through it, and there was scarcely much left that was worth carrying back. He went to the next trailer and found one old wool blanket stuffed in a suitcase in the top of a closet. He rolled it up and put it in his pack.

The last trailer that Sam checked seemed a little nicer. He found two more blankets and a Buzz Lightyear pillow. What a classic. He tied the items to the top of his pack and headed back to camp. McCrory was sitting up, and Jennifer was tending to some of his dressings. Sam gave Jennifer the pillow, but she insisted on McCrory having it. *I guess you can't stop a doctor from doctorin'*, he thought.

Most everyone spent the day trying to relax. Sam sat down, leaned against a tree with the sun beaming down on him and soon fell asleep. Too soon, Daniel was shaking him awake telling him it would soon be nightfall.

Sam looked at Daniel and said, "I know you're not going to like this, but I want you to stay and help Jennifer with McCrory." He looked at Sam, and Sam could tell he had hurt his feelings. Then he said, "Look, that woman was the love of my life when I was your age. I lost her to these men thirty years ago, and I'll be damned if I am going to lose her again. Now if I didn't think this was important I would probably ask someone that hasn't been by my side through this whole ordeal."

He looked up and seemed somewhat appeased. "Yessir," he said, still somewhat dejected.

Sam called Walt and Charlie over and ran through the plan with them one more time. "Follow the Arkansas River south until just beyond the bottleneck of where it and Highway 28 almost meet. As the land widens between the two, stay right in the center avoiding main roads and anything that looks like people. We will be waiting on a ridge north of the airport. We need you there by 05:00. Is that clear?"

"Yes sir," Walt said with a two finger Boy Scout salute.

Rolling his eyes, Sam turned and walked over to where Jam and Garrison were relaxing. "Are you fellas about ready?"

Sam unloaded everything out of his pack except for ammunition, the med pack and several small explosives he had collected over the years. He had four grenades with some trip wire. Four bricks of C-4 with detonators, timers and detonating cord. It was a small stash, but it would be enough to wake everyone up in the morning. He said goodbye to Jennifer and gave her a hug, and she held him tightly before practically pushing him away. He could see tears in her eyes as she turned and started tending McCrory. Sam had never understood women, but he sure wanted to try to understand that one.

They took the horses back across the north end of the valley and worked their way south. By nine, Sam could see the lights of the airport and they stopped on a ridge about two miles west of Smeltertown. They dropped down into a small canyon half a mile north of the airport and secured the horses. In about eight hours the first division would be knocking on the front door. The second division should be just beyond Poncha Springs, ready to kick the back door in and Sam with his men will have secured the airport.

The ridge from where they sat provided a beautiful view of the area. The moon at this elevation, no matter how small, provides an abundance of light on a clear night. They could see men moving occasionally around the tarmac and in some of the buildings. The apartments that housed the soldiers lined the Airport Road on the south side of the tarmac. A ravine with a creek created a good place to stay concealed to the north of the landing strip.

They moved on foot to the ravine and crawled up to within a few feet of the fence. Jam pulled a set of wire cutters from his pack and started working on the fence, taking two sections out and providing a large path through it that would allow three horses to pass at a time. The razor wire at the top was proving difficult even for the unusually large arms of his. Once the fence was down, it was several minutes after midnight. They had a while before the team arrived, so Sam decided to do some more recon around the airport. He sent Charlie to retrieve the horses and wait on the cavalry. Sam slipped through the fence and crawled through the grass, working his way around behind the hangars. Jam maintained a position at the hole in the fence with a rifle in case Sam was compromised.

Once at the back wall of the first hangar, Sam found the rear exit. He put his ear to the door to see if he could hear anything. Apparently they had all the patrols around town and several in the woods, but virtually none around the airport with the President arriving in a few hours. Sam thought that maybe they had seen the first division and were already reacting to it.

Sam turned the knob slowly on the door and cracked it just enough to look through. The lights were all out, and everything was quiet. He slipped through the door letting it shut behind him. There were exit signs over two doors: the one he had just entered, and one across the hangar on the opposite side near the front. The exit signs provided just enough light to see what the Sheikh was hiding there. The hangar was about the size of two football fields side by side, and as far as Sam could see the place was full of weapons of war. There was a multitude of crates containing Stingers, Javelins and other shoulder launched missiles. In the front of this array of war toys were four hummers with .50 cal machine guns mounted on roof turrets. In front of the four hummers were two Abrams tanks.

If the bad guys got a chance to open this up, Sam's cavalry would have no chance. The abundance of weapons was staggering. The south side of the building was one big gun rack that apparently held each soldier's AR-15, or whatever long gun he was assigned. There were numerous M249 SAW's and several sniper rifles, including several Barrett 50 BMG's. Sam found a gear bag someone was using to keep their tools in and emptied them into a trash bin. He took the bag over to a crate that read M72 LAW and popped the latch with a hammer, taking three of the LAW rockets and placing them in the bag with as many grenades as he could carry.

He found a plastic crate marked "C 4" and pulled at the latches, prying it open with the claw end of the hammer. Inside were a dozen bricks of the explosive. He took eight bricks and found as many detonators with det cord. Sam looked at his watch and thought, *time flies when you're having fun.* He checked the rear door and slipped out into the moonlight. He peeked around, the side of the building and saw some men moving around obviously preparing for the day.

They turned and headed south, away from the building and toward the hangar closest to town. They entered the hangar through a side door and moments later the enormous front door started to rise. Inside the hangar, Sam could see a helicopter being prepared for travel. *This is not good*, Sam thought. He picked up his bag of toys and ran low for the fence.

Jam had moved back into the bushes and was leaning against a small tree. He made most things look small. Sam opened the bag and his eyes widened. "Awe Sam," the big guy said. "You shouldn't have. I didn't get you a thing." Sam was in battle mode and not in the mood for jokes. He just looked at Jam calmly, placing his finger over his mouth and whispered,

"Shhhhh. It's about 04:00. Everyone will be waking up soon." Sam placed the C-4, the detonators and the det cord in his pack and turned to Jam and whispered, "I am going to take these toys and set some surprises for those young men over in the apartments and I think the Sheikh may be going somewhere. They are prepping that chopper to leave. Don't let it! If I am not back by 06:00 start without me."

Sam left the rockets and grenades with Jam and took off back around behind the hangars, heading south toward the apartments. Behind the hangars was a small irrigation ditch that let him move easily across the open field by staying below the line of sight from people around the airport.

Sam arrived at the south end of the airfield at approximately 04:30 and started planting his Good Morning America surprises along the south side of the apartment buildings. He casually walked down the sidewalk with the pack over his shoulder and bent over, placing the devices between the air conditioning units and the rear wall of each apartment building. He set the devices for 05:55.

Sam gradually worked his way over to the east side of the airfield where the corrals and stables for the horses were. He let the latch open on each of the corrals, and leaving the gates open allowed the horses to wander out on their own accord. Sam checked his watch and it was 05:15. He moved around behind the corrals and started heading north again to circle back around toward the hole in the fence. He stepped past one of the stable doors and someone said, "Hey!" Sam froze for a second with his heart leaping out of his chest. It had been so quiet and easy up until now and he had gotten careless. He was unsure of where it was coming from and he slowly turned, trying to locate who was calling him out this early in the morning. He replied, "Hey back." He saw a shadow and started walking toward the stable. Just inside the door was an older man sitting on a stool smoking a pipe. He looked at Sam as if he were analyzing a snake trying to figure out whether it was poisonous or not.

Sam turned and said, "Yessir, What can I do for you this morning?"

"I don't believe I've had the pleasure of meeting you young man. I've maintained these stables for years, and I know pretty much everybody here that is worth a damn and I don't know you."

"Well I'm new here," Sam replied.

"Hogwash!" he said. "You ain't new anywhere. And I'm bettin' you are about to cause a ruckus here."

"Now why would you say that?" Sam was just about to reach for his Glock when the old fella responded.

"Cause I've been a cowboy all my life, son. Even when I was a marine, I was a cowboy. It's a way of life, but I guess you know that. We tend to recognize one another. You're not one of these fellas. I imagine I'm going to clock out here in a few minutes and I am going to get on my horse and quietly leave early. I'm going to ride old Ben to my house, kiss my wife good morning, and watch the fireworks from my front porch up on that mountain over there. I hope you don't have a problem with that."

Sam smiled at the old man and said, "No sir, I don't. In fact, if you run into anyone else you don't know tell them Samson said to let ya through."

He tipped his hat and said, "Thank you, sir. Be careful. These boys are pretty stupid, but stupid people playin' army can still be dangerous." He turned and shuffled back into the stable, and Sam could hear him leading a horse down the wooden floor and out the back door.

CHAPTER 50

Not long after the President's request, Kevin was able to acquire a list from General Services Administration of federal buildings in New York and Washington that were not equipped with RF jammers. There were eight. Of those eight, only two had received major renovation since 2008. Kevin knocked on the President's office door.

"Come in," President Bradshaw said. "Glad you are here. I have just gotten off of the phone with the Air Force Command and have made arrangements for AWAC's to buzz New York and D.C. for the next two days pulsing the frequency Gene provided."

"Thank you, sir," Kevin replied. "By the Fourth, all the federal buildings that have had renovations since 2008 will have been equipped with RF jammers, and we have contacted the director of the U. S. Marshals Service. Deputies have been assigned and have made contact with the building managers in each one and assumed control of the RF jammers per your order. They will make sure the RF jammers are working and will turn them off during the two days the AWAC performs the fly by. Once the AWAC mission is completed, they will turn the RF jammers on and stand guard, providing security until the devices are located and removed."

"That is very good, Kevin. Have you had any updates from out west?"

"Yessir, I have some sad news that two of our agents there performing surveillance were tortured and murdered, with one being injured badly. A Marshal has also been killed, but the integrity of the mission still remains. Nothing has been compromised as far as we know. As of my most recent report, my injured agent is in the care of a doctor, and the Marshals have control of the mission at this point. Their plan is to have the airport secured and in their control when we arrive. If it is not secure by 08:30, we will not land until it is. Air Force One does not need to land in the middle of a firefight."

The phone rang, President Bradshaw walked over to his desk and lifted the receiver. "This is the President," he said.

"Good morning, Mr. President. I am curious if you are still coming for your visit on the Fourth?"

The President indicated to Kevin that the voice on the phone belonged to Mahannad. "Yes sir, I would not miss it for the world. Sounds like we'll have a really good time."

"Funny you should say that. We have had some interesting things going on around our quaint little valley, and I am wondering if you are entertaining second thoughts about the agreement we have made?"

"What kind of interesting things?" the President asked.

"My intelligence reports suggest there is a group of armed men approaching Salida from the southeast. Even more disturbing, in the last two weeks several of our security patrol members have quit reporting. That wouldn't have anything to do with your arrival now would it?"

The President winked at Kevin and replied, "Sir, with all due respect I would never contest your superior force and risk losing the millions of people in New York. I am thinking they may be a rebel force from the Neverland region that you should have no problem dealing with. At this point in the rebuilding of our government, we neither have the manpower nor the financial resources to provide for an adequate military."

The Sheikh paused for a moment. "Then answer me this, Mr. President, why have you authorized the flight plans of the AWAC's for the next two days?"

The President was busted. Thinking the game was over, Kevin lowered his head in disgust and frustration.

The President quickly said, "You did not receive my message?"

The Sheikh said flatly, "No."

"We sent a courier late last week informing you of the test flight we were running on some of the military jets we thought the United Nations would be able to use. I sent a memo to the Air Force Command to pull several of the more modern jets out of mothballs to be brought up to speed with maintenance and test flights. The AWAC's are merely one of several that we thought would be crucial to the mission of the UN."

The Sheikh was silent for a moment. "Very well, Mr. President, I will take you at your word for now, but be assured you will not win if you decide to contest me."

"That will not happen, sir," the President replied.

The President set the receiver down and looked up at Kevin. "I guess we have another mole, somewhere between here and Air Force Command. We have no time to be concerned about that now. I think we should keep moving forward with the current plan. And I was curious, did we ever identify the towers we needed to shut down the pager network?"

"Yes, Gene did that when we initially found out about the pagers," Kevin replied.

"I think it's time to isolate that bastard from his so called intelligence. Kill the towers," President Bradshaw replied.

Kevin nodded and said, "Will do, sir. Also, if you do not mind, I need to know at this point what is your plan for the Fourth?"

The President was standing behind his desk. He paused for a moment and looked at Kevin with the expression of a warrior about to step onto the battlefield for the last time. "We are going to walk up the streets of Salida and shout to the world that the United States will not be intimidated. We will not even tolerate those that attempt it. If the Sheikh doesn't surrender he will die, and I will not hesitate to pull the trigger."

"We will prepare Air Force One, sir."

President Bradshaw said, "Don't. Let's take a military jet, something that will hold plenty of gear and an armored vehicle."

Kevin nodded. "I agree sir, we will make the arrangements and I will pick you up in the limo here at 03:00."

Kevin turned and left the office, then hurried to find Gene. Gene was in the tech lab with Jerry eating a sandwich, and Jerry was examining some of the explosive residue from the site of the monument.

"Gene, I need you to disable the cell towers we identified that transmit the pager signals. We have another mole and we believe it is too late in the game to deal with our plan being compromised," Kevin said.

"Ten-four good buddy. We'll get right on that."

Kevin looked at Jerry shaking his head. “How much coffee has he had today?”

Jerry laughed, “Way too much.”

Gene replied, “That’s right! Mucho java caliente!”

Kevin gave Gene the “look.” Gene said, “Okay, okay, settle down. We’ll get in our little Prius and go blow up a tower.”

Kevin added, “Also we need to make sure everyone is ready for Salida. Anything can happen and Odin wants to take a military transport with an armored vehicle. We all have a lot to do, so y’all get moving.”

“Aye aye Captain,” Gene said as he hustled Jerry out the door.

Kevin pulled his pager from the holster on his belt and texted a message to Agent McCrory.

Hope all is well, buddy, hang in there, we are going dark in a few minutes and you will not hear from us until wheels down.

Moments later the pager vibrated and McCrory responded,

Will do, see you soon.

The next day, Kevin, Gene and Jerry met at Andrews Air Force Base running through checklists of equipment for the mission the following day. Kevin had secured a C17 Globemaster. The C17 has been in use since the early 1990s and was designed to deploy troops and equipment in places no other transport planes could land. Not only can they take off and land on a football field, they can carry 180,000 pounds at over five hundred miles per hour. Capable of inflight refueling, the C17 Globemaster can potentially fly anywhere in the world. Currently the United States has a depleted inventory due to maintenance, in addition to lack of parts and supplies.

With only seven currently in active duty, it was difficult for Kevin to acquire one on such short notice. Andrews AFB maintains two on a regular basis, and one was just completing a planned scheduled maintenance, so Kevin was able to jump to the front of the line using the stroke of the President’s credentials.

“How did the cell towers go yesterday?” Kevin asked.

Gene grinned and said, "Down."

Kevin shook his head. "I guess I asked for that one."

"Yup," Gene replied as he turned walking toward a different hangar.

"Where are you going?" Kevin asked.

"You'll see. Be back in a minute."

Kevin watched Gene and Jerry walk through the side door of the hangar and shortly the bay door in front started to slide open. The sound of a motor turned and exploding through the door coming directly at the rear of the C17 was a beast of an armored vehicle that looked like something Batman had driven in his last movie. Gene spun the steering wheel and turned the vehicle, sliding up to the back ramp of the C17 just short of where Kevin was standing. Gene and Jerry both opened the doors of the beast and were grinning as if Christmas had come early.

"What the heck is that?"

"In 2015, the Russians came out with an armored vehicle called the Punisher. This is the American version, basically the Russian version on steroids. Rated at one thousand horsepower, two hundred and fifty more than the Russian version, seats twelve people comfortably and with the triple turbo diesel it can run down a highway fully loaded at eighty-five miles hour for a range of five hundred miles. On top is a remote control mini-gun that pops out of the roof automatically when engaged and rotates three hundred and sixty degrees. The windows of course do not roll down but there are shooting ports on either side in case you are in a running gun fight. The vehicle is equipped with a snorkel kit and is almost completely submersible. It is for the most part unstoppable." Gene pumped his right fist twice on his chest, crossed his arms and said, "Boom!"

Kevin, Gene, and Jerry loaded the Punisher onto the C17 and strapped it down preparing it for flight. "Guys, I came prepared to spend the night here on the plane. Since we discovered that someone in the line of command that the President is dealing with has questionable loyalty I do not trust anyone on this airfield with a plane the President will be on and we will have two escorts that will break off after we land and refuel at Colorado Springs. They will be on standby, no more than fifteen minutes away."

"Now that we are fairly sure that the bombs are stopped, why don't we just bomb the crap out of Salida?" Jerry asked.

"Three reasons. One, the President wants to make an international statement that you do not mess with us. Two, he wants to make sure Mahannad is taken down. And three, maybe, just maybe since Neverland is pulling our butts out of the fire on this he can use this to improve relations making the country whole again." Kevin replied.

Gene said, "Well I'm going to run home and get my bags. I want to spend the night here as well. I always loved sleep overs"

Kevin looked at Jerry and with a smile said, "Wanna go to the dance?"

"Why not? if I don't go I'll never forgive myself. I'll ride back with Gene and get my things."

Kevin and sixteen other agents drove the President to Andrews Air Force base at 03:00 in the morning. After performing a series of additional checklists, they loaded two more regular armored limos on the C17 and strapped themselves in for takeoff. By 05:00 they were wheels up with escorts over Virginia. Kevin sat next to President Bradshaw, and as the C17 leveled out, he stood and prepared the President for the next few hours. Handing the President a bulletproof vest, he insisted he put it on under his suit coat.

"Sir, this is where things are going to change for a while and why I am here. You may not agree with some of the things I tell you but trust me. We are basically going to be flying into a war zone, and I need you to stay right next to me and hopefully most of the actual fighting will be over by the time we arrive."

"Kevin, thank you for all you have done," The President replied.

"Thank me when it's over."

President Bradshaw stood up, called everyone on board around him and said, "I think we need to stop for a minute and say a prayer for this country, for what we are about to do today, and most of all for the men on the ground paving the way for us."

Everyone bowed their heads for a moment of silence and the President finally said, "Father, we come to you humbly and ask that you watch over our friends fighting this evil today. We pray it is not too late to turn this country around. We also humbly ask that you place a hedge of protection around each and every one of your warriors. We ask these things in Jesus' name, amen."

"Amen," repeated the group.

CHAPTER 51

Sam quickly crossed the airfield on the east side and followed the ravine back to where Jam was guarding the hole in the fence. As he came up the ravine, Sam could see that the thundering hoards had arrived, and Patton was waiting patiently to lead them into battle. The chopper was warming up on the east side of the airfield, waiting for takeoff. Sam leaned over to Jam and said, “Get a rocket and go get that chopper!” Jam slung a LAW over his shoulder, turned Kong and headed east paralleling the runway, letting Kong’s legs loose on that open bluff.

Sam checked his watch, and it was 05:45. They slipped through the fence and quickly spread out in a long line from east to west facing the apartments. Once they were in position, it was only seconds before simultaneous explosions erupted all through the apartments across the landing strip from where the horses anxiously held their ground. Patton sensed the excitement as his feet pranced, and he knew they were about to run. Patton liked to run. The lights of the airfield were bright enough to silhouette the men in fatigues as they came running from the houses to the east and saw the large hoard of men on horseback. Walt and Charlie each shouldered a LAW rocket and directed a volley at the front of the apartments, sandwiching the enemy between the burning buildings and massive explosions caused by the rockets. Many coming from what was left of the apartments were staggering, shocked or wounded and lying in the grass as their apartments burned. Soldiers who had been patrolling the town were being driven toward the airport by the first division and saw that they had nowhere to run. They quickly surrendered.

Sam looked to his left and saw the helicopter attempting to take off. It was moving up and to the east, starting to climb above the tree line when a streak of light emerged from the trees on the bluff to the north. Traveling like a bolt of lightning, it struck the helicopter in the tail rudder, throwing it into a violent spin. It spiraled downward and crashed with a loud explosion, erupting into flames just shy of Salida. Sam could see Jam riding Kong down the bluff from the light of the explosion with his AR-12 raised and firing. Sam pitied any fool that would stand in that man's way.

They advanced the horses slowly, looking for more resistance. A line of over a hundred cowboys on horses moving aggressively on an enemy had to look pretty intimidating, and many had yet to fire a shot. The shock and awe of the bombs exploding while they were sleeping took those who had survived totally out of the fight. As the apartments burned and men surrendered, they all heard the rumbling sound of American muscle on two wheels. The first division with Joel and his motorcycle gang had arrived, and they were buzzing the city looking for a fight.

Sporadic skirmishes were occurring throughout the area, but the enemy was generally overwhelmed by numbers, attitude, and ability of the American patriot. It appeared these "soldiers" were the typical Republican Guard type that surrendered when they saw the nature of a true American soldier. They were typically used to dealing with innocent civilians whom they bullied and abused. The few that rode as the assassins had better skills than these foot soldiers, but they still had a long way to go before they could wear the boots of an American soldier.

Once the area was secured, Sam pressed the button that slowly opened the enormous front door of the hangar where the weapons were kept. As they gathered the forces, the second division arrived from Poncha Springs and helped in the cleanup. Sam started to relax and the sun began bringing light to the battlefield. He could see that some of the men from first division had opened the corrals, let the horses out and were using the fenced area to temporarily house the prisoners of war.

Looking at his watch, Sam realized how quickly time had passed since this started at 06:00. Air Force One would be arriving in a few minutes, and the runway was still cluttered with men, horses and debris. Sam called out to Walt and Jam, and they went to secure the tower and see if there was any radio traffic from the President's jet. They climbed the stairs to the main deck, and the Air Traffic Control office was empty. The view was spectacular from the tower, and they could see the entire valley. The lights on the radio came to life as Walt powered it up and put the headset on.

"Air Force One, do you copy? I repeat Air Force One, do you copy? This is Salida Regional Airport, all is clear, the area is secured." Silence, no response. Walt repeated the message and paused for a moment. The old speaker crackled and popped as the pilot of Air Force One responded.

"Yes sir, Salida Tower. Message received. We read you five by five. We should be coming into view within the next two minutes."

The three of them stood there in silence as they watched a Military Transport Jet escorted by two F-16's pop over the top of the Rocky Mountains with the Sun Rising behind them. The President had obviously opted to fly an alternative jet here, and it seemed very appropriate. The speaker crackled to life and the pilot decided to have a little fun.

"Tower, this is Ghostrider, we are requesting a flyby."

Walt replied, "By all means Ghostrider, light us up."

The Transport buzzed the tower followed by the F-16s, and he gave the men on the ground a wing wave, and the men went crazy cheering. The C-17 made a wide arc and aligned itself for the approach. A minute later it was on the ground taxiing toward the tower as the F-16s pulled off and headed east. By the time the jet came to a stop, Jam, Walt and Sam were standing at the base of the tower waiting on the President. The cargo doors started opening, and they moved around to the back of the jet. The doors hit the ground, and President Bradshaw walked down the platform escorted by at least a dozen Secret Service agents. He stopped at the edge of the platform and asked,

"Who is the Marshal in charge?"

"I guess that would be me, sir."

"Job well done, Marshal. Do you have the Sheikh in custody?"

"No sir, the first division contained and secured the Palace Hotel where he is staying, and because of the timing we wanted to make sure the airport was secure before we tackled another mission." Suddenly a rumble of engines roaring at the east end of the airfield began to approach the presidents jet. Everyone turned and saw a procession of Harley Davidson motorcycles coming toward the crowd of warriors gathered around the President. The men started cheering and chanting, "USA! USA! USA!" Sam laughed as he watched Joel leading the group with an American flag mounted to the back of his bike, a pretty remarkable scene.

Joel pulled up beside the C17 and said proudly, "Sir, we are here to serve as your escort if you would have us."

The President laughed and said, "Certainly, I would love for you to lead us into town."

It took only a few minutes for the President's men to unload the limos and the Punisher. An agent approached Sam and said with his hand outstretched, "Hello I am Agent Landrum, Kevin Landrum. Thank you for all you have done."

"Well, you're welcome, but it's not over yet."

Sam and his men arrived at the Palace Hotel to find numerous guards dead or dying in the street. Two dozen Harley Davidson motorcycles were on their kickstands, and the rest of Joel's friends had secured the perimeter around the hotel. Sam spun the AR-15 from his back and let it hang in front, preparing it for duty carry. He preferred the versatility and surgical precision of the AR when faced with long hallways and large rooms, and if the need arises, transitioning to a secondary weapon takes less than a second.

Jam led the way as point. Sam followed, then Garrison, with Walt bringing up the rear. Sam asked some of Joel's people to control the exits and elevators as they entered the building. They cleared the first floor easily. It was mostly lobby, offices and conference rooms. The second floor was more of a problem with many more doors and individual rooms. Several people were found in closets, bathrooms and other various places. They asked several for information and realized quickly that we were wasting their time. They would rather meet Allah or just flat lie, as if after thirty years in law enforcement Sam expected anything less. Each person was handcuffed and passed down the stairs to the bikers, and the search team continued to advance through the hotel.

The third floor was somewhat different. The stairwell door opened into a reception area, and there were two very large doors at the other end. They cleared the reception area and advanced toward the doors. The doors were not locked, and Jam pushed hard on one, opening it to the wall. Sam pushed a wedge from his pack into the doorjamb to hold it in place. Jam quickly peaked around the door and looked at Sam shaking his head no. He turned the corner and walked through the door, looking at two young boys lying on the floor together with gunshot wounds to the head.

Jam said, "He's already gone. He wouldn't have killed his toys if he were going to stay." They cleared the room and secured it, leaving several of the first division in the suite and at the elevators just in case they had missed something. As they were about to leave the Sheikh's floor, a thought occurred to Sam, and he turned and walked back through the enormous double doors. Sam went to the Sheikh's desk and started rummaging. "Whatchya doin, man?" Jam asked.

"When Daniel and I were observing the town during surveillance, he told me of the original installation that they had built out of an old mine shaft. It is somewhere on the east side of the valley north of where we were camped. They call it the Sheikh's Fortress. He never told me specifically where, but if the Sheikh was running for his life, I am sure that would be his next stop, if nothing else but to supply his caravan with food and weapons."

Sam and his team continued to search the suite going through everything with a fine tooth comb, and still the location of the fortress eluded them. Sam realized the location of the fortress was not to be found in the Sheikh's suite. He turned and headed out of the suite and down the stairs to the lobby where most of the Sheikh's staff was still being held. Sam had them all stand in a line and he proceeded to analyze each prisoner. Each one he passed looked him in the eye with deadly intent and a smirk of disgust. As Sam neared the end of the line, he saw a man that seemed a little different than the others. His eyes had doubt, and as Sam looked at him he looked away refusing to make eye contact. He wanted out of this trouble, and Sam was going to give him an opportunity.

"Jam," take this man into the office.

The man screamed, "No, please, I beg of you!"

"Sorry little fella," said Jam, playing the perfect bad cop routine he had picked him up, threw him over his shoulder and walked into the office like he was carrying his next meal.

"Please, do not hurt me!" the man pleaded with tears in his eyes.

I think I picked a good one, Sam thought.

"What is your name?" Sam demanded.

"Abdallah, Abdallah Kahlil," he answered without hesitation.

"What is your title?" Sam asked.

"I am an Imam, an assistant to the Sheikh Mahannad," he replied.

"Abdallah," Sam said somewhat respectfully. "I am going to give you one shot at this. Answer my questions truthfully, and I will speak for you to the President and see if we can get a pardon. If you refuse or lie, I am going to pretend you told me everything in front of the others out there and leave you with them."

Abdallah stiffened and hung his head low with his chin against his chest. "I will do what you ask."

"Where is the Sheikh?" Sam asked. Abdallah looked terrified but gave no answer, so Sam nudged him a bit and repeated his words with much more conviction. "Where is the Sheikh?" he demanded.

"He left me. I was his favorite assistant. He told me so, and he left without me," he said sadly.

"Where did he go?" Sam asked.

"At about five-thirty this morning we received a message that the force to our south was much larger than we were originally told, and that another force to our west was closing in as well. He sent for the helicopter, but I am afraid it was destroyed so he had the men prepare horses for us. He sent me to my room to pack, and when I returned he and his men were gone. He killed those two wonderful boys."

"Where did they go?" Sam asked again, beginning to lose patience.

"We have an escape plan that if something catastrophic happens we are to try and get to the fortress in the mountains," he responded, still not telling what Sam wanted to know.

"WHERE!" Sam demanded.

"Northeast of Smeltertown there is a valley that you follow and it leads you to a trail up high on a ridge called Aspen Ridge. Follow the ridge trail for about five hours and you will see a valley to your west that is the most beautiful valley. The Fortress is at the head of that valley."

Sam called in two of the men from first division to see that Abdallah is housed separately, at least until they confirm his story. Sam walked down the street to where the President's entourage was waiting. The President was standing in the street shaking hands with the many men who participated in the mission.

"Mr. President," Sam said. "We have determined that Muhannad and his men have fled on horseback and we now know his destination. Sorry to be short, but if we are to catch him we need to leave now."

"I understand, Marshal. We will wait here for your return."

Sam's thoughts now were only of Jennifer. They were heading directly for her.

CHAPTER 52

Sam looked at his team, Walt, Jam, Charlie and Garrison and said, "Are you gentlemen up for one more ride?"

Agent Landrum said, "With the President's permission, I would like to go."

President Bradshaw smiled and said, "I would be disappointed if you didn't. I think I will be fine with this army around me."

Sam looked at Agent Landrum and replied, "Can you ride a horse?"

"I'm from Texas," Kevin said laughing.

Jerry said, "Okay, I'm in as well. Kevin dragged me out here, and I'm not going to miss the ending."

"Garrison, can you find these men two horses? And gentlemen, I hope you have some fighting skills. I think this is gonna get nasty. Oh, and bring some extra ammo!"

They retrieved extra weapons and magazines full of ammunition from several of the Secret Service agents, and by then Garrison had acquired two horses for the new team members. They all bid farewell to the President, and were on their way.

The Sheikh and his men had about a three hour head start, and the posse had not even cut their trail yet. About two miles northeast of Smeltertown, Sam crossed a trail covered with fresh tracks, and they were moving fast. In their haste, they were not concerned with hiding their back trail, and they were heading directly for the camp and Jennifer. Sam urged Patton on and he agreed to go faster. What a magnificent horse. The others were trailing behind, but Sam could not wait. Seconds may mean the difference in life or death. The posse cut a path winding their way up the valley at breakneck speed, and still Patton pushed on relentlessly.

As they approached the clearing where they had camped, Sam saw no one at first. He paused for a moment looking around, and there, over by a large Ponderosa pine, was the Buzz Lightyear pillow. Sam led Patton over to the pillow and saw McCrory, leaning up against the tree on the other side. Fearing the worst, he rounded the large trunk of the tree and the agent was crying.

"I'm so sorry," he said. "Jennifer saw them coming and had just enough time for her and Daniel to drag me over here. They ran to their horses and distracted the Sheikh's men while they tried to get away, but the men overtook them within a few hundred yards. I'm sure they've been made captive or they would have been back by now."

"McCrory," Sam said, "you will have to stay here until we get back. How long have they been gone?"

"No more than two hours," he replied.

"Good. We are gaining on them." Sam hit the trail again slowing a bit to look at the tracks. Sure enough, after about a quarter of a mile there was the sign of horses tangled in a struggle as they twisted and turned sideways.

They spurred our horses on again knowing the odds were against covering a two hour gap in a day's ride. Sam stopped at a creek to let the horses rest and drink, pulling out his map of the area. He saw that they were on Graphite Ridge. Staying behind them was no good. If they got to the fortress first, even just minutes ahead of them, they would be locked out with no way of breaching the enormous door. They had to beat them there. Graphite Ridge joined Aspen Ridge, both coming together and running north. To get down into the valley where it seemed the fortress was, they had to go a mile beyond the valley and take a trail back down into it. The bluffs to the west of the ridge prevented a direct route. This valley to the west of Aspen Ridge had to be the one Abdallah spoke of. If they dropped down off of the ridge and traveled hard straight north, they would have a chance of getting there first. Sam showed the map and the plan to the men, and they all agreed.

They bailed off of the ridge, plummeting down the bluff that was still manageable. Once at the bottom, they found a game trail that led straight north, and floored it. Patton was really stretching it out now. This trail ride was one to remember, more like motocross on a horse.

They kept traveling north as fast as the trail would allow, paralleling Aspen Ridge. Occasionally as they would hit open meadows, Sam would check the ridge to see if he could get a glimpse of the Sheikh and his men, but they were undoubtedly still far ahead. By midday, he caught a glimpse of something metallic reflecting in the sunlight on the ridge just ahead by half a mile. He pulled the reigns up on Patton and brought him to a halt. He turned and told the men that they were close, less than a mile to go. The enemy was high on the ridge with a better vantage point, however they did not know the posse was there.

The trail they were on came to a fork with the right fork leading up at an angle toward Aspen Ridge. Sam sent Garrison, Kevin, Jerry and Walt on the lower path to see if they could find the fortress first and possibly defend it. Sam made a decision to move back up on Aspen Ridge with Jam and follow the Sheikh and his men, trapping them between the two forces. "If you can make a stand and prevent them from entering the fortress, we have a chance. Hold your ground, and we will win the day."

The duo took the trail back up to the ridge, and as the ridge opened up before them, Sam realized that we were not more than a few hundred yards behind them. The tracks were very fresh, and they had to be careful not to overtake them too quickly. Two men may not fare well in a confrontation with a dozen assassins. They rounded a bend in the trail, which was very straight for a great distance, and they could see the group with their horses still slowly trotting. Sam held back on the reigns, and they moved the horses off trail just in time as the last assassin turned to see if anyone was following. They cleared a turn in the trail, and once they moved out of sight the duo closed the distance by half, sprinting the horses for almost a hundred yards. Bringing Patton to a slow trot then a walk, Sam peered around the curve to make sure they were not running into an ambush.

The trail was empty for a long stretch and Sam determined they must have taken another path down into the valley. He dismounted and crept through the woods over to the ledge to see if he could see any sign of them. Looking out across the valley was beautiful. The afternoon sun was shining, and he could see the fortress door hiding in the shadows on the mountain wall from here. A large meadow led up to the door with trees on either side, and he grew concerned for the rest of the team when he heard hoofs scraping the rocks below.

Sam looked down, and less than one hundred feet below him were the Sheikh and his men. The assassin behind the Sheikh held a tether that was tied to Jennifer's neck. She was bound with her hands tied behind her back and her mouth was gagged. Behind her was another assassin escorting Daniel who was not bound or tethered for some reason. There was no stopping the procession as they climbed down the tiny goat trail into the valley.

Sam returned to the trail where Jam waited. He stood beside Patton, hesitating to step into the saddle. He looked at Jam with doubt in his eyes.

"What should we do?" Sam asked. He was at a loss. He had never been put in this situation before. Patton rubbed his forehead against his chest looking for a rub and then he slightly nudged Sam, pushing him back.

Jam chuckled, "He's telling you what you should do. Your mind is clouded by that beautiful woman down there. You should do what you're good at, what you always do. Go right at 'em!"

CHAPTER 53

The two trail weary warriors stepped up into the stirrup and settled into the saddle. Sam rotated the AR-15 letting it hang in front. He did a double check of the Glock and Ruger. Jam likewise took a moment checking his gear and moving his twelve gauge into place. Sam led the way down the trail and could hear the heavy hoofs of Kong following. They were sitting ducks in an arcade game coming down that trail, and Sam's goal was to get to the bottom and finding some cover before the assassins could get on target. Patton breezed right down the trail with only a couple of stumbles at the switchbacks. Kong, however, balked a bit at the turns but finally figured it out, and was making the switchbacks look easy by the time we got to the bottom.

Once they were down, Sam whispered "Let's split up and stay about fifty yards apart. Use the trees as much as possible. Avoid the open. I think now they at least know you and I are here, but have no idea about the rest of the team." Just as they started moving apart, a bullet struck the cliff face wall where Sam had been standing and pieces of rock and dust peppered their backs. The two men both urged their horses quickly into the thick trees of the valley. Sam dismounted and started advancing through the brush slowly. Another shot fired close by and he ducked realizing the bullet was meant for Jam this time. He listened quietly for a minute trying to hear the crack of a twig, the unnatural sound of movement by man in the wilderness. Suddenly he heard the sound of whispering voices, twenty yards in front of him at best.

Those who have never hunted do not realize how sound carries in the woods. Movement is the other cardinal sin of hunting. Game cannot see you if you are still. The slightest movement is very perceptible in a still forest. Sam heard them first, and now he could see them moving their hands and their heads as they whispered to each other. They remained low, not presenting him with a clear shot. He waited, and patience was a virtue. One of the men slightly raised his head as he turned to move to Sam's left, giving him a clear shot for a split second. The forest echoed with the explosion, and the man dropped disappearing into the ground cover.

Sam ducked and crawled to the next tree, changing positions. He raised his head slowly above the undergrowth and saw a man looking to Sam's right in the direction of Jam. Jam has his merits being big and strong, but lacked stealth and agility. The assassin started to raise his rifle in Jam's direction, and Sam squeezed the trigger. Down goes another assassin.

Suddenly the fireworks started at the edge of the meadow. The team had obviously found the fortress door, and with a perfect field of fire had waited patiently for the Sheikh and his assassins. Sam moved forward advancing toward the meadow as the firefight continued. As he got closer, he could see the Sheikh holding Jennifer's tether. He was crouched low behind his men as they carried out his work for him. He was the kind of man who always had someone else do the dirty work. He had someone else do the fighting and someone else to do the dying. Sam could see Jam to his right trying to get his sights on an assassin. One of the men moved to the left, and he soon found out there are no seventy-two virgins.

That was the final straw that caused sheer panic in the Sheikh. He stood, dragging Jennifer with him. He ran north, following the wood line of the meadow. The Sheikh's hostage was unfortunately doing exactly what he intended, for no one wanted to take a risk of shooting and accidentally injuring the woman.

The team at the fortress door was holding their ground, so Sam followed the Sheikh hoping for an opening to shoot. He found a trail and followed it up through the aspens and into the pines. The firefight continued below but had slowed as each side was starting to conserve ammunition. The Sheikh topped the ridge, and Sam had his moment. Just as he started to squeeze the trigger the Sheikh moved, and Jennifer was in the crosshairs. The ridge high above the fortress was true high country containing beautiful vistas where you could see for miles, yet very dangerous and oftentimes lethal.

The Sheikh had nothing left, yet he had everything. In less than a day, he had gone from being the potential leader of the world to high on a lonely mountaintop holding a tether of a woman for whom he was about to die. Sam walked up the ridge toward him, and as the sole of his boot ground lose gravel the Sheikh turned quickly with a gun in his hand, leveling it at him.

The Sheikh's hand shaking, he threatened, "Don't come any closer or I will kill the girl."

"Let the girl go and I won't kill you!"

The Sheikh pulled the trigger, and the bullet ricocheted at Sam's feet.

Sam continued walking toward the Sheikh, rotating the AR-15 to his back. Sam paused for a minute and said, "You have nothing. You live an empty life. Your religion is empty, and your false god has failed you. The Sheikh pointed his gun again and pulled the trigger. The shot missed wide left. Maintaining his sights on Sam, he started moving left toward the edge of the ridge and dragging Jennifer who was looking at Sam pleading with her eyes.

Sam took another step toward the Sheikh and suddenly heard the loud crack of a rifle. His legs collapsed under him as Jennifer screamed. Sam realized he was hit. His left leg had a horrible burning sensation as he rolled to his side, lying on his belly to see the assassin who had slipped up behind him.

"Daniel?"

"You stupid old fool," he said. "It was so easy to play your game, winning your trust and betraying you in the end. I will be greatly rewarded for saving my Sheikh and sending you to hell."

"Why did you wait so long," Sam said through clenched teeth and pain. "There is no reward for being loyal to the Sheikh if he lost."

"The minute I saw that he escaped and was riding through your camp I knew he would win. I made my choice. You had me nailed from the beginning, but something made you soft and forgiving. I took advantage of that. I waited to see who won," Daniel replied.

"It ain't over yet!" Sam said gritting his teeth from the pain.

Daniel started to raise the rifle leveling it at Sam's head, and suddenly rounds peppered the rocks at the edge of the ridge. The men below had finally taken care of the Sheikh's assassins and must have seen Daniel shoot

Sam from behind. They started firing at him, and the range was too great for any amount of accuracy, but it served a purpose.

Daniel took his attention off of Sam for a split second, allowing him to draw the Ruger. Sam fired three rounds from a prone position, placing two to the chest, one to the head. The .357 creates an enormous amount of trauma and wound cavity. If by chance the intended target survives the initial impact, he would eventually bleed out in a short amount of time. Daniel reeled backward. His body turned back toward Sam, still arguing with the fact that he was already dead. He stumbled forward and then fell sideways over the edge of the ridge, his body rolling and twisting as it careened down the mountain. The Sheikh yanked on the tether pulling Jennifer close, hiding behind her as he walked backward across the ridge looking for any escape.

Sam slowly stood, ignoring the pain in his bloody leg and walked forward.

"Sheikh, this ride is over."

The Sheikh looked over his shoulder and then back at Sam and said, "You cannot catch me on that leg of yours, and you will not shoot me as long as I have this woman. That is why you are weak. That is why your country is weak. They tolerate everything, even their own demise." The Sheikh was obviously buying time as he continued to back up, pausing at a rock formation and momentarily glancing behind it over his shoulder. He then pulled Jennifer behind the rocks and disappeared.

Sam limped over to the formation and looked around the rocks only to see a trail leading down off of the ridge. The Sheikh was thirty yards down the goat trail, pushing Jennifer ahead of him. To his left was a cliff face and to his right was a two hundred foot drop. Shooting him at this point would guarantee him falling over the edge and dragging Jennifer with him, so Sam continued to follow. With each step it felt like a hot knife stabbing into the wound. Fortunately, the bullet had passed clean through muscle and had not struck a major artery, or he would have already been dead.

The Sheikh was definitely gaining ground, and he was well over fifty yards ahead of Sam as he pushed forward, realizing that unless he did something different not only would the Sheikh get away, but Sam could lose Jennifer again, this time forever.

Sam dropped to his knees, unslung the AR-15 and lay in the grass. He pulled the ACOG scope up to his eye and watched as the Sheikh continued to push Jennifer down the path. He carefully aimed, and the Sheikh paused for a moment to see if Sam was still pursuing. The Sheikh did not see him lying in the grass with the rifle propped over the top of a rock. He was looking for a limping man still pursuing and must have assumed that Sam had either quit or fallen. He started smiling just as the setting sun reflected off of the lens of the scope. Sam squeezed the trigger. The Sheikh realized his fate a split second before the bullet entered his left eye. The Kufiya that he wore flew from his head as the top of his skull exploded upward. His body went limp, crumbling to the ground. Sam pushed himself up using the rifle as a support and limped slowly toward Jennifer who had fallen and was kneeling in the grass not far from the Sheikh. Sam heard a sound behind him, and it was his posse riding hard toward him on horseback.

Sam limped to where Jennifer knelt, exhausted and crying. He cut the straps of leather that had bound her, and she passionately wrapped her arms around his neck and kissed him long and hard. She paused only as his leg started to give and immediately became a doctor again. Jam, Garrison, Walt, Charlie, Kevin and Jerry… Sam's team, all stood there grinning as he went from being the big bad bear to a whimpering little cub with an owie.

CHAPTER 54

Morning broke, and Sam woke early having slept soundly in spite of the wound and the growing stiffness. It was a peaceful morning, and he lay there afraid to move, content in sharing the embrace of the lost love of his life as she snuggled close, stealing the blanket and what little warmth was left in his cold, tired body. It was going to be a good day. On the ground at his feet was his enemy, the terror that threatened to destroy the United States. Around him was a loyal group of friends, and they were all in the Rocky Mountains, the most beautiful place on earth. They gathered their gear, and Sam helped them as best as he could, but had to relinquish his man card when Jam helped him into the saddle. The cold ground had made a hard bed for a wounded man and seemed to make his muscles much older and stiffer than usual.

They broke the camp about midmorning with the Sheikh in tow, lying across the saddle of a spare horse Walt had retrieved from the dead assassins. They rode slowly and deliberately, embracing the day and relishing not having to be anywhere or do anything – a luxury they had not enjoyed in a very long time. Around two p.m., they had made it back to the original trail along Aspen Ridge and were enjoying the gorgeous country when they began to hear the rumble of horses riding in their direction. Too tired to run and not caring whether they were good or bad, they kept the horses walking at a leisurely pace. The thundering posse rounded a curve ahead, and Sam smiled, pleased to see the Clayton brothers, Jensen, Johnny and Tim leading the pack with President Bradshaw himself riding tall in the saddle beside them. Somehow the President had found a hat, boots and a pair of jeans somewhere in Salida to wear. They slowed to a walk, and the President came forward and saluted the team.

Sam's posse returned the salute, and Sam said, "Mission accomplished, sir." The entire group cheered, ringing a chorus of voices never heard at this altitude in the Rocky's.

They arrived back in Salida that evening. Waiting at the bridge was Theresa, Elise, Tiffany and Sara. Theresa and Jennifer had a joyful reunion that included long hugs and many tears, and all the girls cried. Sam rubbed his eyes as they were leaking a little as well. Probably allergies, or maybe he was just tired.

Sam let the girls enjoy themselves as he dismounted and hobbled over to a rocking chair on the front porch of the Palace Hotel and slowly eased himself into a somewhat comfortable position, attempting to keep the weight off of his wounded leg.

The President approached a news crew from Washington. They had somehow found out about the story and were waiting for the President to make a statement. He rode over to them on his horse and began talking, taking advantage of a pretty impressive political moment in light of the past few months. He looked squarely at the camera, tilted his hat back and said, "I am not going to spend a lot of time here answering questions tonight. I have a wonderful team of people here that have spent a great deal of time and effort working toward a goal of stopping terrorism in its tracks, working tirelessly over the last few months overcoming amazing odds. This unselfish group of men and women recognized that the need for the defense of this country demanded immediate attention, and in the spirit of patriotism joined forces with many others sacrificing more than they needed to because of our government's failure to provide for the common defense, and to ensure the domestic tranquility for our own citizens. I will elaborate on this entire story later and answer as many questions as you want in the coming days, but these warriors will be celebrating victory tonight, and the press will leave them alone. Is that understood? One thing you can tell my friends back home: the United States is safe. The Constitution is intact and will remain that way. Those who conspired against it and the security of this country will soon be arrested and punished appropriately." The reporters were visibly shaken by the President's statement.

He then took his hat off and said to them, "America is free because of warriors like these and many that have died to make America what it is. If we do not accept the fact that sometimes we must take a violent path, then we will lose our freedom and everything that good men like these have died for. These warriors stopped an evil that would create a life that is not living but merely existing beneath those who would rule with tyranny and violence." President Bradshaw nodded at the crew, thanking them for their cooperation. He ended his statement saying, "Happy Independence Day, y'all!" He then turned his horse away from the reporters and rode him to the porch of the Palace Hotel. He dismounted, tied him to a post, walked up the steps and sat down next to Sam in a rocking chair where they both sat in silence watching as the moon climbed high into the sky over the Rocky Mountains.

CHAPTER 55

Their bare feet touched in the soft white sand as they gently rocked, slowly dancing under the setting sun on a deserted beach. The rhythm of the waves lapping at the shore played a musical tune that only the two could hear. Sam looked into her beautiful eyes and gently pulled her close, bodies touching as their hearts took them back to a time long ago. Jennifer put her head against his chest and quietly said, "This dream can never end." Sam turned her in the sand as they danced. He wrapped his arms around her, and embraced his dream as reality.

CPSIA information can be obtained
at www.ICGtesting.com
Printed in the USA
LVOW07s1941020517
532927LV00003BA/943/P

9 781942 451488